HANDY ALL THE WAY

Richard

with dear wishes

Peter Walwyn

*For Bonk, my partner in
everything for over
forty years*

HANDY ALL THE WAY

A TRAINER'S LIFE

Peter Walwyn

metro

First published in Great Britain in 2000
by Metro Books (an imprint of Metro Publishing Limited),
19 Gerrard Street, London W1V 7LA

All photographs are from the author's collection,
unless otherwise indicated.

The extracts from George Lambton's *Racing at Home and Abroad* and
Michael Church's 'Derby Day' are reproduced with thanks

British Library Cataloguing in Publication Data.
A CIP record of this book is available on request from the British Library.

ISBN 1 900512 99 8

10 9 8 7 6 5 4 3 2 1

Typeset by MATS, Southend-on-Sea, Essex
Printed in Great Britain by CPD Group, Wales

From quiet homes and first beginning,
Out to the undiscovered ends,
There's nothing worth the wear of winning
But laughter and the love of friends.

Hilaire Belloc

I remember Captain Machell once saying, 'I don't like seeing a trainer walking briskly about with a smile on his face and whistling. I like to see him with his head and shoulders bent; then I know that he is thinking about his horses.' There is much truth in this: a trainer's mind should be full of his horses, to the exclusion of everything else.

George Lambton, Racing at Home and
Abroad: British Flat Racing and Breeding

CONTENTS

PREFACE

When I retired from training, several people in the publishing world came to me and asked if I would write my memoirs. I hesitated because I wondered whether anyone would read them; but after giving it some thought I decided I would take up the challenge. My wife and I have had – and are still having – such a wonderful life that it seemed only right to try to share some of that enjoyment with others. I was encouraged, too, by the request from Julie Spencer of *Hunting* magazine to write some articles for her; this I have thoroughly enjoyed doing, taking the opportunity to emphasise the connections among all our country sports.

I decided to call the book *Handy All the Way* as that was always the way I liked my horses ridden, especially when I had a jockey riding for me who was not used to my methods. The two books about racing which I adore reading myself are *Men and Horses I Have Known*, by George Lambton, and *Sods I Have Cut on the Turf*, by Jack Leach – each a microcosm of its author's life and times, with in Jack's case also a lot of humour. I still re-read *Men and Horses* about once a year, as there is always something I have forgotten. To try to emulate, or even get close to, either of those books would be impossible. But, while statistics are soon meaningless, because of inflation and the passage of time, I want those who pick up this book to feel, as they read through it, that they share in our triumphs and disasters.

Peter Walwyn
Lambourn, June 2000

1

'I'M DYING FOR A LARGE DRINK'

Derby Day was here
The thoroughbred in bloom
The hopes and dreams of many men
Were shown this afternoon.

If you were in the Queen's Stand
Or out there on the Downs,
Or riding on the funfair,
The magic came around.

The scene could run forever,
As only the players change,
You make a bet, they shout 'They're off!'
You turn another page.

Michael Church, 'Derby Day'

Wednesday 4 June 1975 – Derby Day.

That feeling of excitement as we woke up was not due to nerves. It never worried me having good horses – far more troublesome to have bad ones and the difficulty of finding races for them – but to have a runner which we thought could win the Derby gave one a very strange feeling. We had had two seconds in the Derby before, with Shoemaker and Linden Tree, but as we had broken the Epsom hoodoo by taking the Oaks with Polygamy in 1974, after three seconds in that race, I was very hopeful that we could bring off the Blue Riband this year with the second favourite – Grundy.

The most wonderful day of my life, bar my wedding day, was that glorious fourth of June 1975. The tradition and history behind the Derby, as with the Grand National, are so powerful that I get a cold shiver down my spine every time I go to Epsom, one of the foremost shrines of racing. That Wednesday morning we arrived about nine-thirty in the morning, having driven down from London; we have our own little traditions, and always went up to town on the Tuesday evening to go to the Twelve Club Derby dinner dance, a very enjoyable event, with family and friends, before tucking into bed at our club for the last night before the great race. The next morning, too, had its own ritual, which took our minds off the big event: a call in at the Cavendish Hotel to collect the papers and enjoy a delicious fry-up breakfast and a lovely relaxed get-together, with our greatest friends.

We were able to do all this because, before the days of the M25, any runner I had in the Derby did his last canter round the paddock at home on the Tuesday; then, after a feed at midday, the horses left for Epsom in the afternoon by the super-efficient Lambourn Ridgeway transport, so that by the early evening they would be in the security of the racecourse stables at Epsom. Before the days of motorways it was not advisable to leave it until Derby day itself to get your horses to Epsom because of the traffic and risk of mechanical breakdown.

In the quiet of early Wednesday morning we were able to take our horses down the path to 'Boggy' Whelan's yard, about half a mile below the racecourse stables – he rented the yard from Lady Helen Smith, the daughter of Lord Rosebery, and both of them were great friends of ours – and have a trot back up in peace and quiet. Ladas and Sir Visto, among the Derby winners owned by Lord Rosebery's grandfather, rest in their graves in the grounds of the house, the Durdans. 'Boggy' was always the soul of kindness and helpfulness. After their trot the horses had a pick of grass at the back of the stables before being securely locked up again. I never thought there was any need to canter the horses round Epsom. We have a superb replica of the Derby course beside the Wantage road from Lambourn, and Grundy had sailed up, round and down its unique gradients with such ease ten days earlier that we felt certain he would act on the course.

Epsom, like Aintree, has a magic about it on its big days, and whenever possible we try to walk the course, whenever we go. On Derby morning every year I take a posse of mainly young people right round the Derby course, along with the funfair and stalls, and tell them a bit of the history of the place. In 1975 Jeremy Speide-Soote, who was then taking over as my assistant, asked if he could come on my tour with us. We started off with a stall, where there was a lady guessing our age and weight. She announced that Mark Smyly, our assistant, was only 22 years old, and 9 stone; when we all shouted 'nonsense' (he was actually 32, and weighed 11 stone), it turned out that he had given the lady £5. I take the tour right round the funfair (though I have not yet attempted the 'big dipper'!), and finish off by passing the rows of clairvoyants and their splendid caravans, with patterned and flowered windows, and the odd Mercedes or BMW parked discreetly nearby. One of these welcoming ladies – they are all called, originally, 'Gypsy Rose Lee', 'Rose Lee Gypsy', or 'Lee Gypsy Rose' – invited Jeremy Speide-Soote in to have his palm read and his future told. When he came out, he said that she had told him, 'You are going on a long journey.' I said to Jeremy that she was quite right: I had not yet told him that he was going on a very long journey the next day to Catterick, where we had several runners.

After our wandering tour, those that had come with me – and the number varies each year – meet up in the trainers' car park for our traditional Derby lunch, starting off with pheasants' eggs and champagne or white wine; it is what we call a 'pick and flick' lunch, as we do not use plates, knives or spoons. This is a ritual which we still celebrate every year and hope to continue for a very long time yet – I have threatened my wife that I will appear on Derby day even in my wheelchair! There is something magical about Epsom Derby day. It is, and always has been a day for everyone, it does not matter what clothes you are dressed in from morning suits down to singlets and shorts. It is very different from Royal Ascot.

We had studied all the papers that morning, and they all seemed hopeful of good things from Grundy – as, of course, we were. In fact, I was feeling fairly confident, as Grundy, on form, had a better chance than the favourite Green Dancer who had not beaten two of our less good horses, Record Token and No Alimony, all that easily in previous races. One of our owners, Jim McAllister, walked by and I gave him a fairly punchy answer to his question about the horse's chances, assuring him that Grundy was in top form, and that I thought he would win.

I had already, before the picnic, walked down to the racecourse stables, as one always did, to see Tony Driscoll, our travelling head lad, and check that all was well with the horses. The first three races seemed to fly by and soon Jeremy Speide-Soote, Nick Gaselee and I were saddling Red Regent, No Alimony and Grundy for the big race. Red Regent had only won handicaps but was in superb form, and we had luckily got Brian Taylor, a very popular and competent rider, in the saddle. No Alimony had won the Craven Stakes and Predominate Stakes and was fully entitled to run, with Joe Mercer riding, although I had told his owner Louis Freedman that he would be very lucky to beat Grundy. The form pointer here was that Grundy had beaten No Alimony first time out as two-year-olds at Ascot the previous July.

All the preliminaries went well, and our superb blacksmith, Tony Hailstone, had come to the races specially to check the horses' racing plates. All was in order; there was nothing else I could do.

I had watched Polygamy's Oaks the year before in Lord Derby's box, and asked Rick Parker Bowles, a good friend, whether I could keep the luck flowing by going up to the same vantage point to watch the race now. There was a large crowd up there, but I was able to find a niche in the left-hand corner.

The race itself gave me no anxiety, and two furlongs out Red Regent, running a superb race and helping, involuntarily, to make a good gallop, gave way for Grundy, who had been ideally placed all the way, to draw away from the Prix St Alary winner Nobiliary. Having deafened the occupants of the box with my shouts of encouragement, I tore down the stairs to meet our hero quite a long way beyond the winning post. Here Bonk joined me. She had watched the race on the first floor, beside people she did not then know, John and Carley Newman. As the horses passed the post, they saw a girl they did not recognise get on her knees in the last furlong; afterwards they asked me, is it usual for your wife to watch races on her knees?

We could not believe our luck. The crowd around the unsaddling enclosure was enormous, and I remember a member of the press asking me what my plans were. My reply was short and sweet: 'I'm dying for a large drink.' We were asked up to the Royal Box in an ancient lift to be congratulated by the Queen; a great honour, and a big thrill as she is so keen on her racing.

Our only other runner that afternoon was Taros, in the Diomed Stakes, but here Pat Eddery had a rare lapse, for which one quickly forgave him, and finished only fourth, in a race which we should have won. Bonk then drove Mark Smyly and me home, all of us in rather a daze. Just outside Esher, Mark and I were longing to spend a penny. We found a public loo and, walking in, were faced by a large scrawl on the wall: 'The future of the world is in your hands!!'

At that time I thought it was.

2

A COUNTRY LIFE

The Walwyns are a very old family. The first recorded Walwyn was Sir Philip, of Walwayne's Castle, Pembrokeshire, who was reputed to be descended from Gualguain, a son of a sister of the legendary British hero King Arthur. The name is composed of two British words, *gwal*, which means wall, and *gwynne* or *wynne*, which means white; this derivation is embodied in the family crest of a wyvern upon an embattled wall or silver tower. It is also local, and the ruins of Walwyn Castle, or 'the castle with white walls', are still to be seen in Pembrokeshire, where it gave its name to a parish near Haverfordwest.

Sir Philip Walwyn was sent in the reign of King William Rufus, with eleven other knights under the command of Bernard Newmarch, to fight in the conquest of Brecknockshire, and built a castle at Hay-on-Wye, the ruins of which also survive. The whole family were heavily committed to that part of Wales, and it was a descendant of Sir Philip's, Sir Elias, by whose means Prince Lluellin of Wales was taken prisoner at the bridge at Builth Wells in 1282, and run through with a spear. Although it was a very long time ago, I still feel a little guilty that a relation of mine was responsible for the death of such a fierce patriot. A later Walwyn was reputed to be standard bearer to King Henry V at Agincourt.

My grandfather James was born in 1838, and served at the Second Relief of Lucknow under Sir Colin Clive in the Indian Mutiny; I still have in my dressing room his campaign mirror, which would have needed two bearers to carry it. He retired as a colonel in the Royal Welch Fusiliers to a lovely small estate near Monmouth called Croft-y-Bwla. When I visited the house for the first time in 1999, the old elms up the drive had all died and the whole house and what would have been an immaculate stable yard had about them the air of decay and lack of care which would have made my ancestors turn in their graves!

My father, Charles Lawrence Tyndall Walwyn, always known as 'Taffy', was born in 1883, and as the second youngest of six surviving children was brought up in that idyllic countryside at a time when neither tractors nor barbed wire had invaded the land and spoiled the scent and the jumping for so many hunting enthusiasts. He went to school at Wellington, where he won books for divinity, which he always used to laugh about. Thereafter he enlisted in the army, first as a second lieutenant in the Carmarthen Artillery, Western Division, at Pembroke Dock, Milford Haven, on 17 July 1900. At the beginning of the Boer War he was appointed to the remounts; on 22 January 1902 he was promoted to lieutenant, and his first job was to recruit some mules for the army in South Africa, and take them from New Orleans to Port Elizabeth. He lost four out of four hundred on the way, which at the time was a record. I still have photographs in my father's scrapbooks of the mules being put into slings to get them off the ship.

Father then commanded the Riding Troop, later the King's Troop of the Royal Horse Artillery, at Woolwich, and was subsequently range officer stationed at Hougoumont Farm, near Tidworth in Hampshire. He rode in army show jumping teams at San Sebastian in Spain, in Berlin, Chicago, Paris, and New York, and won many competitions, as well as winning many point-to-points on cheaply bought horses. (In those days free time was much more available in the army!) While stationed with his battery of horse artillery at the Curragh Camp, he helped to start the show jumping at Dublin Horse Show, and rode winners at Punchestown and in point-to-points in Ireland. Tom Masson, a great trainer and top show rider, described my father to me as having hands like velvet. When I said to Tom that you were lucky to be born with good hands, he just tapped his head and said, 'They come from here!'

In 1914 he was sent from Dublin via Kingstown, now Dun Laoghaire, to Le Havre; his troop fired the first two thirteen-pounder shells in the First World War. As commander of 'E' Battery, he rode his famous show jumper and point-to-pointer Rifle Brigade as a charger throughout his part in the war. On 14 January 1916 he was awarded the Military Cross, followed by the Distinguished Service Order a year later, and was three times mentioned in despatches. Eventually he was seriously wounded, and it was while recuperating, in December 1917, that he ventured into the War Office in London, as far as a mere major dared tread, and apparently slammed the table and told the Director of Cavalry that, in his opinion, 'The standard of riding in the Royal Regiment is deplorable; the erstwhile cavalry barracks at Weedon are now empty; I suggest that a riding establishment be set up with the object of training young officers and NCOs to teach riding in their units in place of the Riding Masters and Rough Riders of yore. I further suggest that I should be Chief Instructor of such establishment.' Almost miraculously, it was so. He was sent back to the front at the end of December 1917, and a year later, in the aftermath of the armistice, was posted to command the Riding Establishments at Woolwich. He was recommended for brevet colonel, but was too junior, and instead received the OBE in December 1920.

In the early months of 1919, the cavalry training barracks at Netheravon and the Riding Establishment at Woolwich were combined into a new unit at Weedon. My father chose four Horse Artillery officers and a few sergeant-majors and sergeants to form his opening team of instructors, and sent them on a course for two or three months with a couple of riding masters from Woolwich to imprint on them his methods and technique and to learn the kind of riding school drills that they would have to teach. The riding masters then returned to Woolwich. The course that my father set up in this way became the nucleus of all subsequent military riding tuition, and it is still carried on at the Royal Veterinary Corps establishment at Melton Mowbray.

The young soldiers were all encouraged to go hunting whenever possible, but it had to be done in spare time, and with the proviso that they were back in barracks before reveille. In addition, each soldier was allotted twelve 'bisques' or leave permits which could be taken during the course for any event connected with the horse. The Grand National was a free-for-all, and a special train to Aintree was provided.

While he was at Weedon, he was asked to find a point-to-point horse for the Prince of Wales by his friend and the Prince's George Drummond. He had a lovely horse who the Prince bought, called Rifle Grenade. After finishing second in his first race, the Prince proceeded to win his second point-to-point on Rifle Grenade at the Pytchley races near Great Brington on 16 March 1921. His family and advisers stopped him riding in races very soon after that, but my father was sent a letter, which I still have, as follows:

27th May 1921

ST JAMES'S PALACE S.W.

My dear Walwyn, I apologise for not having written to you before, but we have been away for the last ten days and it was quite impossible to do so. I have discussed our conversation with the Prince of Wales, and he has asked me to write to you and say that he would like to present you with the horse Rifle Grenade. His Royal Highness feels that as you made the horse which gave him so many good rides he would like very much to think the horse went back to you. He therefore hopes you will accept it.

Believe me,

Yours sincerely,

Lionel Halsey

What a wonderful gesture.

In 1923, my father rode the winner of the Grand Military Gold Cup at Sandown Park, White Surrey.

After three years at Weedon, my father was posted back to St John's Wood, then to Aldershot and Newport, and then in 1924 to India to command the 61st Native Mounted Territorial Brigade at Sialkot. On his return he was promoted to lieutenant colonel and posted to Edinburgh to command the 22nd Field Regiment Royal Horse Artillery. The best local hunting was with the Eglinton and Winton, and it was while following hounds that my parents met; they married on 1 March 1931.

When my father retired from the army just after I was born on 1 July 1933, at Hastings near Folkestone in Kent, we went to live in a lovely rambling Cotswold stone house near Chastleton, not far from Moreton-in-Marsh in Gloucestershire, with hunters, two grooms, and 30 acres of old ridge and furrow grass fields. So many people, when writing their life stories, are inclined to say that details of their childhood are tedious. I disagree. What fun I had at home during the years of the Second World War, even as a rather unadventurous and backward boy (very recently one of my boyhood friends told me that when I was very young I was known as 'the tapeworm', because I was so thin). I was the only son of both my parents, although I have a wonderful half-sister in Jean, known as 'Jinnie'. Jinnie is eight years older than me, and is the daughter of my father's first wife, who was glorious looking from her photographs, and very sadly died of tuberculosis. After leaving school, Jinnie studied physiotherapy at Orpington in Kent, and then went to work for Sir Morton Smart in London at his remedial practice, helping to keep the jockeys and other sportsmen fit. After a time she gave up physiotherapy and turned to horse sculpturing, becoming a renowned and much-admired artist.

Both my parents were keen followers of hounds. Before the Second World War they had hunted two days a week with either the Heythrop or the Warwickshire, and they loved jumping the fences. My mother, who was every bit as enthusiastic as my father, rode side-saddle beautifully and went extremely well, sailing along jumping big fences on lovely quality horses, often away from the main stream. Although they seemed to me quite elderly, they were very active, and gave us all the fun they could. They were very loving and protective, to the extent that I might have been described as being rather precious, and a bit wet; but they also encouraged their children in every country pursuit, and the first recollections of sport I have are of sitting on my beautiful pony Kitty Brown and being taken by my 'nanny', a dear friend who is still very hale and hearty, on a leading rein down to watch the nearest covert being drawn by the diminutive figure of Percy Durno, the charming huntsman of the Heythrop hounds.

My father always prided himself on the fact that he never in his life paid more than £300 for a horse, and he made very few mistakes, either buying horses or dealing in them. He was put in charge of buying the Heythrop Hunt horses for Lord Ashton of Hyde, newly appointed master in 1934, and apparently made a great success of it as little Durno was always superbly mounted.

At the age of about twelve I was allowed a four-ten shotgun, and was soon crawling about on hands and knees, stalking rabbits with my first brown and white springer spaniel 'Barney' at my heels until nightfall, and then lugging handfuls of dead rabbits home while my parents were yelling from the terrace that supper was ready. Preparatory school was Amesbury near Hindhead; I was never any sort of scholar, and even worse at games, but it was a nice school and I made lots of decent friends. One of my jobs was to look after and feed a great big angular red setter called Rufus, belonging to General Montgomery as he was then. Montgomery was great friends with the Reynolds family, who owned the school, and were also friends of my parents.

This sort of life went on throughout the war, with hunting with the Heythrop in the winter holidays; the pack had to be run on a shoestring but it was of course essential to keep it going to control the numbers of foxes. Despite failing to shine at prep school I managed to squeeze through my Common Entrance to Charterhouse near Godalming. This was a very different cup of tea from Amesbury. There were and are very few people there from the same kind of country sporting background as myself; certainly, unlike so many other public schools, there was no pack of beagles. It was a fine sporting school, however, for all games; Peter May, later captain of England at cricket, was head boy. I enjoyed history, and German, and loved going up to the art school where there was a very good teacher, Ian Fleming Williams, who encouraged me to paint whenever I could. I was no academic, but survived long enough to scramble through seven ordinary levels in school certificate in my last term, and became a house monitor. Curiously, though, I met hardly anyone at Charterhouse who has been a friend since, possibly because I came from so different a background from many of my contemporaries, and my way of life since has been very different from theirs.

Then came the call-up for compulsory National Service. I had, according to the army doctors, a bad back, with one vertebra which the doctors did not like the look of. This never bothered me, either then or since, but it ruled out any thought of getting a commission and dashed my hopes of going into the Scots Greys, a regiment of which a great friend of my father's, George Todd, was colonel. (George Todd's daughter Caroline later married Bob Brooks, with whom, before his tragically premature death, I had many happy times rabbit-shooting near his farm at Churchill in Oxfordshire; their son Charlie himself became a National Hunt trainer, taking over the famous yard of Fred Winter at a very young age. He became a good friend and valued colleague of ours in Lambourn. On retiring from training in 1999 he wrote a most entertaining book called *Crossing the Line* about his life, including his disgraceful arrest by the police for alleged involvement in the fixing of races.)

It is a pity that there is not National Service nowadays, even for a year, as it would sort so many young people out, in both their manners and their dress, and teach them the sort of discipline which so many parents nowadays never think of. Even for myself, having benefited from an exemplary upbringing, it was quite a culture shock, having hitherto been slightly shielded from the realities of the outside world. As Gunner Walwyn 22589717, in my first posting to the Royal Artillery Basic Training Regiment at Oswestry, I suddenly realised that I would have to get on with people from every walk of life. Startling though it was at the time, I think this has stood me in good stead since. I hope I understand a little how the ordinary person's mind works, and certainly I have built some wonderful relationships with those who have worked with me and for me.

After this I had a brief spell with the Royal Signals at Rhyl camp, before again twiddling my thumbs in frustration during a period with very little to do, when the powers that be did not know what to do with me. I was posted to 68th Training Regiment Royal Armoured Corps at Waithwith lines, Catterick camp. Some good friendships date back to this period: it was here that I met up with Simon Walford and his sister, now Jessie Harrington, as well as Tommy Pilkington, who has just completed a taxing term as Senior Steward of the Jockey Club. Simon and Tommy were in the training wing for potential officers, and I saw quite a bit of them. My main job, as ablutions orderly in charge of the latrines, was scrubbing the loos with soda, and washing the concrete floors. Then I was promoted to be a squadron clerk, but I usually found my ablution duties over by 10 a.m., by which time I could get down to the NAAFI and read the *Sporting Life*, which I ordered each day! The tedium was further alleviated by a spare ride in a nearby hunter trial, in an army team under Colonel Mike Edwards-Heathcote, afterwards master of the Old Berkshire hounds and uncle of Nicky Vigors, who trained at Lambourn and is now doing very well as a stewards' secretary for the Jockey Club.

In the course of being shunted around different camps I appeared in front of several army medical boards, including one at Millbank in London, but each time my hopes of being allowed to try for a commission were met with flat refusal, because my back was so bad; they rated me P3, the lowest rating you can get. It was then decided I should be sent to the Intelligence Corps depot at Maresfield Park camp near Uckfield, possibly because I had learnt German to 'O' level standard at school. On passing out in Field Security, I was sent to Klagenfurt in Austria, where I spent a fascinating year; able to speak a bit of the language, I ended up as a full corporal, wearing civilian clothes most of the time and being driven round in an unmarked car all over the province of Carinthia. It was then lovely unspoiled countryside, with the farmers' wives and workers still cutting the corn by hand or with ancient threshers and binders. The farmers used to go into Klagenfurt on market day and zig-zag their way back home in their carts, having spent several hours in the local *Gasthaus*. Although I got on well with the Austrians I met, I never found one who would admit to having fought against the British in the war; they all assured me that they had been on the Russian front!

On 11 October 1953 I was discharged from my National Service. I still have the testimonial to my conduct, which reads:

> During the time that Corporal Walwyn has served with this Unit, he has always shown himself to be a hard working and efficient NCO. He is extremely popular with all ranks, and has the knack of getting on with people of all walks of life. He always puts the best into his work, and undertakes all his tasks cheerfully. There is no doubt he will be a success in whatever occupation he undertakes.
> W. A. Self, Captain
> Field Security Carinthia
> Intelligence Corps

3

ALL BOOZE AND BETTING

Throughout my National Service I was hankering after some sort of a country life and, spurred on by the exploits of my hero and first cousin, Fulke Walwyn, the leading amateur rider of his day and then a top National Hunt trainer, set my sights on becoming a racehorse trainer. Fulke was the very best trainer of jumpers there has ever been, and a number of his big race triumphs were legendary. He was also very good with the few flat racehorses he had, training Aldborough to win the Doncaster Cup, and taking two-year-old races at Royal Ascot as well. More than this, he was a wonderful man; he loved young people, was the greatest fun and always ready for a party. He and his wife Cath held permanently open house and were adored by all their staff. My parents were at first less than enthusiastic at the thought of my training – all booze and betting! – but when I insisted I was set on it, they did everything they could to get me the right grounding. This consisted of an interview with the well-respected and successful Newmarket trainer Geoffrey Brooke, the introduction being performed by my father's friend Geoffrey Freer, the senior Jockey Club handicapper.

In 1922, on coming out of the army, Geoffrey Brooke had been assistant trainer to his brother-in-law Atty Persse. Geoffrey's sister Emily had been a famous actress, and there was a story told about her which showed that she had lost none of her skills. She told Atty she was going to London one day, and just after she had gone there was a telephone call from a woman with the most awful American accent, asking if she could come round evening stables that night. Atty thought this might be a possible new owner, and accepted. The woman arrived, swathed in furs, in a great big Rolls-Royce and proceeded to lay down the law for hours about horses and racing. Atty got more and more cross, but it was only after this witch had left that he realised that his own wife had completely pulled the wool over his eyes. I wonder how many of our wives could have the same effect on us?

After staying with Atty for about thirty years, and always asking when he was going to retire, in 1949 Geoffrey had taken the bull by the horns and, having little capital, started out on his own account by becoming private trainer to Major Lionel Holliday. The Major was a difficult man: he always used to say, 'My trainers arrive on bicycles, and leave in Rolls-Royces!', and there was a certain amount of truth in this as he had a very good breed of racehorse (he had won the Oaks with Neasham Belle), but his trainers had a shorter time with him than most football managers do in their clubs.

The Major had an obnoxious head man called Meaney, who used to ring up his employer and tell him how many bottles there were outside the trainer's door each morning. It is very lucky that my head men have never done that!

Geoffrey Brooke's partnership with this irascible character came to an abrupt end when he was rung one evening by his employer.

'What happened to my filly last night at Ripon? One of my friends said she didn't run very well, and did not look very well either.'

Brooke replied, 'I did not know you had any', and put the receiver down. Needless to say, after that divorce was inevitable, and in the summer of 1952 he launched out on his own; relying on his friends to help him start up as a public trainer, he found no shortage of patrons. In November the following year, he accepted me at Clarehaven Lodge as his first pupil assistant, and there followed three of the most formative years of my life. For the first year I had no car, only a bicycle. I started off doing my two horses like any stable lad; then, progressing under the guidance of a wonderful head lad, Bob Ruttle, I started to learn my craft. Bob was the most extraordinary little man, over fifty but weighing under 7 stone and as fit as a flea. He would ride anything (one of his characteristic expressions was 'Ize can ride 'em!'), and used the most fractious filly as his hack, setting off each horse in turn of a string of thirty, at the bottom of the canter, without a care in the world! When not in the yard with his horses, he was always mending rugs and doing odd jobs, to smarten the place up and save money for the 'Guv'nor'.

After a few weeks I was promoted to head lad in the bottom yard, a collection of ramshackle buildings at the far end of the big paddock, with a sea of mud in front of the boxes, and a lot of wild Irish apprentices under me. Now, in addition to looking after three horses myself, I was rapidly learning the art of feeding horses. Many of those under my care were cheaply bought or modestly bred two-year-olds that were being put through their paces to no mean tune, in order to exploit their modest capabilities; as a result they had to be coaxed to eat anything at all in the daytime. A little bit of grass in their feed was always a help.

I was also learning how to manage problem horses. We had one which used to worry, so we put him in the bottom box, next to the railway line. By the time he had had six steam trains go past him in close proximity, he soon stopped worrying. Another little horse we had down there was nicknamed 'The Dropper', as he used to deposit his lads with the utmost regularity. He used to walk his box, but we fixed that by putting him into a very long, narrow box, where he could not turn round and had to be backed out the same way as he was led in.

Geoffrey Brooke was a wonderful trainer, especially of two-year-olds, and they were always ready to win first time out. He used to let them stride along before Christmas over three furlongs on a nice gallop called Railway Land, just down the Norwich road from Clarehaven Lodge. This gallop faced towards home, which is always a help; I think most horses race better in that direction. He and his wife Betty were kindness itself, and underneath his rather bluff exterior there was a heart of gold. Although my lodgings were not always the best, the hospitality I received at the Brookes more than made up for that; I always had a marvellous breakfast in the house, usually rushed, after possibly leading a horse home for two miles from Racecourse side, our stables being on the other side of town. My appetite was rapacious, and there was always a mountain of delicious fry-ups left behind by other guests, who had come to see their horses work or were staying in the house. There were often dinner parties, too, to which I was asked as a spare man. At these occasions I just sat and soaked up the conversation as the great and famous aired their views on racing. One such was Michael Beary, a brilliant jockey with beautiful hands who had retired to train, albeit unsuccessfully, and was making a comeback. He had been stable jockey to Atty Persse when Geoffrey Brooke was at Stockbridge, and used to come to ride out with us at Clarehaven. Enchanting to listen to, with his engaging Irish brogue, he lived at a rate of knots, always staying at Claridge's when he was in London and thinking nothing of extravagance. He loved his hunting, and was as much at home riding over hurdles as he was on the flat.

Stories about Geoffrey were legion. We had a good-looking girl in the yard called Jill, who used to ride out a dear old horse called The Blessing. Gradually she started to put on weight, and her sweater started to get tighter, with more and more buttons left undone. Geoffrey was asked what the reason was, and he replied, 'The Blessing is carrying a seven-pound penalty, and I think the straw bale gave way at the wrong moment.' When someone questioned him as to who was responsible for getting Jill pregnant, his reply was: 'I think it was the work of a syndicate!'

Tim Forster, of whom I shall have more to say later, succeeded me as assistant at Clarehaven, and recalls the arrival of a yearling from the sales one day when there was no empty box for it. Bob Ruttle asked Tim to go to the house in the middle of the afternoon and find out from the Guv'nor where the newcomer should go. The great man was having a siesta on the sofa in the sitting room, with a paper over his head. When asked the question, he raised the paper and said, 'I've just bought two more this morning, so you had better find somewhere for them as well.' And then he put the paper back over his head, leaving Tim to embark on a quest for spare boxes elsewhere.

In my first season in Newmarket, 1954, my bottom yard notched up seven winners before the top yard had got off the mark, but of course we had the small, cheaply bought, precocious horses. It was not long before animals were being moved around, and the horses with problems sent down to me, while my pride and joys were being ridden up to the more prestigious and important top yard, which was much more amenable to the owners. In most cases they were personal friends of the 'Guv'nor', and I couldn't have met a more delightful lot of people.

Gradually the bottom yard was transformed with mown lawns and rose beds, and it was time for promotion. My initiation into a racing stable had been fascinating, and learning the art of feeding and managing a set of horses gave me the best possible grounding. After a year without a single outing in charge of a horse to the races, I felt I wanted to learn more, and gladly took up Bob Ruttle's suggestion that I start to take the horses to the minor second meetings, sometimes by train, from the old station at Newmarket, and sometimes by horsebox. The train journeys were the most fascinating: a lorry would pick up all the food and clothing for the horses very early in the morning, and the horses themselves were led down to the station, a mile and a half away, usually in pitch darkness, along the walking ground beside the Long Hill gallops. What would have happened if a horse had got loose I dread to think, but all went well, and I can't remember this happening even once. The train was usually what was called a 'special', with its own engine, a carriage for the travelling head lads, and a guard's van on the back. Horses always travelled well that way, as the guard's van gave the convoy stability, and the horses were not being swayed about, like they were on the roads of those days. Until the motorways came along this was by far the best way of travel, and horses that went to the races by rail seemed to run better and keep their form. No racecourse has yet installed a weighing machine, but I believe a lot of the weight loss that occurs when horses go racing comes about during the travelling, with the bad travellers shifting their legs around to get a better balance.

For two more years I spent the summers travelling horses all round the country, being able to slip away for a short holiday and hunting with my parents in the winter. I was also offered a few rides in point-to-points. On my first time out at Marks Tey I told my parents I was riding, and they very loyally came to support me. As I was legged up in the paddock, my mother (having, as she afterwards admitted, taken a tranquilliser called 'Oblivon') looked up at me and said, 'You won't go too fast, will you?' I hadn't the heart to tell her that this was not quite part of the plan! On another occasion I was at Moulton for the

Newmarket and Thurlow point-to-point when Alan Lilingston, then at Cambridge, asked me to ride his thirteen-year-old Caherdaniel in a race as he had been offered the ride on the favourite, belonging to a famous point-to-point owner in those parts called Mr Howgego. The old horse I was to ride had serious leg trouble and had not run for three years, and I was told not in any way to give him a hard race. I tucked him in early on, but at every fence he jumped spectacularly, landing nearly up with the leaders. Eventually, obeying my instructions to the letter, I decided it was time to pull Caherdaniel up going down the hill. I started to take a pull at him, but it took three turns of the plough to accomplish the feat, and I could only hope that the stewards – who included Geoffrey Brooke – were looking elsewhere. The following week, ridden by Alan, the old horse bolted up in the Members' race at Cottenham, with Alan on; but though I had everything I could spare on him, he started at long odds-on, so I didn't win a fortune.

After a couple of years, the question inevitably arose of where my future lay. My grounding had been impeccable, and I was now capable of doing most jobs in the yard, with the exception of one I cannot do to this day: plaiting a horse's tail. However, this is very seldom done in flat race stables, and I am against plaiting manes for racehorses; a well pulled mane looks just as good as a plaited one, especially when, as in so many cases now, the plaits (usually far too many of them) are secured with elastic bands instead of thread.

I was then approached out of the blue by my first cousin, Helen Johnson Houghton, Fulke Walwyn's sister, to hold the trainer's licence for her at her yard at Blewbury in Berkshire, which she had kept going since her husband Gordon had been so tragically killed in a hunting accident in 1951. He was the most promising trainer of his era, and held in very high esteem, although sadly I never met him. At that time women were not allowed to hold a licence to train racehorses, and so the licence would be granted to either the head man or an assistant trainer, although the real trainer was the woman. In this way Helen had had Colonel Dick Poole and then Charles Jerdein to help her. Charles was very bright, but now felt he had done it long enough; and it was at this point that I was called in. It was a very great honour and the chance of going several rungs up the ladder.

I did not know my cousin at all well, but her reputation as a horsemaster was becoming legendary, as was her very short fuse. I was probably lucky, but we got on very well and had great times together. When I joined the yard she had about twenty horses, mostly ordinary, except for the moody Gilles de Retz, who had won the Two Thousand Guineas the year before; although he was a very good horse on his day, he was not certain to show his form in each race he ran. Helen was an excellent judge of yearlings and expert at assessing the well-being of her horses, and very little was missed at her evening stable inspections. Gradually I learned the intricacies of running a stable – organising the galloping grounds, mole catching, and all the other many and varied facets of the job – as well as keenly studying Helen's art of placing horses. She was a genius at this, with an eye as sharp as a needle for spotting conditions races; in those days, too, the handicap ratings were decided by various different people at different courses, so that we could find out which were kinder to our horses.

After four more very happy years, at the end of which the stable had expanded to over eighty bulging boxes, I felt it was time to dip my toe in the water, and try the art of training myself.

Having been in Newmarket for three years, and then at Blewbury for four, I decided in favour of a base in Berkshire. The good hills and undulations of the downs mean that horses do not have to be extended so much as they do at Newmarket;

because it is so level there, much more work is done with horses off the bridle, and certainly there are far more flat-out gallops with, as I have so often seen, lads riding the heads off horses, with their sticks flailing. Only the laziest of horses needs the whip on the downs, and as they necessarily have to be hit in races, the less they are hit at home the better. Nevertheless, I always like riding out with a stick, mainly to correct the horse I am riding – and possibly to use as a balancing pole! – if, for example, it shies when a pigeon flies out of a hedge. Noel Murless always said that he loved downland training, and had only accepted the offer to train at Newmarket because of his health problems.

By this time I no longer had only myself to consider. At Kempton on Boxing Day 1958 I was briefly introduced by 'Tory' Dennistoun, who afterwards married John Oaksey, to a very pretty girl called Virginia Gaselee. She was always known as 'Bonk', long before the name had its modern connotations. It was something to do with her and her brother Nick's grandfather, who always referred to them when they were very young as 'the two Bonks'. Her father, as I afterwards discovered, owned a tug firm on the Thames, and was master and huntsman of the West Kent hunt. I can't think why, possibly because I was so busy, but I did not see her again until after the Grand Military meeting at Sandown the following year. I was friendly with several of the officers of the 11th Hussars, who had sent down a team of horses from Carlisle to run, and after racing was over we all went off to dinner, ending up at the Stork Club, then one of the most fashionable night spots in London. It had been a long day, and I was fully occupied with helping Helen with her training, but I do remember dancing with 'Bonk' a lot, and thought she was adorable. For her part, she says that she had a crick in her neck afterwards, from dancing with someone as tall as me.

The following March, 1959, I went to a bitterly cold Cheltenham, and there on the lawn was this pretty girl again, looking wonderful, as she had just been skiing. I asked her to have a drink, but when I got to the bar, rather like the Royal Family, I had no money on me! So she had to buy me the drink, and I felt that my chances of seeing her again would be remote. However, I was luckier than I perhaps deserved. We arranged to meet again on Good Friday, at the flat of a friend of hers in Farm Street; from there we went on to the Berkeley Hotel, where Bobby Harvey was playing all night on the piano. It was magic, and we had dinner – which in those days cost a white fiver – and danced the night away. London was deserted, and I knew I had found heaven on earth! We kept meeting a lot after that, and were able to announce our engagement on 19 September.

We decided to get married in early 1960. The night before the wedding on 5 January 1960, I stayed in London with Tom and Tessa Luckock, the sister and brother-in-law of my best man, Tim Forster. We decided to go and see a well-recommended film, *Beloved Infidel*, starring Gregory Peck and Deborah Kerr. It was about F. Scott Fitzgerald and Sheilah Graham. Scott had died of a heart attack, practically broke, and his wife Zelda ended up being trapped on the seventh floor of a sanatorium, when it burnt to the ground. The whole film was horrific, as there was row after row, and both parties were heavily on the booze. We came away thinking that it was not a great recipe for marriage!

Tim became one of our greatest friends, a companion in all our triumphs and disasters. He never got married, but the girls always adored him, and he had a succession of very pretty and delightful lady friends. Having done so well from his yard at Letcombe Bassett, training a host of winners, including an incredible three in the Grand National, he decided to sell up and move to Downton near Ludlow. Shortly afterwards he decided to retire; he had not been well for some time, and, having battled courageously with serious illness for many years, suddenly became very ill, and died in 1999. He had handed over his immensely successful stable to Henry Daly, a worthy successor to the Captain in training horses with great skill.

Sadly, both my parents had died in 1959 – it was a terrible shock to lose them both so quickly – but my parents-in-law-to-be wanted their daughter to have a proper send-off, and I believe about three hundred guests helped us celebrate. On the morning of the wedding, which took place in the local church at Plaxtol in Kent on 5 January, Bonk stepped in a dog turd as she got out of bed. I told her that was lucky. In fact she has been in the mire ever since, married to me.

Bonk and I spent our first night at the Savoy Hotel, well subsidised, I believe, by the manager Miles Thornewell, a great friend of my father's in the army. As we walked in we were confronted by Robin Abel-Smith, a charming man with an irrepressible twinkle in the eye. He asked us what we were doing there, and when we replied that we had just got hitched very generously offered to buy us a bottle of champagne. Knowing him, with all his panache, I rather doubt whether he paid for it – but it was very kind of him!

From the Savoy we set off on a somewhat chilly but relaxing honeymoon in Tunisia, returning to a sweet two-bedroomed cottage called Little Breach, on the Cholsey road out of Blewbury, which my mother had found for us. I found that I had enough of a legacy to think of starting training – though as yet I had no offer of any horses – and Bonk and I spent much of the year looking around for a suitable base. In the autumn of 1960 we eventually found a small stable to start from. We had so many friends in Lambourn that we thought the area and facilities were right for us. We had looked at Bockhampton Manor, a lovely old house; but it was too far from any gallops.

We had looked at The Old Manor at Upper Lambourn, a very pretty yard and a nice house – but at the last minute the owner, Geoffrey Champneys, decided not to sell. Then we found Windsor House in Lambourn: a Georgian house, two cottages including a hostel, and thirty boxes. It had always been a lucky yard, first with Sir Charles Nugent and then with his grandson Hugh. The Nugents were ardent Catholics, and started the first chapel in the village, in an upstairs room in what we afterwards had as the lads' hostel, in the cottage on the end of the yard.

In the Second World War the house and stables were requisitioned by the army, and taken over by American airborne soldiers of 101st Division, 501st Regiment. The officers lived in the house, the NCOs in the hostel, and the soldiers nine to a box in the stables. There are still signs of the celebrated Tortoise stoves in the boxes. The troops did weapons training and shooting on a range in the paddock across the road, and the lawn beside the road was used for unarmed combat, with trenches and barbed wire right up to the far boundary. An instructor who returned recently said he remembered breaking four soldiers' arms during the practising for D-Day!. The unit left from the Membury airfield where the M4 service station is now. Around 200 of them flew out on the eve of D-Day, 5 June 1944 and sadly twenty-two of them never returned. There is now a brass plate on the wall in the yard to commemorate their stay.

After the war Tom Rimell moved to Windsor House from Kinnersley, where he had trained Forbra to win the Grand National, leaving his son Fred to take over there. Old Tom in his turn sold Windsor House to Syd Mercer, a cunning old fox who had started his career with Tom Coulthwaite, the trainer of three Grand National winners, at Hednesford. Syd, like Geoffrey Brooke, trained for Lady Wyfold, and rang up Geoffrey in despair one evening. He had a lovely well-bred filly of Lady Wyfold's who had won her first two-year-old race at

Birmingham in a canter. He was then training at Guy's Cliffe near Warwick, and he said that the gallops were not good enough to train a top-class filly. Would Geoffrey take her over, as he felt he could not do her justice? In return, would Geoffrey let him have the old handicapper The Blessing? Of course Geoffrey agreed, thinking he might train a star; but when the filly arrived in Newmarket, it turned out that she made a noise like a roaring bull and was gone in the wind. Needless to say she never won another race, whereas The Blessing went on winning for years and years.

Syd's abilities extended to curing warts, and he certainly fixed some I had on my hands with a lick from his tongue on to a far from clean hand which he then wiped on my own!

Having bought the stable from Syd for the then considerable sum of £12,000, it was then our job to try to fill it. The first person to offer me a horse was Percival Williams, then master of the Four Burrow hounds in Cornwall. At his wife's home in Herefordshire he kept just two mares, one of which was Aunt May, bought with a legacy left to him by an aunt of that name. We were asked over to Herefordshire by him and his lovely wife Barbara to see Aunt May's first foal. I remember well going into a field on a hill in the pouring rain and seeing this insignificant yearling gelding by Roc de Diable. But when Percival waved his handkerchief, the little horse did stretch out his toe; he could certainly move. Having accepted Be Hopeful, as they had named him, to train, we drove away, and I said to my wife that at least we ought to be able to train him quite well, as it was the only horse I was likely to be offered! Little did we know then that he would eventually win twenty-seven races, including one at Deauville, ridden by Lester Piggott.

Already in the yard at the time we took it on was a lovely gelding by Mossborough called Don Verde. He was a liver chestnut, always, I think, the nicest colour for a horse, with good limbs. His owners, Captain Philip Dunne and his son Martin, had had him in training with Syd Mercer and he had run once with promise over hurdles, finishing third. They asked me if I would keep him on, and he certainly seemed a reasonable prospect.

Also in the yard already, and a great asset to us as newcomers, was Syd Mercer's head lad, Ray Laing. He was a brilliant feeder and adept at breaking in the yearlings, and stayed with us for seventeen years, the backbone of the yard, until he decided that the pressures of an expanding stable were too much for him.

Before we could expect to fill the yard, we had to get it into shape. It had been somewhat neglected before we moved in, and I have always felt that if the staff and yard are scruffy, there is every chance that the horses will be as well, as there are no standards to keep up. This is hardly likely to attract owners. Why should anyone walk into a shop with grime and cobwebs all over the windows? Even in the house there was no central heating of any sort. Syd Mercer had assured me that the heating worked well, but when I asked to see the boiler, he replied that he had lost the key . . . there was a coke boiler, but it was completely useless, and full of rust. However, by sorting that out and renovating the shabby lads' hostel, we soon got the place looking a lot tidier.

Until you start training on your own account, it is impossible to realise how much difference there is between being an assistant, even with considerable responsibility, and running your own show. However much help you give to someone else, whether your advice is taken or not, the ultimate decisions are taken elsewhere. Now, all the decisions lie with you. Where do you run? Who rides? Is the horse fit enough? Has he schooled enough? The answers to all these questions, and many more, only come with a great deal of thinking, which no one else can do for you.

When anyone starts training, even with massive backing, which I never had, it is hard to visualise that one is capable of training top-class horses, which after all is the real purpose of the exercise. When we started, we felt that our main job was to train winners; any thoughts of really high-quality horses were a mirage, and far from our thoughts. As Robin Oakley, a keen racing man as well as until recently the BBC's political editor, has written, 'To outsiders the racing world appears a hard-bitten one, full of unscrupulous operators seeking to exploit the system. In truth, racing people are often straight and almost always gnawed with self-doubt. So much can go wrong with racehorses, such powerful but fragile beasts.' Running a racing stable is not so much like conducting an equine gymnasium as like operating a private health clinic – except that you cannot charge the same fees. 'A happy trainer', says Sir Mark Prescott, one of the best in Britain today, 'is a bad trainer; a few profit mightily: most struggle to survive.' I don't quite agree with that, and although I have never been motivated by money, the satisfaction of doing a job well, and getting adequate reward for it, is gratifying enough.

I still have my first wages bill: a total of £19 18s 2d, for four employees. I believe that we paid the lads in the hostel £5 and that they paid us £2 per week for their accommodation. This shows you what successive bad governments and inflation have done to our economy. The amounts seem ludicrously small now; but with taxes so much higher now, few people in this country are any better off now than they were in those days.

When we started training in Lambourn, there were two good flat race trainers in the village: Peter Nelson, at Kingsdown, and Freddy Maxwell, a great little Irish character, who had moved from Blewbury in the spring of 1959. 'Maxie' was great fun, and rode beautifully, riding work on his horses nearly up to the time he retired. He was a brilliant trainer of every sort of horse, from

Merry Madcap, a talented sprinter who won the July Cup in 1965, to Fighting Charlie, who won two Ascot Gold Cups, and Pandofell. He and his dear wife Nora were very supportive when we first came to Lambourn. At a drinks party we had at Windsor House 'Maxie' was looking at our pictures, and came across a portrait of one of my ancestors called Thomas Tyndall. He asked what his profession was; when I replied that he was a merchant from Bristol, he replied, 'I would have made quite a good merchant myself!' And he surely would, with his great charm, sense of humour and stories of how he started out in racing. Maxie was always immaculately dressed, and one day we had a drink with him when he was still dressed in his plus-fours. When I asked him where he had been shooting, all he said was 'Near Cirencester', and when I asked him 'Who with?' all he said was, 'There were just two of us, me and the other fella.' His other great fascination was the croquet lawn, where he was very hard to beat.

As for the jumpers, my cousin Fulke Walwyn's string stood out, with about sixty horses – a large string in those days, when there were far fewer horses in the village than there are now, and the whole atmosphere was much more relaxed. Brian and Mary Marshall trained at Berkeley House, and became good friends of ours. Brian had been a top-class rider, with two Grand Nationals to his credit, and Mary had been a very stylish international show jumper. Among the guests at a party one night was a dear old girl, Nan Birch, who struggled on training at a very pretty house and yard in the middle of Lambourn, now incorporated into yet another housing estate. Brian turned to me and asked who she was with. I replied, 'I think she is with her first husband called Kennedy, who she has just remarried.' All Brian said was, 'Ah well, they didn't have to walk the course, did they?'

Our first runner, on 10 October 1960, was a light-framed little horse called Port Stride in a handicap on the flat at Warwick. To our amazement and delight, he finished second. We then decided to run Don Verde in a novice hurdle at Worcester on 22 October. John Lawrence, now Lord Oaksey, had been down to school him and he seemed a natural jumper. John, who qualified for the Bar but then decided that race-riding and journalism were more to his liking, has a brilliant brain, and is one of the most successful amateurs we have ever seen. Horses really ran for him, and he was a very good judge of pace. In the race he kept Don Verde handy throughout; the horse jumped well, apart from a blunder at the second last, and drew away easily to win by eight lengths. This was unbelievable; actually to train a winner with my second runner! Although we have had nearly 1,900 winners since, in England, Scotland, Ireland, France, Italy, Germany and the USA, the feeling of first seeing one's name in the paper the next day as a winning trainer was hard to better.

And yet, so many people are involved in the preparation of a horse that I always think it unfair when only the trainer's name appears, as it is only thanks to the hard work of a team that results occur; even the youngest apprentice is partly responsible. How proud the whole yard felt to see that all our joint efforts were coming to fruition.

4

HOPPY

Be Hopeful arrived at Windsor House in November 1961, as a mud-covered yearling in a battered old horsebox. Percival Williams had come in the box with him, and as the horse was led down the ramp he handed me an envelope. To my amazement, when I opened it up there was a cheque for £500. I was so surprised that I asked him what it was for. He said, 'I know it's very hard starting a business, this will help if you put it against my account.' It was a wonderful gesture which we'll never forget. In those days it was a whole year's training fees in advance, because of course there wasn't the dreaded VAT, and I had started by charging £9 per week. How many owners today would countenance paying in advance, even for a substantial discount? Some are very slow, choosing to forget that the trainers have to pay their staff or they would have a walkout or strike on their hands.

It was several days before Be Hopeful's coat started to appear out of the mud; at first, naturally enough, everyone laughed at him, and no one wanted to look after him. Gradually we started to break him in, and from the very start he used to throw himself all over the place with exuberance and ignorance. Just after he was ridden away for the first time and I had sent him off trotting up the Upper Lambourn road, I drove along in the car to see how he was coping, and found him lying motionless in the road. In one of his turns he had thrown himself over. I thought him dead; but he had only winded himself, and just then he shook himself and got up. Luckily the rider too was perfectly all right. Even in those days the horse was as tough as old boots, and I cannot remember him ever leaving an oat. By the end of March he was cantering away, and we could see what a wonderful mover he was. Some horses move well, but cannot quicken, and just keep going at the same one pace; but we soon realised that Be Hopeful, although very backward, had a bit of speed too.

Whenever we have had backward horses, I have always found that if we have the chance, it is a very good idea to send them back to their owners for a month or two in the spring, to get the new grass. This helps them to relax and come to themselves. I am not so keen on horses going back to their owners in the winter. The owners love it as they feel they are saving money, but in fact they are being penny wise and pound foolish. A thoroughbred should always have a rug or rugs on at night, but their owners often omit to do this, and to make matters worse often leave them stuck out in a bitterly cold field all day, when after the first half hour or so all they do is to stand at the gate, longing to come in again. If animals do go home in the winter, they should go straight after their last race, and be back before Christmas. The later they come back in, the longer it takes for their coats to come through – and the longer it will be before they are racing fit. Often an owner would ring up straight after his horse returned, and ask when the horse was going to run. Horses are not got fit to run overnight; there must be at least a month of cantering before the trainer will dare to do any more with them.

Randall, the old stud groom at Aramstone, Mrs Williams's estate in Herefordshire, did not know much about racehorses, but was a wonderful old-fashioned stockman, and Be Hopeful's holiday did him good. The horse was such a character that we became very fond of him. When the string pulled out in the morning he would buck and buck for the first few minutes: the rider just had to stand up in his stirrups, secure himself with a finger through the neckstrap, and grin and bear it. We nicknamed him 'Hoppy', and he was known by that title the whole time he was with us.

When we moved to Seven Barrows there was an old duck pond by the back door. We dug it out, filled in the base with hard core and put rails and boards round it, converting it to a secure lungeing ring and sand pit. This became a magnet for Hoppy; as soon as he had finished his exercise, his saddle was taken off and he was led to the enclosure. With the alacrity of the most dedicated Catholic priest, he was on his knees like lightning, and rolling over and over. Some horses take to it like ducks to water, and I always liked to see them roll over completely; if they will do this, they are on good terms with themselves and free from pain. If a horse will not roll right over, he is often feeling some deep-seated ailment.

Not everyone took to Hoppy's playfulness. We had a lad for a short time who afterwards worked for Fred Winter called Harry Foster. Harry was so frightened at the horse's bucking that he did not obey his instructions and jumped off on to the road outside Windsor House, where the string used to take a turn at the beginning of exercise. Inevitably, he broke his ankle, and was off work for a year. He then sued me, although I had paid his wages for the full time. His complaint was that the horse was dangerous, but the whole case fell through. Some called Foster a hero, but that wasn't a word I would ever have used of him. Meanwhile Be Hopeful had scored seven of his eventual twenty-seven wins.

That summer we gradually got Hoppy cantering again and thought we ought to get a run into him as a two-year-old. The race we selected was the Rays Plate over five furlongs at Windsor on 3 November. The going was described as dead, but I remember it as being bottomless. In the gloom of a November afternoon, Be Hopeful started to run on from halfway, and although unplaced, showed enough to make us think he would win races. Derrick Morris rode him, and I had told him on no account to give the horse a hard race – he was not ready for it – but to teach him his job. He was a good lightweight and a pretty good judge as well, and was very complimentary about him.

After the race Boggy Whelan, a grand little man who was training a small string at Epsom with great success, came up and asked me, 'What was that you ran? I'm going to back him every time he runs.' It was a very profitable move, and I believe the old horse made him a lot of money over the years, as he was always a reasonable price.

Hoppy went home for another short break in the winter and came back muddier than ever but looking stronger. After being placed third and then second in his first two races in 1962, he opened his account in a conditions race at Warwick over one mile worth £207, ridden by Paul Tulk. Later that year he won again, in a seven-furlong handicap at Salisbury. This was the first time that Joe Mercer had ridden him, and he rode him to win four more times, although I never felt that he held him up quite enough. Hoppy had a very short run, and could be held until the last furlong.

The following year, 1963, he won at Warwick over seven furlongs and at Lewes (which sadly closed down the next year) over a mile, both times with Lester Piggott up. Lester got on with him very well, and at Lewes in August we suddenly realised how much the horse loved downhill tracks. I was very fond of Lewes, with its undulations, and many good horses were trained there, at the top of the town near the old prison, by Jack 'Towser' Gosden, including Charlottown, the 1966 Derby winner. He had retired by the time the horse triumphed at Epsom, but had the doubtful pleasure of seeing a horse whose career he had mapped win nicely.

The small courses, like Lewes, are so important to British

racing, with the variety of one- or two-day meetings they offer; very few racegoers want to go to a course for many days on end, unlike the United States, where meetings go on for a month on end and there is in effect centralised racing. Unless we have a lot more all-weather racing, which God forbid, the grass courses won't stand much more racing because of the damage caused and the repairs that have to be undertaken afterwards. It is not that I am against all-weather racing; it caters well for moderate horses, and indeed I was asked to be on the original committee which went to Laurel Park and other American courses with Ron Barry and others on a feasibility study. We found that all-weather racing was indeed perfectly feasible, but were concerned at the injuries to horses' legs that might result, as indeed they do in the States. Of course, the American regulations allow trainers to run horses on medication, some brands of which are allowed to be administered on the morning of the race. This means that the horses are virtual junkies, kept on medication to mask their injuries while they are in reality chronically lame, with the symptoms suppressed to make them feel at their very best. That is why, I believe, there are so many fatal accidents on US tracks. By contrast, the British regulations on medication mean that horses can only be raced when they are sound, even on the all-weather tracks, which makes for a much more edifying spectacle.

From 1963 Be Hopeful won every year for a decade, especially loving Epsom, Brighton and Bath. He won twice in France, at St Cloud and at Deauville – our first winner at that enchanting course. Of all the places to win races abroad, Deauville stands out. Nowhere else do you get the same holiday atmosphere, with lovely long beaches (not always all that clean, I might add), with polo as well as racing, and a casino thrown in, and probably the most delicious food and wine in the world. We have had some of our happiest moments at that lovely Normandy course.

On the track itself, the round course is pretty tight, but there is a good straight mile course as well, and it was here that Lester Piggott drove Be Hopeful into the lead in the last furlong to win the Prix du Calvados by a short head. For days afterwards, people kept coming up to congratulate us. I could not really understand why, until I realised that the owner of the second horse, Minstrel Son, was unpopular with a lot of people – although I always got on with him myself.

We were at the Newmarket July meeting in 1973 when Be Hopeful, ridden by Frank Morby, won at Brighton, beating Tender Heart, trained by John Sutcliffe junior, the winner of that year's Hunt Cup at Royal Ascot. He was then fourteen years old and as sound as a bell of brass. After the race John Sutcliffe came up to me and gave my hand a big shake. All he said was, 'Isn't it about time that you retired that old bugger?' We were very fond of John. He was a very astute trainer; his horses never went unsupported, and he was always reputed to have a large bet when he fancied them.

That September I went off to the sales in America at Lexington, and on the way home called in, as I always did, at Nydrie, Danny Van Clief's stud in Virginia. The first time I stayed there, I was put into a very comfortable attic with a nice big wooden bed. In the middle of the night, there was an almighty splintering noise, and one side of the bed frame collapsed. There was nowhere else to sleep, so I just stayed where I was, with the bed at a rakish angle. In the morning the Van Cliefs' charming black butler, Ben, came in and commiserated with me. 'Never mind, sir,' he said, 'one screw will put it right.' My reply was, 'Ben, I think too many screws have put it wrong!'

When Bonk picked me up at London Airport on my return, she had a very long face. It turned out that our beloved Be Hopeful had been doing a very steady canter on the all-weather on Faringdon road, when he suddenly cracked a hind cannon bone. Although they got him home in the box, he could not be saved, and they had to put him down.

These were very sad times. Hoppy would not have harmed a fly, and was such a genuine character. Alan Bailey, who looked after him, was as upset as we were; we all loved him, and he had done so much to get us going. When his owner, Percival Williams, died, he did me the great honour of leaving us a lovely Lionel Edwards picture of Be Hopeful in the yard at Windsor House, which now hangs in pride of place in my sitting room. He had run 115 times, won twenty-seven, and been placed many more times.

What a horse!

5

SEVEN BARROWS

On an easy day in the early spring of 1964 I decided to go for a long trot, right out to Seven Barrows, a distance of about two miles each way. This estate had a remarkable history, with the ancient stone age burial grounds from which it took its name just across the road. These mounds had, it is thought, been built as memorials to famous people rather than as actual mass burial grounds, although when they were excavated in the 1850s, the archaeologists had found in one chamber the bones of a chieftain surrounded by arrowheads, and in another the bones of an ox and a lurcher-type dog.

On this morning I was riding a lovely-looking horse called Flambeau, which we had bought for Martin Dunne and his father Captain Philip Dunne to replace the unlucky Don Verde. Don Verde had given us our first three winners over hurdles in 1960 and 1961, and had been leading at the last flight in the County Hurdle at the Cheltenham Festival when he had a crashing fall. The vets advised getting him home in the horsebox, although he appeared in a bad way, and he died on the way home. This was very upsetting; like Be Hopeful, he was a horse that had really started to get us on the map. Flambeau himself had had a heavy fall in a steeplechase at Newbury, and at this point was just getting going again before cantering.

Opposite the front gate of Seven Barrows I met Cerise Candy – Derrick's wife, mother of Henry – out with their string. She and Derrick were much older than Bonk and me, but we had become good friends. Now she greeted me, and suddenly said, pointing

at the buildings I was passing, 'Wouldn't you like to train there?'
The property had belonged to the Candys for the last few years,
but as they already had their yard established at Kingston
Warren they did not train there, but let the stables to Derrick's
cousin David Hastings. I replied that I would love to, but did not
know if I could afford to buy it. I did, however, ask her whether,
if ever it came on the market, I could have first refusal. We were
coming near to bursting at the seams at Windsor House, and in
those days there was no scope for expansion at the yard in the
village. We rented a few boxes over the road at Downs House,
but felt that there must be somewhere nearby which would suit
us. Seven Barrows, we knew, would suit us very well – if we
could afford it. David Hastings already allowed us to use its
private gallop, but it was a long way out of the village, and the
gallop itself stretched away from Windsor House, meaning a
two-mile return journey.

Nothing came of this conversation for some months. Then, on
4 August, we went to Wolverhampton, where Q.C., owned by
Percival Williams, was running in the Wolverhampton Derby, a
poor replica of its Epsom counterpart – when Q.C. won, his prize
money was just £382 2s! The Candys were leaning against the
iron rails fronting the straight when they called us over, and
again I was asked if I was interested in the place. I repeated that
I definitely was, and asked why they wanted me to go there.
They both replied that they would like to have us as neighbours.
Again I said that I would love to have first refusal. Again
nothing happened for a while. Then in November I received a
formal letter from Derrick's solicitor, saying that Seven Barrows
was for sale, naming a price, and asking whether I was
interested. I rang up straight away and went to London that
afternoon. When I asked why the price was so reasonable, the
reply was that the property needed a lot doing to it as it had been
let go and was in a bad way.

Seven Barrows had a long and complicated history. It had been part of the Craven Estate, owned by the Earls of Craven since the time of King Charles I, when Lord Craven, horrified by the sights of the plague and longing to find somewhere healthy to escape from the hordes of people dying in the houses and streets of the capital, rode out of London and found this spot in a fold on the downs. Here he built a magnificent mansion, Ashdown Park, which has now been renovated to a very high standard. The Earl was one of the great magnates of his time; romantically involved with the King's sister, Anne of Bohemia, he financed the European wars of Charles I, and his estate stretched right from Uffington near Wantage, to Hamstead Marshall near Newbury.

Seven Barrows was originally a sheep farm, with a barn and well, so that it was very useful in bad weather to the farmers bringing their sheep to the fairs in Lambourn. Brady Nicholson lived in the house and was judge of the important coursing meetings held at Ashdown and still further afield at Newmarket. Call-overs for the coursing were held the night before the meeting at the Red Lion hotel in the centre of the village.

The first racehorse trainer at Seven Barrows was Charles Jousiffe, an ebullient character who broadcast his fancied runners all over the course. He trained Kettledrum, the winner of the Derby in 1861, who had been sent to the stable of George Oates at Stork House, once the smartest yard in Lambourn, because his owner, Colonel Townley of Burnley in Lancashire, had heard that the Berkshire downs had the finest old turf in the country. Kettledrum's rider in the Derby, Luke Snowden, died the following year aged 22 and is buried just outside the west door of Lambourn church. Jousiffe is known as the 'father of Lambourn racing', and the lych gate outside the church was built in his memory. The outstanding horse that he trained at

Seven Barrows was Bendigo – not an easy horse to train as he ran only sixteen times in five seasons. He did, however, win the Cambridgeshire (and finish second in another running), the Lincoln Handicap, the Hardwicke Stakes at Royal Ascot, the first Eclipse Stakes, the Jubilee Handicap and the Champion Stakes. He was a very good-looking horse, but with no pedigree, and hardly bred a single winner.

After Jousiffe, the stables at Seven Barrows were run by Garrett Moore, an old-fashioned horsemaster who had ridden The Liberator to win the Grand National in 1879, until the lease ran out at the turn of the century. Then the stables fell empty. Bert Randall, who started off as an amateur and used to ride the champion mare Sceptre, until he got the sack for riding some terrible races on her, used to live in the house. One of his guests was Geoffrey Freer, who remembers Randall keeping a hack and riding over to the gallops to meet Charlie Morton, who trained at Letcombe Regis, to ride work, and then riding again afterwards. Geoffrey also remembered one morning when a gypsy woman came along as their gardener was sweeping the front drive. At that time there were cattle sheds where the pair of cottages are now, and the girl asked if she could go into one for a few minutes. She came out shortly afterwards, with a baby in her arms.

After the First World War, Harry Cottrill, who had been brought up in Cheshire, rented the yard, having previously hunted, ridden in point-to-points, and financed these pleasures by making and dealing in hunters. He then returned to Cheshire, establishing a small stable of jumpers at Tarporley. He once attended the famous hunter sale at Islington and was accused of only being a racehorse trainer, whereupon he made a bet that he would buy a yearling the following year which would not only win the hunters' championship, but also win the first important two-year-old race at the first big flat race meeting of the year, the

Brocklesby, then held at Lincoln. He succeeded in doing both; and he used to jump a five-barred gate at Seven Barrows each morning in front of the string on his hunter to show the staff what could be done. He was a very shrewd judge of a horse, and trained winners of both the Two Thousand Guineas and the Oaks.

In 1937 there was a terrible fire at Seven Barrows; the boxes, being mainly wooden and creosoted, went up like tinder, and five horses were killed. Several others, having been turned loose in order to save their lives, roamed the downs for several days, but even those that had been burnt recovered their form quickly. Indeed, within a fortnight Cottrill, being the sanguine character he was, had the stable up and running again and winning races at Royal Ascot.

When Harry Cottrill retired the stables were again rented, first to Ronnie Bennett and the steeplechase jockey Bill Payne, before David Hastings took over the lease in 1958. He was a cousin of Peter Hastings-Bass, and had come from East Ilsley. In 1961 the whole Craven estate came on the market for the first time in centuries, and Derrick Candy was able to buy both Kingston Warren, where he was training, and Seven Barrows, where David Hastings remained as tenant of the stables.

Having had a survey done, which showed the property to be well worth the price being asked, we bought the place, with three hundred acres. It was quite an undertaking, but bearing in mind how fast our string was increasing, we thought it worth while. We had been very happy at Windsor House, probably the nicest house in the village, but the opportunities of Seven Barrows, with its scope and variety of exercise facilities, offered too good a chance to miss for people like ourselves who wanted to get on in life.

And there was certainly plenty to get on with. The house had rain water running down the inside walls, as the gutters were never cleaned out, and the whole building wanted redesigning, while the lads' hostel next door was so full of rats that the Pied Piper of Hamelin would have been quite at home there. In fact it was uninhabitable, and had to be pulled down. But the exercise grounds have always been superb, with the most wonderful mile and a quarter gallop in the world, up Faringdon road. It has not got a single dip in it, and is very stiff, so that if the work riders go too fast early on, the horses are walking by the time they get to me at the mile post, where I always stood. Sadly, these gallops too had been neglected, and were over-run with moles. I learnt to become quite an expert trapper. There is only one way to catch moles, and that is in a spring claw trap. You do not dig the trap into the mound; you find with a cane the run between the mounds, and (always using rubber gloves) lay the traps in the tunnels, first wiping earth over them. When you have your mole caught, and he is always dead, you know he cannot do any harm, and after the first year, when I caught over four hundred, we had hardly any more trouble with them.

We had to build first a hostel for the staff, and a cottage right beside the back drive for the head lad Ray Laing; these were Colt houses, very adequate, but obviously, being wooden-framed, with a slight fire risk. Then we gutted the main house and moved in, during the August Bank Holiday of 1965. We had little in the way of curtains or carpets, and lived in only two rooms, but it is one of life's certainties that if you can move into a house with the builders right round you they work a great deal faster. The other thing I have learnt is that architects are an expensive luxury, and as far as I can see have never lived in the sort of house which normal people want to live in. In my view one is far better off choosing a good builder, who may also be a surveyor, and knows what can or cannot be done.

We had our first Classic placing in 1965, a third in the One Thousand Guineas with Mabel, a filly by French Beige, a good tough stayer trained by Dick Peacock, out of Aunt May, who was also dam of Be Hopeful. She had won two of her four races as a two-year-old, including a nursery handicap at Ascot, and this year also won the Yorkshire Oaks. In all that season we won twenty-six races and over £14,000, not a bad figure for those days, as we only had about thirty boxes in the yard.

We rode the horses out to the new yard at the end of the flat race season of 1965, and they were very soon settled. The thirty-five boxes were of good size, but with chalk floors, which, though they have the advantage of draining well, are always being dug up by the horses. In the old days, with labour aplenty, there would have probably been some expert on hand who knew how to lay chalk, and bang it in with a rammer, but in the absence of such a specialist we decided to put in brick floors, laid on sand, with the bricks right up against each other. In some boxes we used concrete, but there is always the worry with concrete that it becomes slippery; in those days we did not have the benefit of the rubber floors invented recently and now made by an excellent firm called Lightfoot.

At the same time as preparing the stables, we had to prepare accommodation for the staff. There were three cottages which we gradually renovated, and by the time we moved the horses in, the hostel was ready. I have always believed that in an isolated establishment a hostel for staff is essential. It brings more of a community spirit to the place, and I have always felt that happy staff in good accommodation help to make happy horses. Of course, hostels are expensive to maintain; one has to subsidise the costs enormously, but unless you have domestic staff to cook and clean, the whole place quickly goes to rack and ruin. Left alone, young stable lads will burn the furniture, stain or set light to the bedding, and cause all manner of casual damage. They need constant supervision, as was done in the army. If I found anything broken on our regular inspections and the culprit did not own up, I used to make the lads pay for the damage collectively. This usually did the trick and the offender would come forward pretty quickly.

At Easter 1966 we had our first winner from Seven Barrows: Crozier, who had finished fourth in the Horris Hill Stakes at Newbury, running on nicely under Wally Swinburn at Doncaster on 9 April. The horse was always a bit kinky, but had lots of ability. Robin Hastings and I had bought him for 960 guineas from the stud of Lord Brocket, run by Vincent O'Brien; he was by the unfashionable sire Zarathustra, which may go some way towards explaining why so good a horse slipped through their net. Crozier ran a dismal race in his second outing at Sandown before winning three in a row, and justifying our bold decision to run him at Royal Ascot by running a good second in the King Edward VII Stakes. He was our first runner at the Royal course, a meeting I have always loved: the showpiece of English racing, and run at the right time of year, in the middle of summer. We were the more satisfied with Crozier's performance as the horse that beat him was Pretendre, a slightly unlucky second in that year's Derby, when Paul Cook, newly appointed stable jockey to Jack Jarvis, let the cunning old-timer Scobie Breasley up on his inside. (Years afterwards, May, Scobie's wife, made the famous remark at Newmarket that suggested less than total adherence to the rule forbidding jockeys to bet. After the Middle Park Stakes had been won by a 100–1 youngster, Hittite Glory, trained by Scobie, Jim Phillips, Senior Steward at the time, asked May at the post-race celebrations: 'I do hope your husband had a bet?', whereupon she replied 'Oh no, Scobie has not had a bet since he gave up riding'!)

At the end of the 1966 season we had had thirty-seven winners, thirty-nine seconds and thirty-four thirds – a satis-factory outcome, as in an average year a trainer should have roughly the same amount of winners as placed horses. In a really good year the short heads usually go your way, and the winners outnumber the placed horses by a large margin.

In 1967 we had our first winner in France, at Le Tremblay, a good racecourse near Paris, sadly now a building site. This was Apex II, a great big angular colt who had won nice two-year-old races at the back end of the previous season at Newmarket and Ascot. I had found this conditions race for him as it would have been asking a lot of him even to run well at Royal Ascot, which was taking place at the same time. I rang his owners, Lord Galway (Simon) who had bred him, and his wife Tessa, and asked if they were going to Ascot on the Wednesday; when I told them we had Apex in at Le Tremblay there was a sudden change of plan, and long-lasting celebrations afterwards. Also this year Winter's Quota, a precocious two-year-old, won his fifth race of the season, again at Le Tremblay; and Be Hopeful and Lester Piggott gave us our first winner at Deauville. Back at home Crozier, ridden by that marvellously fit little jockey Frankie Durr, won the Doncaster Cup, beating Hermes, winner of the Dante and Great Voltigeur Stakes the previous year. All in all, the year had seen us take another step up, with forty-five winners – and the McCalmont horses arriving.

Major Dermot McCalmont was a famous Irish owner–breeder, whose star horse before the First World War had been The Tetrarch, a brilliant unbeaten two-year-old – and surprising sire: although he won seven races of no more than six furlongs, he bred three St Leger winners. Dermot McCalmont had his horses in training with Geoffrey Brooke, who was retiring, and in the spring of 1967 he rang and asked us to have lunch with him after the Guineas meeting at the Cavalry Club in Piccadilly. When we arrived, all he said was, 'Unless you are as thick as a brick wall, you must know why you are here.' We then went over to the Irish Derby to see the bloodstock at his lovely

Ballylynch stud. It was arranged that the horses would be split between Doug Smith, who had been his jockey, and us, and that they would come over in the autumn.

Gradually we built more boxes on the site of an old yard which had been pulled down just after the war, when the place was not very full. We first built twelve traditional boxes on the old foundations, and then, as numbers were expanding ever faster, decided on building a barn-like structure with a high roof and excellent ventilation, to make the whole operation more viable. We built more storage for hay and straw, but kept the feedhouses in the same place in the middle of the complex, so that feeding was all done from one place, saving a lot of time and motion. At this time we were using Australian oats, with a high protein content. They looked a little insignificant, but had a very thin husk, so that when they were put through the crusher and lightly bruised they came out very well. Sadly, thanks to our wonderful Common Market regulations, which the British seem to interpret far more strictly than any other member state, a surcharge was brought in not long after this on produce from non-Common Market nations, which made the oats a prohibitive price.

But our boxes were full, and more and more good-class horses were coming our way. We were happily settled at Seven Barrows.

6

HUMBLE DUTY

It was in the autumn of 1964 that my old friend Charles Smith-Bingham asked me if I would take a two-year-old filly called Smasher belonging to his mother. Jean, Lady Ashcombe, was a fine-looking woman with wonderful taste, always beautifully dressed; she had also had several husbands and trainers – including that charming man and brilliant trainer, especially of jumpers, George Beeby, who had sent out her Brendan's Cottage to win the 1938 Cheltenham Gold Cup – and we were a bit frightened of her at first.

Smasher had been bought as a yearling, as she was well bred, to make a broodmare, and had been in training with that great character Atty Corbett at Newmarket. Atty quite rightly said quickly that she was no good; Jean took offence, and Charles asked if I could train her. A striking filly, almost black, she was long in the back and the most wonderful mover; but, like so many, she could not quicken one iota, and although placed several times, over every distance, failed to win. All the same, she did a wonderful job for us, because I let her lead Mabel in her work. Mabel was the first top-class filly that I had trained, and was third in her first start as a three-year-old, in the 1965 One Thousand Guineas.

One does not need a top-class lead horse, contrary to what most self-styled experts think. In fact, too good a lead horse can disappoint and sour a good horse. This is what happened to Premonition, trained by Captain Cecil Boyd-Rochfort. He had won the St Leger as a three-year-old, and as he looked a top-class

four-year-old in the making, it was decided to find him a lead
horse. The horse chosen was Osborne, a useful mile-and-a-half
handicapper, who had won at Ascot in a faster time than
Supreme Court, the winner of the King George VI and Queen
Elizabeth Stakes, on the same day.

Their first run together was in the Yorkshire Cup; Osborne,
ridden by Royce Burrows, a very good work rider in the stable
at home, led, and eventually finished fifth to Premonition.
Burrows said to the lads in the yard that he would have won if
he had been off – that is, if he had really tried. They laughed at
him, but he was eventually proved right. The two met again at
the end of May, in the Paradise Stakes at Hurst Park. Again
Burrows made the running on Osborne, and entering the last
furlong his horse was still on the bridle, while Premonition was
being driven for all he was worth by Harry Carr. Burrows
looked round for his stable companion, saw that he was gaining
very slowly and dropped his hands, and eventually Premonition gained the upper hand to win narrowly. There were howls
of protest from the press and public, and Boyd-Rochfort was
fined £200 by the stewards for failing to give Burrows explicit
orders. He was a wonderful trainer, but rather more cunning
and devious than he made out.

The failure of Smasher did not put Jean off, but in fact whetted
her appetite, and she asked Charles and me to see if we could
find her a nice filly at the October sales at Newmarket in 1968. I
always liked the October sales; they always produced the
highest percentage of useful horses, and I believe have produced
far more high-class winners than any of the other sales.
Although not so fashionable as the sale now known as the
Highflyer, they are much more of a working man's marketplace,
and certainly the best place to find value for money.

I had just arrived at the sales complex and crossed off the
withdrawn lots when I met Ray Barnes under the archway

1. My grandfather, Colonel James Walwyn, in 1908 on Paddy, bought off the Bristol boat for £35 in 1907 and sold in 1910 for £60

2. My father, Major Taffy Walwyn, jumping the stone wall at Punchestown in 1912

3. My father in the paddock talking to Edward, Prince of Wales, before winning the Grand Military at Sandown in 1923 on White Surrey. The Prince of Wales bought Rifle Grenade from my father – the first horse on which he won a point-to-point

4. Aged seven, on my donkey Jessica with my sister Jinnie; taken at our home in Gloucestershire

5. My wedding day, 5 January 1960, at Shipbourne Church in Kent, with my best man, the late Tim Forster, who later became a renowned trainer of jumpers, including three Grand National winners

6. Coming out of the church with my wife Bonk – whose childhood nickname did not have the connotations it does today!

7. Bonk aged eighteen with her brother, Nick Gaselee (who later trained Party Politics to win the Grand National), at their home near Plaxtol, just about to go off hunting

8. Bob Ruttle: head man at Geoffrey Brooke's stable, where both Tim Forster and I were assistant trainers. He was an early mentor

Facing page:

9. Taxynthus, given to me by Tim Forster (ridden by Tony Goswell), winning at Doncaster in 1962; during my early career as a trainer I enjoyed training jumpers, but my main business has always been training flat-race winners

10. At home with Bonk and the dogs at Seven Barrows

11. Bonk riding out Royal Pardon on the Faringdon road gallops in 1963

12. Hunting with the Vale of the White Horse; on the left is our old friend Mrs Nancy Barker, master of hounds. My wife is on Bowgeno who had been fourth in the Grand National

13. Lester Piggott on Be Hopeful, coming in after winning at Deauville, August 1967; the wonderful Be Hopeful was my first 'flagship' horse, winning no fewer than twenty-seven races for us

14. Bonk on Frontier Goddess (who later won the Yorkshire Oaks) in the paddock at Seven Barrows in 1969

15. Lucyrowe wins the Coronation Stakes at Royal Ascot in 1969 by an official twelve lengths (the maximum number the board could put up!)

leading to Somerville Paddocks. He was a friend of ours who had introduced me to Peter Goulandris, then just getting into the bloodstock business in a big way, and managed for him. Peter went on to own Shoemaker, our first Derby runner, and second to Blakeney, in 1970. Ray said, 'I've just seen the most glorious filly, in the left row of boxes just in front of us.' We looked her up in the catalogue and saw that she had been bred by the Tuthills and Whiteheads at their famous Owenstown stud in Ireland; she was by Sovereign Path, a very good, tough miler, out of Flattering. I got her led out, and she had the look of eagles. She was a grey and very athletic, and had something about her that just asked you to go and look again.

I was once asked to write an article on the conformation of horses by Dorian Williams, famous master of hounds, judge of horses, schoolmaster and show-jumping commentator. I thought about it for some time, puzzling over how to put into words what one looks for. First of all, think about judging a good-looking girl. We all have our different ideas, but good legs must be the priority. It's the same with a yearling; if a horse is correctly made, with a leg at each corner, like a table, and not too crooked, it has every chance of being an athlete and therefore more likely to stay sound. After that, look at a horse with a good head. George Lambton, who bought the old Aga Khan his foundation stock for his fantastic stud, always said, 'If a horse has a good head and outlook, forgive him again and again, because he will come good in the end.' I have always found that, like most of what he said, this was wonderful advice, and usually correct.

The yearling sales are a fascinating aspect of the racing scene in the autumn. The main sales are held in the best sale ring in the world, Tattersalls at Newmarket. Many buyers go round the studs beforehand and look up the horses in the sale catalogue at home, before they come up to the sales. Before the sale you can try to pick out those that catch the eye, on pedigree, but it is not until you get to the sales that you start to separate the best from the rest. So many animals that look good on paper are disappointing when seen in the flesh: either light of bone, or with crooked legs, and therefore difficult to train.

One marvellous thing about the Newmarket sales is that the majority of your opponents are in sight. The buyers can look and see who else might be bidding, knowing that many of them may have more money to spend (I have often been the underbidder). Some will disguise their intentions, and there will often be a vendor's reserve on the yearling, so that only when the auctioneer announces, some way into the bidding, that the animal is for sale do you know that the horse is really on the market.

We felt, having looked at some other fillies, that this grey was the star of the show. We eventually bought her for 17,000 guineas, a large sum in those days; indeed, she was top price of the day. Someone said to Jean, 'I hear you've just bought a filly bred to get three furlongs,' and a vet in the Lambourn practice, luckily not our own, said, 'If I were you I'd get her eyes checked, as I think she is going blind.' Panic! But all was well; on her return we got her checked over, and there was nothing wrong with her eyes at all.

We broke her in our usual way. We have never used cavessons, great big breaking bridles far too heavy for yearlings, and instead use a headcollar under the normal breaking-in bridle, with a canvas lungeing rein strapped round the front to begin with. We started the process with lungeing both ways, and then putting the breaking roller on. This has a padded girth strap, and a breast-girth, so that the horse cannot buck its way through the equipment and get it off. Some horses are very quiet, and take to it readily, but others, when the girth is squeezed up tight, roar like bulls and squeal with anger. This exercise must be done in an enclosed area, boarded paddock or ring, otherwise the horse can get away from the handlers. It always needs at least three people to do this operation properly, otherwise there could be an accident. I am also a great believer in long-reining, where the yearling men put the youngsters into long reins and drive them from the ground. This is hard work, but means that the horse has a bridle with reins behind him from an early age, and this helps to form the mouth, without a rider to heave on the reins. Once the yearlings had been backed and ridden away, we always gave them lots of time, getting a good lead horse to take them walking and trotting in figures of eight over the place to get them balanced before we started cantering at all. It is most important to use a sensible lead horse who will behave properly and not whip round; horses are very imitative animals, and if the lead horse misbehaves or is a bad mover, it will inevitably affect the youngster. When we got Humble Duty ridden away after about one month, she seemed very pre-cocious, having taken to the whole process quickly and easily.

We had had a great start to the season. Our Derby hopeful, Shoemaker, had won the Classic Trial at Sandown and the Player Wills Classic Trial in Ireland and looked to have a reasonable chance in the Derby. When we started working the two-year-olds, we picked out Humble Duty together with a sweet filly by Pall Mall called Rose Arbour, and the two of them soon showed promise. Rose Arbour belonged to a wonderful woman called Pam Mackinnon, whom I remembered from her days as joint master of the Heythrop hounds when I was a boy; she wore a green hunt coat, the same colour as the Heythrop hunt staff, and sailed along at the head of the field, looking very elegant, and was nicknamed, quite rightly, 'the green goddess'.

We took Pam to Deauville one day in August 1970 to see Rose Arbour run, flying from Blackbushe in Hampshire in a remarkable old aeroplane called a Rapide. There were fourteen of us, and we had a stewardess; I believe the flight cost £5 return each. The filly finished fourth, and we had a delicious alcoholic lunch. On the return journey, poor Pam grazed her leg badly on the rather steep steps of the plane, and by the time we got back to Seven Barrows the wound looked quite nasty. Bonk took her upstairs, and shortly afterwards shouted down to me, 'Darling, will you get some disinfectant, please?' Thinking that one of the dogs had left a mess (which happens quite frequently), I duly fetched a bucket and some Jeyes Fluid and took them up – to be greeted by howls of laughter. What Bonk really wanted, of course, was some Dettol for Pam's injury.

We decided to run Humble Duty in the five-furlong maiden fillies' race at Sandown on 26 May. There were fourteen runners and she was drawn towards the far rail, a good draw. She was always right up there, and ran on well to win by a length. Duncan Keith, a dour and down-to-earth Scotsman, got off her and said 'top class but only half fit' as she had blown up a bit in the last furlong. She progressed well after that, and we aimed her at the Queen Mary Stakes at Royal Ascot, the first big two-year-old fillies' race of the year. The ground was very firm and, although having every chance, she could finish only third to Farfalla. However, she came back with sore shins, and so with hindsight we were very pleased with her performance, as there had been a clear reason for her defeat. We still thought her a high-class filly, and had to get her right. We treated the shins with a mild tar blister; this has the effect of bringing up a scurf on the legs, which takes a few weeks to settle down, and we gave her all the time she needed to recover.

Sore shins is the most baffling complaint that a horse can have. The symptoms become apparent when you run your hand down the front of the forelegs: the horse is quite sore on one or both legs, below the knee. No one knows exactly why some horses are vulnerable in this way; some say immaturity, but Tim Forster's old horse Baulking Green, a champion hunter chaser, got them so badly each time he ran that he lay down in his box for several days afterwards from the pain, even aged fourteen. Treatments vary. Some people leave the legs alone; the Americans use a technique called freeze-firing, which leaves marks that show up for the rest of the animal's life. I believe that blistering is the right solution.

We brought Humble Duty back into strong work slowly. She had a hard race on her comeback in the Lowther Stakes at York, and though she got up in the last furlong to beat Pisces and Mange Tout she blew hard after the race, and was probably a bit rusty after her lay-off. In her last run of the season, the fillies' championship, the Cheveley Park Stakes at Newmarket, she turned the race into a procession, leading all the way and winning by two and a half lengths from her old rival Farfalla. After that she really looked the part of a genuine Classic winner, but could have no pretensions to getting more than a mile.

That autumn Jean Ashcombe gave a party to celebrate Humble Duty being champion two-year-old filly. Jim Cramsie, our great friend and songwriter, made up a calypso, which was sung with great gusto. Part of it went as follows:

. . . and Dickon Lumley – now Lord Scarborough
Said it's very odd what fools some people are
For I hear that someone lashed out in style
For something which will only get a quarter of a mile
To Seven Barrows the grey filly soon found her way
The responsibility of Pete and Ray
And if any of you think this is the slightest bit risky
You've simply just not reckoned with Bonk and Frisky.
Now just to show she had got what it takes
Humble Duty firstly won the Anne Boleyn Stakes
But in the Queen Mary she was only third

Meeting Farfalla, who went like a bird.
But Messrs Smith & Van Clief, they had had their fun
For the next time together these two horses run
Humble Duty took the honours, in the Cheveley Park
Having previously won the Lowther at Yark.
Congratulations, Jean, are now due, I feel,
Not forgetting Duncan Keith, who held the steering wheel
And one can only wait for nineteen seventy
Wouldn't it be nice to win the 1000g?

Before the Classics, though, we had to get through a horrid wet winter. It was bitterly cold, and most fillies hate cold weather, however many rugs they have on; if it is wet as well, very few animals thrive. We had infra-red lights in Humble Duty's box, night and day, to try to bring her forward. We had also been very fortunate in that Louis Freedman, owner of Lucyrowe, our top-class filly of 1969, had very generously offered in the summer to help us build an oblong covered ride in the field behind the stable yard. It was a furlong round, with wooden boards sloping outwards to help riders avoid hitting their feet on the sides. The actual width of the ride was 15 feet, and a paddock was left in the middle for grazing. These rides don't make a single horse go faster, but they do help in maintaining exercise, especially in bad weather; now we were able to keep cantering Humble Duty, and selected other horses, all the time, as the grass gallops were very heavy, and young animals get pulled about in that going.

Humble Duty did not thrive at all in the spring, and was well off her food. She was working well, though, on the bridle, and Jean and I decided to give her a race before the One Thousand Guineas, in the Fred Darling Stakes at Newbury two weeks ahead of the Classic. She looked awful, but I felt a race might just help to bring her on, especially if it wasn't a hard one.

Duncan Keith had started the season off with our first winner at Kempton, Darlington, but then had a severe recurrence of his weight problems. In previous seasons, after suffering severe fractures of the leg, he had been sent to the RAF rehabilitation hospital at Roehampton to recover his strength. However, the doctors here got him doing a lot of swimming, and of course that put on muscle and therefore weight which was very hard to get off. Now he rang me out of the blue in early April and said, 'I can't go on, the weight is killing me.' He was a good, dependable jockey, and I knew I had to give him a chance; so I sent him to Dr Darragh in Ireland, an expert on weight loss for athletes. In the meantime I had to find alternative riders and assuage the owners' concerns; fortunately, at this stage they were eating out of my hand, so that wasn't too much of a worry. My first priority was Humble Duty and the Guineas. I rang up Lester, the obvious Classic jockey. The conversation was brief and to the point.

'What do you ride in the Fred Darling and the Guineas?'

'Don't know.'

'Will you ride Humble Duty in the Fred Darling?'

'Yes.'

There were only three runners at Newbury, including Highest Hopes, who loved soft ground, and was fully fit; she had won the Ascot fillies' trial the week before in heavy going, ridden by Jimmy Lindley, a wonderful substitute for Joe Mercer, Dick Hern's stable jockey, who was at that point languishing in an Indian gaol as a result of being arrested on accusations of smuggling jewels while riding there for the winter. Lindley took the ride again for the Fred Darling, and the race was amazing, both jockeys coming into the last furlong with their fillies on the bridle. Neither let out an inch of rein; my orders to Lester had been, 'Get as close as you can but do not put her under pressure or hit her, as she will go backwards after the race if you do.' So many good fillies have been ruined in the spring of their three-year-old career by being given one hard gallop or race when they weren't up to it. I wasn't going to fall for that one! Eventually Highest Hopes' superior fitness just told, and she won by a length.

After the race I asked Lester in the unsaddling enclosure what he thought, but with all the press howling around, he just said, 'Ring me tonight.' I rang him and said, 'What do you think?' He said, 'I'll ride her in the Guineas, and she'll win!' Suddenly we felt we were climbing the mountain.

The day before the fillies' Classic, Lester had an easy win in the Two Thousand Guineas on Nijinsky. Afterwards I leant against the rail in the weighing room and asked him again what he thought. 'She'll win all right,' he said. Then he got to the heart of the matter: 'What's the owner like?' – in other words, would she be generous? I reassured him on that point, and he gave one of his hard-to-fathom smiles.

The next day is difficult to remember. Everything went well; Alec Head's filly Gleam made the running, but at the Bushes two furlongs out the motionless figure of Lester was suddenly seen to let go of the reins, and coming out of the Dip, Humble Duty quickly drew clear, to win going away by seven lengths, the easiest One Thousand Guineas victor in living memory – and our first Classic winner! It was unbelievable. Even though most of the Classics are now sponsored, the traditional names are still used and still carry the same force.

The occasion is immortalised in the famous picture of Humble Duty's very elegant owner leading her in, which appears in this book. Bonk said, 'That's a very lucky suit,' and Jean wore it every time the filly ran that summer. Afterwards she gave it to the Victoria and Albert Museum as an example of the way ladies dressed in those days, and it is still displayed there to this day.

From the Guineas onwards the filly really began to thrive,

eating and putting on weight. Her next outing was the Ebbisham Stakes at Epsom's Derby meeting, then a top-class fillies' race, though now sadly only an ordinary handicap. Again she was very impressive, skating home with the minimum of fuss, and in the process welcoming Duncan back to race-riding with an excellent win. Under Dr Darragh's treatment Duncan's weight had been controlled, and he had been so keen to get back in the saddle that he got fit again very quickly. Then came Royal Ascot, where she won the Coronation Stakes over a mile in a canter, beating John Dunlop's Black Satin by three-quarters of a length. Black Satin had previously won the Irish One Thousand Guineas easily, so this was a very good performance. Our filly had started at long odds on, and after the race Jean Ashcombe's brother-in-law, Jack Thursby, came up to me and said, 'Well done, but that wasn't a working man's price.' As Jack had never been known to do a single day's work in his life, we thought his comment was a bit superfluous.

Humble Duty was now at the height of her powers, and her next goal was the Sussex Stakes at Goodwood. She won nicely, though she was 11–8 on, and had a comfortable win. However, we were beginning to get hints that she would not go on for ever. The first signs of temperament were beginning to appear, no doubt inherited from her grandsire Grey Sovereign. She was still eating and looking fine, but was becoming reluctant at times to jump off in her gallops, so that I or someone else had to go down to the start of the gallop to lead her in. Some trainers would respond by putting blinkers on, but I have always felt this is an insult to a top-class horse, although I have often used them at home. In any event, she was very well, and good enough to beat the high-class four-year-old Gold Rod in the Wills Mile at Goodwood at the end of August. But everything she had done after the Guineas had been a bonus, and I had decided that her final race was to be the Queen Elizabeth II Stakes a month later at Ascot. She did not fire at all, and finished a well-beaten fourth to Welsh Pageant, who made all the running.

When fillies start getting obstreperous, they are really telling you that they have had enough; and when they start to lose their enthusiasm, they are telling you that it is time they went to stud. I believe that you can get too greedy with a good filly. A mare can have only something like ten foals in her stud career, whereas a top stallion at a stud like Coolmore will cover 150 mares or more in a season. So nothing you do with a filly should prejudice her chances of making a broodmare, and in most cases the top-class filly should go to stud at the end of her three-year-old career, unless possibly the owner is elderly, and has little chance of seeing her progeny run.

We had a friend called Abe Hewitt from America, whom I was always quizzing about the American way of racing. Why, I asked him, were so many American fillies hard raced, and yet went on to produce top-class horses, while so few top European racemares or fillies produced much of any consequence? I cited Petite Etoile, Dahlia, Pawnese and Humble Duty as examples – though Humble Duty did not have a long enough stud career to have a real chance. He replied that the American fillies hardly ever had to race against colts because there were so many races at all ages for fillies and mares, so they don't get squeezed dry. A case in point was Empery's dam Pamplona II, who won fourteen races from nineteen starts in Peru and Argentina, including the Peruvian Triple Crown, and still managed to produce Empery, trained in France by Maurice Zilber and ridden by Lester to win the Derby. Luckily our race planners have since remedied the situation by opening up many of our best races for fillies to include mares of four years old and over.

We retired Humble Duty to Charles Smith-Bingham's Attington Stud in Oxfordshire, but sadly she had no luck as a broodmare, producing only a leggy colt by Tudor Melody. I bought him cheaply for a group of owners, but he never thrived, and after he had been placed twice we sold him to South Africa. Humble Duty then died while foaling. It was a sad end; along with Lucyrowe and Frontier Goddess, she was one of the three best fillies I ever trained.

The other tragedy about Humble Duty was that her wonderful owner was later killed in a ghastly air crash on the way back from a holiday in Majorca, along with her sister Liz Thursby. It was an awful shock for us, as she had been so kind and thoughtful to everyone she dealt with. The only consolation was that we had been able to give her tremendous pleasure in the last few years of her life, and I think she was dreading the thought of growing old.

7

ROCK ROI AND LINDEN TREE

In the autumn of 1969 Gordon Richards retired from training at
Whitsbury. He was criticised for not hitting the heights with his
horses, but was in fact a skilful trainer, on top of his incredible
career as a jockey, winning the Middle Park Stakes with Pipe of
Peace and many other good races. If anything, he was a bit easy
on his horses; but they always looked wonderful, and very well
turned out.

Among the owners who had been with Gordon until he
retired were Colonel and Mrs Roger Hue-Williams; they now
asked me to train for them, and among the first batch to arrive at
Seven Barrows was a two-year-old by the French stayer Mourne
called Rock Roi. He was a fine big chestnut horse with a lovely
temperament, but we had no idea how good he was; all he had
won so far was what turned out to be a very ordinary newcomers' race at Goodwood in September over six furlongs,
which he took by two lengths. To get the measure of him, we ran
him first in the Union Jack Stakes, in those days an early Classic
trial at Aintree. He did everything wrong and could not cope
with the bends at all, but managed to finish third. We still
thought he had ability, and ran him in the Craven Stakes at the
first meeting at Newmarket. The course suited him much better,
but he was not really good enough over that stiff mile; again he
was third. After that we decided to step him up in distance and,
as he had a favourable rating, to put him in the Scottish and
Newcastle Breweries Handicap at Newcastle over a mile and a
quarter, with Lester Piggott on board.

The big danger was a colt from the Arundel stable of John Dunlop called Arthur. He had won his only race as a two-year-old, and had started the season off with an eyecatching third in the Stroud Green handicap at Newbury, where it appeared that Ron Hutchinson was having difficulty restraining him throughout the race before he finished very strongly. At Newcastle, while Rock Roi finished third once again, being given a lot to do, Arthur predictably won easily. I was at Kempton that day, and could not help noticing that every jockey who came into the paddock for races after that wore a beaming smile, as they had no doubt seen Arthur's run at Newbury, and put their punters on for the Newcastle race.

At that time the Arundel stable was regarded as a serious betting stable, and although Arthur's owner, Lady Rosebery, was reported as being surprised after the race, she was the only person who was. Not long after this Arthur Stephenson, that genius of a northern trainer, was had up for some misdemeanour with one of his horses at York. When asked for an explanation by the stewards, he is reported to have said: 'I think you have got the wrong Arthur.'

Lester got off Rock Roi and said to Tony Driscoll, my travelling head lad, 'He is a c**t of a horse,' which was unfair; in my view, the horse was just a bit one-paced and terribly laid back. Next time out, fitted with blinkers to make him concentrate, he ran a very good race at Newbury over a mile and a half, making the running, and finishing a highly creditable second, giving the winner 12lb. After that we ran him over the two miles of the Queen's Vase at Royal Ascot, again in blinkers, which seemed to be working; he looked to have every chance but did not stay as well as the horses that beat him, eventually finishing fourth. There was then a conditions race for him at Chester, a course I love as it does teach horses how to race. Duncan Keith could not do the weight, and so I booked Geoff Lewis for him. I put a pair of blinkers on him to sharpen him up, and he was always handy, hitting the front six furlongs out and winning easily in a record time over the unusual distance of nearly a mile and six furlongs.

It was time to increase the tempo, and we ran him in the mile-and-a-half Warren Stakes at Goodwood, on the first day, the Tuesday. Again he was handy throughout and strode away to win easily. I had left him in the much more prestigious Gordon Stakes on the Thursday over the same distance, and left him at Goodwood overnight, in case the Hue-Williamses wanted me to run him again. Geoff Lewis had won on him the last twice, because Duncan could not do the weight, and when we decided to let him take his chance on the Thursday, there was quite an argument before the Hue-Williamses got their way and had Geoff put up again. Once more Rock Roi answered his critics in fine style with a facile win.

After this we really had to let him show what he could do, and ran him in the Great Voltigeur Stakes at York. Reunited with Duncan, he ran an excellent race, finishing a close second to Meadowville in a slowly run four-horse race. Meadowville was a pretty good horse, who had won the Lingfield Derby Trial – beating an admittedly ordinary horse of ours called Long Till – before finishing fifth to Nijinsky in the Derby. Rock Roi had run a lovely race, quite rightly making the running until collared by the winner in the last furlong.

After that we were lucky to have a pacemaker for him in the shape of King of the Castle, sent over from his previous yard in France by the Hue-Williamses to help us train Rock Roi. We decided to run the pair of them in the St Leger at Doncaster, but everything went wrong. First of all, King of the Castle was not good enough to make the running; and such was the speed of the race that Rock Roi, who got away very slowly, was unable at any stage to get on terms, and finished fifth, beaten about ten lengths by Nijinsky.

Still, at the end of the season we felt that he had done us proud; he had suddenly started to get the message, and given that so many of the best horses of his generation were going to stud at the end of their three-year-old careers, his future as a four-year-old looked bright.

In 1971 we started him off in the mile-and-a-half John Porter Stakes at Newbury, where in a field of twelve he was taking on his old rival Meadowville, and High Line, trained by Derrick Candy. After making the running Rock Roi battled on well, being beaten by these two in the last furlong, by a short head and a neck. This showed that he had progressed the right way, and was probably a better four-year-old than he had been at three. We now felt that he was going to be a top-class stayer, and with that in mind ran him in the Paradise Stakes at Ascot early in May. He won by just three-quarters of a length, but although he had a hard race to beat Alto Volante, trained by our dear friend Freddie Maxwell, his performance was enhanced when Alto Volante went on to win the Yorkshire Cup, before sadly getting leg trouble.

Rock Roi himself was showing increasing signs of arthritis by now. He started pulling out in the morning very stiffly, and we suspected that he did not like firm going. We always let him walk out on his own round the back of the yard to warm up, as if he was in the covered ride he would hold the whole string up when we started trotting – an indispensable stage in exercise, in my view, to check that the horses are moving all right before we give them a canter. His legs had not the slightest hint of heat in them, always the first sign of leg trouble, and he was moving well in his races, so we kept him going. Next time out, in the Prix du Cadran at Longchamp (the equivalent of our Ascot Gold Cup), he ran an excellent race to finish second, albeit a long three lengths behind one of the leading French stayers, Ramsin. On his return from France, however, the arthritis got worse, and we were advised by our veterinary surgeon, Stuart McDiarmid, to put him on a course of equipalazone, also known as butazoladin. This new anti-inflammatory drug (not a painkiller) had already been tried with success on horses in the area.

The dosing instructions said that the drug should not be given less than seventy-two hours before a race; if it were given later, it might not clear the horse's system before the race and thus risked showing up in post-race dope sampling. We planned to run Rock Roi in the Ascot Gold Cup, where he would have a very good chance, as Ramsin was not even entered. Ray Laing discussed with me what dose to give and decided to give him 2 grams daily for three days, as opposed to the recommended dose of 20 grams over a week. His course of treatment ended on the Saturday evening, so that we felt that we were quite safe for the Gold Cup on the following Thursday.

Certainly Rock Roi was moving better as a result of the drug, and to help us even more the going came up heavy. In the race the colt was always travelling well, and, aided by his pacemaker, King of the Castle, and his jockey, that fine horseman and judge of pace George Duffield, drew clear to win easily by four lengths from Random Shot. We were delighted; it was a race which we had always wanted to win, even though its exceptionally long distance of two and a half miles means that victory is the kiss of death for a prospective stallion.

It was on my birthday, 1 July, that the Jockey Club inspector Bob Anderson came up to me at the races at Salisbury and asked if we could have a private word. It was very hot, and the stewards had announced that those in the members' enclosure could take off their coats and ties. I have never taken them off at the races since. The inspector told me that Rock Roi had tested positive with an illegal substance in the samples taken after the Gold Cup. As soon as he said this I suspected the butazoladin, and to everyone's surprise – the horses had run well that day and we had had a winner – I was not in very good form that evening; a pity, as we had June McCalmont staying over with us. When we got back to the yard I questioned Ray Laing as to when he had given the last dose of the drug, and he assured me it was on the Saturday, as we had agreed, leaving more than four days for the substance to get out of the system – well over the seventy-two hours stipulated in the dosing instructions.

I immediately rang the vets, the Hue-Williamses' manager Leslie Harrison, and the Hue-Williamses themselves. The next day I went straight to London and told them of the position. Somewhat to my surprise, they were wonderfully supportive and backed me all the way. Then I had to wait to hear the official news, which came out at the Newmarket July meeting, and set about getting all my evidence together to mount a defence at the inevitable inquiry. I surmised that because Rock Roi was such a laid-back horse, a dour stayer with slow reactions, he had retained the substance in his system longer than most horses would. I rang up Edward Cazalet, a junior QC who was a great friend of my wife, to consult him about legal representation, and he suggested I got in touch with a senior silk, James Miskin. He had no knowledge of racing at all, but like most skilful legal people was able to sum up the whole case brilliantly; armed with his advice, we decided to fight the case, knowing that we had strong evidence in our favour. The Hue-Williamses told us that they would pay for our defence, and appointed a lawyer, Leonard Sainer, whom I did not then know, to represent them.

The inquiry had originally been due to take place in July, but was postponed until 27 August, as we had managed to produce evidence from English and American vets to support our case that the amounts given to the horse and found in his system, and the time lag between the last dose and the race, ruled out even the slightest effect on the result of the race. In the mean time Rock Roi had come out of the Ascot race in fine trim, and I was determined to prove my point that the horse was definitely superior to Random Shot without the merest trace of butazoladin in him. So we decided, to the surprise of many people, to run our horse in the Goodwood Cup. King of the Castle did an even better job here than he had in the Gold Cup, leading into the straight, where Rock Roi took it up and galloped on strongly to win by four lengths, with Random Shot well beaten a further four lengths behind in third place.

This was a big relief, but obviously we still had a serious battle on our hands at the Jockey Club inquiry in Portman Square. James Miskin was at his brilliant best and tied up the Jockey Club forensic scientist, Professor Michael Moss, in knots. He asked what horses were used to determine the excretion rates for racehorses, and was told (as we had ascertained already) that they were using Shetland ponies, turned out in a field. James Miskin argued that the secretion rate of fully fit racehorses would be very different from that of Shetland ponies. Moreover, the American and English vets, including Dr Tom Tobin of the Department of Veterinary Medicine at the University of Kentucky, and Charles Frank, one of the partners in the Ridgeway Veterinary Group, presented their findings that the amount of the substance found in the horse was so minuscule – only 0.004 parts per hundred – as to be incapable of making one iota of difference to his performance. Indeed, the rules were subsequently changed so that the amount found would not now make the colt liable for disqualification.

The hearing went on for five hours until eventually the Jockey Club stewards decided that the rules gave them no choice but to disqualify Rock Roi, on the grounds that the substance found in the samples 'could have altered the racing performance of the horse at the time of running'. The stewards found me guilty under rule 52, and fined me the minimum of £100, but acquitted me from any corrupt practice, and exonerated Ray Laing.

Shortly after this the laboratory decided to investigate secretion rates in racehorses in full training and being fed properly, which vindicated our argument. Furthermore, on 5 November the Royal College of Veterinary Surgeons issued a statement warning veterinarians of the serious consequences that would follow for trainers if any residue of phenylbutazone or any other such anti-inflammatory drug were discovered in post-race testing. The statement went on to say that 'in the present state of scientific knowledge, precise elimination times cannot be given' for these drugs, but the following advice was given: 'If a veterinarian recommends the discontinuance of any such drug not less than *eight* days before racing (even though such a period may be longer than is necessary in many instances) he should be able to feel sure that he has catered for all but the most exceptional case.'

The Hue-Williamses were wonderful over the whole episode; although at times they could be difficult owners to please, when it came to the crunch they could not have been more supportive.

We were all set to run Rock Roi in the Doncaster Cup, but he rapped his near fore fetlock some weeks before, and the wound required six stitches. However, although he was short of work, and we could only get one decent gallop into him in the three weeks before the race, King of the Castle did his usual good job leading into the straight, whereupon Rock Roi took up the battle with first Russian Bank and then his old rival Meadowville; it was a hard-fought contest until he finally asserted himself in the last furlong to win by a length. When he came in to unsaddle there was blood pouring from the wound, which had reopened itself in the race. He had done us proud, and showed what a genuine horse he was after a slow beginning.

In the spring of 1972 King of the Castle went wrong, which was a bore, as he was such an accomplished lead horse. Luckily we had in the yard a dear old selling plater called Butomus, a ten-year-old entire by Botticello whom Duncan Keith had urged us to buy for apprentices and to win the odd race. It now occurred to me that it would be a good idea to lend him to the Hue-Williamses as lead horse for Rock Roi. Although only moderate, he would lead anything up the gallops, and as I have said before, you don't need a very good horse as lead horse; all you need is a willing horse that goes a good even pace. This is especially true up the Faringdon road gallop, the stiffest true gallop I have ever seen, where a selling plater can lead a champion as long as the riders know what they are doing and go a sensible pace. George Lambton, whose dear widow Cicely we used to know, always said, 'Curb your curiosity, especially with fillies.' So many people want to see their horses prove too much at home and wear them out on the gallops; I have never used a stop-watch, or a weight-cloth, and I do not ever think that I ever left a big race on the gallops through asking too much of a horse in its work at home.

Butomus did a marvellous job for us in the John Porter Stakes at Newbury, leading into the straight before Rock Roi put up one of his best performances over a mile and a half, winning decisively in the mud. He was then beaten for speed in the Jockey Club Stakes at Newmarket by the moody Knockroe, a good horse on his day. We were all set now for another crack at the Prix du Cadran at Longchamp, where this time we were taking on Parnell, the previous year's Irish St Leger winner, and easy victor in his two races for his new trainer Bernard van Cutsem. Luckily we had Butomus as our pacemaker again, ridden by the redoubtable Frank Morby, and we were hopeful – but not confident, as Parnell looked the most improved four-year-old in training.

Butomus did a sterling job over the two-and-a-half-mile trip, swinging along at a good pace in the lead and being ignored by all the other runners. I remember Frank telling us afterwards that the horse was enjoying himself so much in front, he still had his ears pricked entering the straight. Rock Roi, given a wonderful ride by Duncan, then took it up and, hard as Willie Carson tried to close the gap on Parnell, held on to win by a length. It was a very well-deserved win – and followed by a most amusing scene, when we went up above the weighing room to a bar with the Hue-Williamses and our jubilant crowd of friends and supporters, to find to our surprise an unoccupied table laden with glasses and champagne and decorations laid out in Parnell's colours. This had obviously been organised by Mimi van Cutsem to celebrate Parnell's win. There was no sign anywhere of the defeated team, and so we took over the whole table. Never count your chickens before they are hatched . . .

Now we were determined to avenge our defeat of the previous year in the Ascot Gold Cup. Our only concern was the ground, which was worryingly firm. The thoroughly reliable Butomus gave Rock Roi a lead, making the running for about a mile and three-quarters until Rock Roi took it up and went for home. However, inside the final furlong Erimo Hawk, ridden by young Pat Eddery, challenged and hit the front. Rock Roi fought back and regained the lead to win by a head, but leant left on to Erimo Hawk in the process. Inevitably there was an immediate stewards' inquiry, and inevitably we were disqualified – for the second year running, which must be a record. It was a bit shattering, because the Ascot Gold Cup is one of the finest old-fashioned races in the country – indeed, it has become even more popular lately, after several years in decline.

After that Daniel Wildenstein bought a three-quarter share of the horse and sent him to be trained by Albert Klimscha for the Arc de Triomphe. I was at Deauville that August and, knowing that Rock Roi was there, asked Albert if I could see him. When I got to his box I saw that his legs were covered in bandages, and I thought this a bit strange, as he had never worn a bandage in all his time with us, except for the time when he had struck into himself before the Doncaster Cup. The writing was on the wall, and sure enough, shortly after that he was returned to us, the Wildensteins saying that Klimscha could not train him on the firm ground in France. On arrival we found him with a severely bowed tendon, and I knew it would be impossible to get him sound again, and his racing days were over; he ended up, I believe, at stud in Australia.

Rock Roi may have been so laid back that it had taken him a long time to grasp what was required of him, but once he had got the message he had been a brave battler. We were sad to see him go.

Among the good two-year-olds we had in 1970 was June McCalmont's Linden Tree, a fine big home-bred colt by Crepello, out of one of her husband's good families. After two runs to gain experience, he galloped on strongly to win the Westley Maiden Stakes at the first autumn meeting in Newmarket. We then let him take his chance over a mile at Doncaster in the Observer Gold Cup, then becoming the big autumn race for staying two-year-olds. Linden Tree battled on well with Duncan Keith to win by a head; and suddenly we had another possible Classic contender on our hands.

In 1971 we ran him first in the Blue Riband Trial at Epsom, but it was too sharp for him and he finished only sixth. It was obvious from this that he was crying out for the full mile and a half, so we aimed him at the Chester Vase. This had been won in the past by Windsor Lad and Tulyar, and was a proper trial, with colts who might have been green beforehand really learning their job around the tight turns.

There were only five runners in the Vase that year, and Levanter, from Ryan Price's yard, was an odds-on favourite, having won the Craven Stakes comfortably. Linden Tree led, and held on to win by a short head from Frascati, ridden by Tony

Murray, with Levanter a well-beaten third. According to Duncan, Linden Tree was peeping and ducking at the starting gate tapes every time he went under them; I had already thought that he might need blinkers, but was reluctant to put them on too soon, as they might have their best effect at Epsom. After this we knew what to do: he would wear blinkers in the Derby.

At home we worked him up the bottom valley gallop with our dear old Butomus as lead horse, Ortis and Rock Roi. This was quite a test; I insisted they all work on the bridle, and the latter two were older horses who both won at Ascot a fortnight later. Linden Tree held his own, and we were thrilled with him. I remember standing outside the house after returning from work and discussing the colt's prospects with Duncan and Paddy Newson; both excellent work riders and judges, they said it would take a very good horse to beat ours in the Derby. What a prophetic statement that turned out to be. Obviously Mill Reef, second in the Guineas, would be a big danger; but we felt Linden Tree had a good each-way chance.

At the Derby Club dinner ten days before the big race I sat at a table opposite Tony Murray, Frascati's jockey. He said to me, 'I'll beat you in the Derby.' Knowing what he did not know, about the blinkers that Linden Tree would wear, I replied: 'Let's save each other a suit,' and he agreed. This was quite a fashion at the time between trainers and jockeys: the idea was that whoever beat the other got a suit from the loser.

Everything went well in the lead-up to the Derby. On the day there was an enormous queue of traffic to get up from Epsom town; a lot of the coaches, laden with food and drink as well as people, were boiling over, and the passengers were getting redder and redder in the face. We saw Ian Balding, Mill Reef's trainer, running past our car, no doubt to get to an important trainers' lunch.

Our worry was who was going to make the running. We did

not want to; but if in doubt Duncan would have to take the initiative. True enough, after a furlong or so Duncan took it up, and went away to make a hot pace. All seemed to be going nicely; then, well into the straight, Geoff Lewis appeared on Mill Reef and went on smoothly to win by two lengths. But were we not proud of our horse! The others were spreadeagled, and Linden Tree had run the race of his life.

I eventually got my suit from Tony Murray, but it took a lot of persuasion . . .

After this we had to go for the Irish Derby three weeks later. Everything went like clockwork in the preparations. We stayed with Andrew and Jane Levins Moore, two of the most enchanting people in Ireland, at their glorious house Yeomanstown, close to The Curragh. When I arrived Jane gave me a big kiss and said, 'Welcome! This is a very lucky house to stay in before the Irish Derby. Fulke Johnson Houghton has stayed here twice, and each time Ribocco and Ribero won.' I said, 'I hate that sort of remark: never count your chickens before they are hatched!' But I loved both the Moores dearly, and Jane was one of the cleverest breeders of racehorses that I have ever met.

Linden Tree was a saucy and rather volatile colt, and we told Tony Driscoll to escort him down across the Curragh to the start to make sure he behaved himself. Once he was safely there, we thought our worries were over. Drawn one (on the outside in Ireland), he went into the stalls early – but just before the last horse was loaded a handler, who had seen his tail hanging over the back of the stall, rushed forward to push it in before Tony could stop him: a completely unnecessary, and in this case foolish gesture. It would be a brave man who would touch Linden Tree's tail in the open. As the stalls opened, Linden Tree was feeling the hand on his tail, and gave an enormous jump and kick as he flew out; then, seeing broad daylight on his left, as there was a large gap between him and the outside rail, he whipped round, getting left a hundred yards. The episode said little for the handler – and not much more for the commentator, who insisted for a long time that Linden Tree was up with the leaders, when in fact he was completely out of the race. Irish Ball, well held by Linden Tree at Epsom, won comfortably.

I felt that June McCalmont must have felt somewhat the same as the Queen Mother after the disaster to Devon Loch in the 1956 Grand National. However, neither lady uttered the merest bleat of complaint, as gracious in defeat as in victory. It is so hard to win Classic races; little did we think that a few years later we would win two Irish Derbies in a row.

Shortly after this Linden Tree sustained a tendon injury, as had his full brother Vervain. This was probably the result of breeding from unsound stallions: both Pinza and Crepello suffered in the end from leg trouble. Linden Tree was bought privately, and went to stand at the Haras de la Louvière stud in Normandy. He bred some winners, but sadly died from lymphangitis while still fairly young. He left his owner a marvellous legacy, however, for his prize money and the proceeds from his sale enabled June McCalmont to buy and build her wonderful house and stud at Martinstown.

8

JOCKEYS

I am lucky enough to have seen a wonderful variety of jockeys through the stages of my training career. The first great jockey who crossed my path (though he was no longer riding by the time I started training) was Sir Gordon Richards, known as 'Moppy' in his earlier days on account of his mop of black hair. I hardly saw him in action, but first noticed him in 1954, the year he retired, down at the start of the One Thousand Guineas, having cycled down to watch the horses set off. In those days there were only a handful of people down at the start, and Gordon was sitting on the eventual winner Festoon, from Noel Cannon's historic stables at Druid's Lodge, with a lovely long, loose rein, and seemingly without a care in the world. I remember Joe Mercer, then an apprentice, seeming to be in a bit of a bate about something, and Gordon saying very quietly, 'Calm down, Joey, everything will be all right.' I remember how impressed I was by his confidence and tranquillity.

Gordon rode for thirty seasons, and was champion jockey for twenty-six of them. Of the other four, in one he was beaten by just one winner, in another he dead-heated for the title, and in a third he had to give up riding with a severe dose of tuberculosis. He was a loose-rein rider and would galvanise a horse in the last few strides to throw it home. Trainers he rode for said that his relaxed air got horses very happy and on good terms with themselves. At one time he had five retainers and played each trainer and owner off against the others , saying that he would win on their horse next week if not this week – and he usually did. I got to know him well in Lambourn, as he was great friends with a farming couple Dick and Ciss Radbourne, and many were the splendid shooting parties we had, with Gordon a fund of entertaining stories over the White Ladies at lunchtime. He was short, dark and very thick-set and strong, but I don't believe he wasted much; in fact aged fifty he could still do 8st 2lb. One year he made the main speech at the annual Derby Club dinner, which is still held at the Savoy Hotel, and entertained everyone standing on a chair. At his memorial service at St Margaret's, Westminster, everyone was in tears as the bells rang when we came out of the church.

Lester Piggott, of course, was a phenomenon. He loved being thought of as very mean, but he had a heart of gold, although until one got used to him one needed an interpreter to understand what he was saying, as he mumbled so much. His work riding was designed to suit himself, and all he wanted to know was the ability of every horse in the gallop. He was inclined to muck gallops up with this trait, pacing them to give himself the best chance of assessing the horses rather than according to the trainer's instructions, but his judgement was seldom at fault. Exceptionally tall for a flat race jockey, he kept his weight down by iron discipline, having only a cup of coffee for breakfast, and no lunch before his supper of a very thin slice of fish or beef.

Lester came into my life in 1957 while I was working with my cousin Helen Johnson Houghton. He and Helen were great friends, and she always asked him to ride for her whenever possible. We had a sharp two-year-old filly called Cameo, and Helen decided to try her with a mixed bunch of about six horses on the straight five-furlong gallop of the Pennings at Blewbury. Helen herself being short-sighted, she had stationed John Goldsmith, an excellent trainer, especially of jumpers, at the top of the gallop to read the work for her. I was on an old sprinter called Courville, and was then about 9st 7lb, far heavier than the others. When we got to the bottom of the gallop, the markers, which were positioned to stop the horses going all over the place, were very close together because of the wet weather, and there was only room for two horses. Lester said, 'Come on, let's go,' so he and I jumped off in front as hard as we could leg it. It was only a furlong or so before my horse dropped out to finish tailed off, but John turned to Helen, and said 'The first two are off all right!' Helen went mad and gave all of us the most fearful bollocking, as we were all supposed to start abreast.

It was when I was with Helen that we had Eph Smith riding for us one day at Windsor. He was very outspoken, but a very sound, strong jockey. He was also as deaf as a churn, and used to ride with a hearing aid built into the side of his crash helmet. The animal, although well fancied, finished unplaced, and as Eph was throwing the reins over the horse's head before dismounting (a very unattractive and potentially dangerous habit), he addressed remarks to us such as 'She's a bastard, she's a cow!' The old lad who looked after her had obviously lost all his money on the race, and I will never forget him looking up at Eph and saying, 'Get off it, you battery driven bastard!'

Lester was an extraordinary jockey and a law unto himself. You could never give him orders – he wouldn't obey them – but he was a brilliant judge of pace, and would get off after a race and tell you how all the other horses had run, even though he had probably led all the way and hadn't seen them in the race from beginning to end! He could have ridden round Epsom, probably the most difficult course in the world, blindfolded. Just before he retired for the last time in 1994 I had a runner at Baden-Baden in a mile-and-a-quarter Listed race, and was desperate for a jockey. Suddenly I realised that Lester was out there; so I tracked him down at the Brenner Park Hotel, rang him up and asked if he could ride, and when he said yes, I gave him some instructions, to the effect that the horse had a bit of speed and needed holding up to come with a late run. I couldn't go myself to watch the race, but apparently he took it into his head to make all the running, and won very easily.

When I started training I considered the finest stylist among flat race jockeys to be Joe Mercer – and it's an opinion I haven't revised since. His brother Manny was a superb rider as well. I remember vividly going into the old weighing room at Ascot with the colours bag, on 26 September 1959, the day our engagement was in the papers; Manny looked up from where he was sitting on his bench, with that beaming smile of his, and said: 'Well done! I wish you every happiness.' Those were the last words he spoke to me. It was a miserable wet day and I was leaning over the rail in the trainers' stand watching the horses going down for the first race when, all of a sudden, we saw Manny's mount Priddy Fair cantering back loose towards the stand. The jockey's body was lying motionless under the rail. It transpired that the filly had whipped round and dislodged him; in falling he had hit his head on the upright post, which was not in those days plastic as they are today, and was killed instantly. I recall the ambulance coming slowly back to the weighing room, bringing with it Joe Mercer, who was very close to his brother, in tears. Racing was abandoned for the rest of the day. Manny was a dashing rider with great style and flair, and surely destined to be champion.

In those days jockeys' crash helmets were only a bit of cloth or cork under the silk, but after several accidents like this the stewards tightened the rules; today the jockeys weigh out without their helmets on their heads, so that there is no incentive to skimp on safety to make the weight.

Joe started riding work for us in 1961, early on in our training days, when he wasn't riding out at West Ilsley for Jack Colling, for whom he had won the Oaks on Ambiguity in his first year with the yard, when still a nineteen-year-old apprentice. Jack had been a top-class flat jockey himself, but was very tall and had to give up because of weight problems; having turned to training he quickly rose to the top rank, although Ambiguity remained his only Classic winner. Joe, who had the best rhythm in a finish I have ever seen, was also a marvellous judge of the form book and a great help in placing horses (and is no doubt now using these skills to the full for Sheikh Maktoum Al Maktoum, to whose manager Michael Goodbody I recommended him). We had a lot of success with him, but with our string steadily increasing and with our move to Seven Barrows, we were thinking of retaining a first jockey. Obviously Joe Mercer wouldn't leave Dick Hern, who had so successfully taken over from Jack Colling, even though they had had a couple of ordinary seasons suffering from what we would now call the virus, so we knew we would have to look elsewhere.

Duncan Keith had always impressed me as being a thoroughly dependable and decent jockey. He had been born in Glasgow in 1939, and had served his apprenticeship with Ted Smyth at Epsom. He had caused one of the biggest shocks of the 1961 season, when he rode High Hat, trained by Walter Nightingall for Sir Winston Churchill, to beat that great filly Petite Etoile in the Aly Khan Memorial Gold Cup at Kempton. Other notable races he won for the Nightingall stable included the Ascot Stakes on Angazi the same year, the Coronation Cup on I Say (1966), the City and Surburban on Hotroy (1967) and the Victoria Cup on Princelone (1967). On Walter's retirement he became available; and, as I inherited Lucyrowe and others of Louis Freedman's burgeoning string from the Epsom yard, it seemed very appropriate that I should take on Duncan too. He was a dour individual, but very likeable, and we got on well. He had the habit with Walter of making the running, and this was very successful, but it took us ages to find out the reason behind the tactics. Walter, it seemed, had been very suspicious, and felt, quite unfairly, that if his jockey was behind in a race, he wasn't trying. Still, it was comforting to know that if we did need a jockey to make the running, Duncan was more than capable, as he was an excellent judge of pace. Sadly, he eventually succumbed to weight problems exacerbated by bad advice on regaining fitness after injuries to his legs.

Keeping weight down while maintaining the required level of athletic fitness is of course a constant dilemma for jockeys, and various famous riders have had their own ways of tackling it. I remember 'Frenchie' Nicholson telling me that when he lived in Epsom, just after the war, he found the best way of getting himself fit to ride before the start of the jumping season was to walk everywhere in several pairs of old trousers, with bicycle clips round the bottoms of the legs, several sweaters, and a balaclava and gloves. I dread to think what his bathroom looked or smelt like when he peeled off the several layers. By doing this, he said, you got fit without putting weight on, which you would do by running or more strenuous exercise. It is a fact that muscle weighs more than fat. For example, a fit three-year-old racehorse weighs no more than it does at two, because the fat which is on the youngster turns into muscle as it gets older and works harder; although a horse looks lighter as it gets fitter, the appearance is deceptive. I discovered this when I started weighing horses. I thought at first that it was unnecessary, but in reality one could often be deceived going around stables, judging by appearance alone, into thinking that the horse had done well or badly recently when the reverse was the case.

One jockey I fell out with was Edward Hide. He had a dear old father and a charming brother, Tony, and used to ride a lot of winners for me in the north. In April 1969 we won the John Porter Stakes at Newbury with Crozier after a stewards' inquiry. Our horse had finished second to Fortissimo, beaten a short head, but a furlong out Fortissimo, ridden by Hide, had wandered off the rail and bumped Crozier. There was apparently a row in the jockeys' room, and Hide had called Duncan a c**t for objecting, but rightly or wrongly, Crozier got the race.

Less than a fortnight after this, we had Lucyrowe running in the One Thousand Guineas. She had thrived since coming from Walter Nightingall the previous autumn, when she had just been beaten by Mige in the Cheveley Park Stakes. I remember that when she came to us she was quite unable to trot: when we were doing our long trotting on the roads after Christmas she used to canter at the back of the string all the way to the top of Blowing Stone Hill, and it took her a long time to settle into the routine. I don't suppose she had ever trotted at Epsom. She was inclined to be a bit free and flighty, but she was a lovely filly of great quality. She had been bought for Louis Freedman by Carey Foster, the veterinary surgeon who had run Sir Winston's stud near Lingfield Park; he was a very good judge, and had also bought another high-class filly in Seventh Bride, who became the dam of Polygamy.

On her first outing for us, Lucyrowe had won the Masaka Stakes at Kempton in a canter, in spite of suddenly coming out with a bad dose of ringworm. This disease is a nuisance, as it pulls horses down and is very painful, as well as being highly contagious. I found the best cure was to wipe a mixture of train oil – really thick sump oil – and flowers of sulphur on the affected places. This took a little time but made the hair grow back at the same time as soothing the symptoms. Fortunately, in Lucyrowe's case the spots cleared up quickly, and we thought after her performance at Kempton that she must have a great chance to win us our first Classic.

Come the day at Newmarket, it was difficult to see what was going on in the early stages, but it appeared to be a very rough race, and Lucyrowe could finish no better than sixth. I came down from the stand very puzzled, as this was certainly not her form. When Duncan got off he was exploding with rage. He had tried to get Lucyrowe settled behind the leaders, but she was running a bit freely, and Duncan told me that Edward Hide had deliberately come across from his draw and intimidated our filly into pulling even harder, so that she ran herself out. We drove home very disappointed, as we knew the filly was in top form, and it was extremely frustrating to have had our hopes of the Classic dashed in this way. There was nothing we could do about the result; but I was determined to show that it was all wrong.

Lucyrowe did really well after Newmarket, and the obvious next target was the Ebbisham Stakes at Epsom, where we were taking on Motionless, third in the Guineas, and then beaten just a length in the Irish equivalent. Lucyrowe won the race with ease, while Motionless was only fourth, though in fairness, she might not have acted on the track or on the firm ground. Then came the Coronation Stakes on a murky day at Royal Ascot; and from the moment Lucyrowe burst into the lead two furlongs out, the race turned into a procession. The official distance was twelve lengths, but I don't think they had a painted board at Ascot in those days with more than that distance on it; I was told the margin was nearer eighteen lengths. It was a great thrill to see this brilliant filly prove us right, and how proud of her we all were!

After Ascot a lot of the horses were laid low with the cough, and so we had to leave them alone for a time. We gave them plenty of time to get over it, but Lucyrowe seemed to come back to form so well that we thought she ought to take her chance in the Nassau Stakes at Goodwood over a mile and a quarter. Duncan was worried that she might pull too hard in a small field, so Louis Freedman allowed us to run his other good filly

Seventh Bride to make the running and keep her company. Seventh Bride had been running in handicaps, and had finished third in the King George V Handicap at Royal Ascot; at Goodwood, having bowled along under Joe Mercer, she looked like winning two furlongs out, but Lucyrowe, under tremendous driving from Frankie Durr (a very good, tough jockey whom we had chosen in Duncan's absence with weight problems), just got up to win by a short head. Possibly I had left Lucyrowe a bit short of work after the cough, but this was a much improved effort by Seventh Bride, as we were to see afterwards.

Lucyrowe then took on the leading miler Habitat in the Wills Mile. Habitat was trained by my cousin Helen and her son Fulke who were having great success for the American millionaire Charles Engelhard. Habitat had won the St James's Palace Stakes in a canter. Duncan could not do the weight, so we engaged the charming and very effective Ron Hutchinson. I felt that dropping back to a mile on firm going we would have a good chance, but Ron waited a bit too long on Lucyrowe and rode a slightly unadventurous race, and Habitat, ridden by Lester, got the better of us by about a length.

We gave Lucyrowe a month off after this, as she had been having tough races in top company; but we still felt that she would get a mile and a quarter, and so ran her in the Sun Chariot Stakes at Newmarket, thinking that if she won this easily we would contest the Champion Stakes. In the event she had a hard race to beat a useful filly of Bruce Hobbs' called Nedda by a neck; so, grateful for all she had done for us, we asked no more of her but packed her off to stud.

Duncan went on battling with the scales until, on the evening of 21 August 1972, he rang me and told me he could not go on riding, as the struggle to do the weight was killing him. It was a very sad day for us; at least he had gone out with a nice winner in June McCalmont's two-year-old filly Cesarea that day at Folkestone. But his sudden decision left us with a lot of thinking to do. We were never short of good jockeys to ride for us, as we were lucky enough to have high-quality horses to train, but we needed a jockey committed to the stable, and we needed a good one. My first thought was to ring up the great master of apprentices at that time, Frenchie Nicholson, and ask him what his current rising star, Pat Eddery, was doing. It had been Peter Bromley, that very astute commentator, who had dubbed him a star; since then we had been watching him very closely, and he had already impressed me with his dash and resolve. Frenchie's reply was that he had been offered two half-jobs for 1973, that is, he would ride for Geoff Barling when Lester was not available, and for Henry Candy when Joe Mercer had a ride for Dick Hern. Somewhat rashly, feeling that the world was our oyster, I asked Frenchie if the boy would like to ride all our horses. He said he would talk to him on the following Sunday morning at the Nicholsons' home, as Pat always came in to discuss the previous week's racing and the next week's plans.

The question had come upon us so suddenly that I had not yet talked to a single owner; now I had to move fast. Knowing that Dick Poole and others were staying at David Wills's estate Knockando in Scotland for the fishing, I was able to put the whole plan on the table, and did the same with June McCalmont in Ireland. Their reply was unanimous: go ahead and book Pat, if Frenchie would let him go. On the Sunday evening Frenchie rang me and said that the boy would be thrilled to ride for us, and the deal was done.

Because of Pat's existing commitments, the arrangements took a little time to reach fruition, but at the Epsom August Bank Holiday meeting he rode us a lovely double on Tranquility Base and Silly Symphony, and we were on our way.

In situations like this you need God on your side; it was a case of either getting a mature, but not improving jockey, or being able to snatch the rising star and mould him to one's way of thinking. I'd rung up our great ally Joe Mercer, always my *beau ideal* of the perfect stable jockey, and told him we were trying to get Pat; all he said was, 'He'll do, we always call him Polyfilla because he fills them gaps.' When I told Frank Morby that I was taking Pat on, he asked simply, 'What are you going to do with this young boy?' My reply, as Frank reminded me recently, was, 'He has plenty of ability, but I would lock him in a box for a fortnight with a goat, to butt some sense into him and make him grow up.' Because of his youthful exuberance, Pat was inclined, as Lester had been many years before, to go up the inside in dodgy situations and cut across with the minimum angle to spare. I remember Gerald Dawson, a great friend and senior stipendiary steward, saying that Pat was in his black book because of a so-called crime he had committed at Newbury; but in all the time he rode for me he never got into trouble. Nor has he ever changed his outlook or way of life. He has never got grand, and to the very end still called me 'Guv'nor' and gave horses just as good a ride as he ever did.

Pat was bred to be a jockey, on both sides: his mother was the daughter of Pat Moylan, a beautiful horseman who rode for the McCalmonts in Ireland when their horses were trained by Bob Fetherstonhaugh, including many of their Irish Classic winners; and his father was Jimmy Eddery, a very effective rider, if a bit unpolished and agricultural in style. At the start of the Second World War Jimmy was called up to serve in the Veterinary Corps at Melton Mowbray. Shortly afterwards he asked if he could go on a seventy-two-hour leave back to Dublin. On getting his pass, he vanished into thin air and never returned – but he had the temerity to buy a box of toy soldiers, which arrived at Melton with a message for the sergeant-major: 'From now on you can play with these!'

Pat was soon gaining in confidence, and our partnership blossomed. He had the most beautiful hands, and could get horses relaxed so that they never seemed to pull with him, either at home or in their races. At the time we had a good-looking filly of Louis Freedman's called Guillotina, and she had been improving all season. After a nice handicap win in a race at Kempton, she ran an excellent second in the Lingfield Oaks Trial, beaten one length by Ginevra, who afterwards won the Oaks. Guillotina came back a bit sore, so we put her away until the going eased. On returning to action after her rest she ran first at Deauville, but never got into the race; then we ran her in the Park Hill Stakes at Doncaster, the fillies' St Leger, and after she had run a lovely race to finish a close fourth we decided to run her in the French equivalent, the Prix de Royallieu at Longchamp. This was Pat's first big race for us, and he rode brilliantly, getting up in the last hundred yards to win by half a length. Since then, of course, Pat has won the Arc de Triomphe four times; but he learned to ride Longchamp very early. It is a difficult course, because the ground falls away from the rails on the far side, and there are three short straights; the Prix de Royallieu finishes at the furthest winning post, which has caught many jockeys out. After her triumph here, we sent Guillotina to stud.

We had also been bringing on a nice big two-year-old chestnut colt by Silly Season, called Lunchtime. I had trained his grand-dam Golden Wedding at Windsor House to win eight races for dear old Peggy Chaplin, whose father-in-law had owned Hermit, the 1867 Derby winner. Golden Wedding had a daughter called Great Occasion, who looked a very promising sort, winning the Golden Hind Stakes at Ascot before going wrong with broken blood vessels; with the benefit of hindsight I'm fairly sure now that she must have had the virus, long before any of us had woken up to the presence of this scourge and the effect it would have on racing.

Lunchtime, co-owned by Colonel Dick Poole and Peggy Chaplin's daughter, was Great Occasion's first foal, and he caught our eye very early on with an inspiring piece of work up the Strip, a little valley gallop on the far side of the main gallops, with one of Nicky Vigors' horses. This one bit of exercise set everyone alight, as he was the most beautiful mover, and looked destined for great things. His first and second races were very easy ones at Goodwood and Ascot in September, and another very easy win in the Dewhurst fuelled our high hopes, prompting thoughts of Classic success. The only cloud on the horizon was the doubt cast by his breeding, for Silly Season was a disappointing sire, and a lot of his progeny were temperamental.

In the spring of his three-year-old career Lunchtime's work was exemplary, and we ran him in the Greenham Stakes at Newbury, a good trial although one which sometimes produces funny results. Certainly Lunchtime behaved in a very funny way, producing his member in the paddock and hollering incessantly, even though there were no fillies in the race. He ran very tamely to finish third behind Mon Fils, trained by the young Richard Hannon. We checked the colt over and could find no fault with him; but come the Two Thousand Guineas he behaved in much the same fashion, and again was well beaten by Mon Fils – and by a lot further this time. But at home he behaved like a hack, never exhibiting any of the signs that he showed on the racecourse. After a further feeble performance, in the Predominate Stakes at Goodwood, where we put blinkers on him, we called in a well-known horse psychologist to look him over. His comment was, 'Perhaps he is under some sort of stress that we don't know about,' prompting my head lad Ray Laing to retort, 'If I am under stress the last thing I want to do is produce my member!'

So Lunchtime was sold to go to Australia, as a stallion, and has done quite well. We were sad to see him go, and if only his temperament had not let him down he could have been one of the best.

9

GRUNDY

We had been training for Carlo Vittadini since 1970, and he wanted his racing manager, Keith Freeman, and me to look out for suitable yearlings for him. In fact we always made a point, whenever we were not too busy racing, of looking around the yearlings coming up at the studs; in this way one is able to quiz the stud manager and stud groom as to what they really feel about the yearlings they are consigning to the sale ring.

One exploratory trip we made was to the Overbury Stud near Tewkesbury in Gloucestershire in September 1973, where we had the good fortune to deal with two very professional people in Tim Holland-Martin and his stud groom Peter Diamond. The Holland-Martins have always been fine horsemen and horsemasters, brought up in a wonderful part of England with superb hunting on their doorstep (the family, who owned Martin's bank, had bought the entire Overbury estate in 1770), and the stud had been started in the middle of the Second World War by Ruby Holland-Martin and his brother Thurston, Tim's uncles; at this time bloodstock was being virtually given away, and they were able to buy several well-bred broodmares for a pittance. When his uncles died, Tim took the stud over.

Grundy's dam Word of Lundy was the third generation of her family based at the stud and had won three races for her breeders before they had her covered by Great Nephew, who had been a useful three-year-old, trained by the wizard Jack Jarvis. He lost his form after finishing second in the Two Thousand Guineas but, transferred to Etienne Pollet, went on to win the Prix Ganay, Prix Dollar and Prix du Moulin, and became the best older horse in France.

I remember watching the yearlings at Overbury being paraded, and thinking that Grundy was very flashy – he was a golden chestnut, with a flaxen mane and tail – but he was a marvellous mover, and had a lot of presence about him. It was not just his striking colouring that caught the eye; there was a swagger about him which I felt was exceptional. Certainly he was both bold and tough: as a foal he had got loose at the stud and jumped out of a paddock, becoming straddled on barbed wire. He cut himself so badly, under his stomach and right up the side of his flanks, that he had to have over 100 stitches put into the wounds; and yet he got over this horrible accident very quickly.

In spite of his colour (flashy chestnuts being widely held to be unreliable), we thought he was a colt to have another look at at the sales. At Newmarket I stood in my usual place, on the left of the rostrum near Carlo, and when the auctioneer was about to knock Grundy down to Bryan Swift for 10,500 guineas, Carlo raised his catalogue for one more bid. Bang went the gavel, and Carlo was the buyer, but immediately Keith Freeman came across and made sure the sales docket was made out in his name, as it was good publicity for him. Bloodstock prices undoubtedly rose fast during the 1970s under the twin influences of inflation and the huge sums of money coming into the market from overseas buyers, but we thought that Grundy, as Carlo named him, was good value.

The colt came to us in the autumn to be broken in the usual way, as I have described earlier. We have always taken a long time breaking in yearlings. A skilled handler may be able, like Monty Roberts, to gentle a horse in twenty minutes, but it takes a month or more to get to the stage of riding a horse away properly and safely, and Grundy was no exception. In fact it took us two months to get him round to our way of thinking, as he was so tough and boisterous that we had to use all our patience. It is essential to have highly skilled and experienced men to do your breaking in; someone with bad hands and a bad temper can ruin a yearling long before he even starts cantering, let alone embarks on strong work. In those days we would have about forty yearlings to break in every year, and we always insisted on having a really steady horse to lead them when they were ridden away. If you have a badly behaved leader, he will teach young horses bad manners; likewise, a bad mover will set the yearling a bad example, as horses are very imitative creatures.

Gradually we got Grundy cantering, and it was obvious straight away that he was a real athlete. He took to it all like a duck to water, and gradually got into fast work. To start with we kept him to half-speed work over about four furlongs, until I sent him down one morning with Cawdor, a fast three-year-old who had just been beaten in the Albemarle Stakes on the Saturday of Royal Ascot, to work from the corner of the plough, a good landmark, up to the brow on the summer gallop of Faringdon road, where I was watching from: four furlongs, on the bridle. Grundy showed enough pace for me to believe that we had a potentially serious racehorse on our hands. What a thrill it was! Unlike so many other trainers, I have never been in the slightest bit worried by having good horses. The worry is training the bad ones: they don't eat, they don't work well, except with horses of like ability, and they drive their trainers mad.

When I saw Keith Freeman at the Newmarket July meeting, he asked how the Great Nephew colt was coming along. I told him that I had worked him that morning with a fast two-year-old, and he had pleased me. He asked what my plans were for Grundy, and I told him that the Granville Stakes at Ascot on

King George day would be very suitable. This is a really lovely event for unraced two-year-olds, which we won four times; it is run at the right time of year, to give trainers an idea of prospects for the following year. All went well in our preparations, and we decided to also run a sweet little horse called No Alimony, belonging to Louis Freedman. I felt that Grundy was the better of the two, but had kept them well apart in their work. Pat chose to ride Grundy, but thought that No Alimony was quite entitled to take his chance. I told Louis Freedman what the position was, and we booked Willie Carson for the other horse. Both jockeys were obviously told to do their best, but in my heart of hearts I knew what the outcome would be.

It was a fourteen-runner field, with Grundy second favourite at 5–1. Halfway round our two runners drew away, and Grundy squeezed through to score a convincing success by two lengths from No Alimony in second place. We had no idea how good the race was, or how good the other horses were, as we had deliberately not wound our two up to their peak, but it was a very promising beginning.

Just after that Grundy had a slightly mucky nose, and coughed for a few days, so we gave him a break. For his next outing I found the Sirenia Stakes at Kempton in August, now a Listed race. He waltzed home in very fast time by two and a half lengths and came home bouncing, and we felt he had to step up a class for his next race. We chose the Champagne Stakes over seven furlongs at Doncaster's St Leger meeting, a recognised Classic trial. Among the other nine runners was Whip It Quick, trained by Ryan Price, who had won the Group Two Coventry Stakes at Royal Ascot. The race was a crawl early on, and Grundy got stuck in a pocket – but suddenly extricated himself in the last furlong and won cruising by half a length. We were delighted, but some of the pundits were not impressed, as Grundy had not done a very good time. As we do not yet have sectional timing on our racecourses, I don't see that it matters; a race is still a race, and the faster they go early on, the slower they go at the end.

Now we had to go for the big time. The two-year-old championship has always been the Dewhurst stakes, run in the middle of October at Newmarket. This year there were only eight runners, including Steel Heart, trained by Dermot Weld and ridden by Lester Piggott, winner of the Gimcrack Stakes at York and the Middle Park Stakes at Newmarket a fortnight before.

The going on the day of the race turned out very soft, as it had rained heavily the night before, and this worried us a little, as Grundy was such a good mover. I have always found the going at Newmarket to be wonderful, with the one problem that it can turn soft with overnight rain; however, Noel Murless, having trained very successfully at both Beckhampton and Newmarket, always said that at Newmarket it never gets deep, because of the sandy undersoil, and horses generally go through it. In the event we need not have worried: he drew away in the last furlong to win with effortless ease by six lengths from his main market rival, Steel Heart. Suddenly we had an unbeaten two-year-old champion on our hands and the world at our feet.

We had had an incredible season, with our little filly Polygamy winning the Oaks, and although the statistics were not published as accurately or as often as now, we knew we must be somewhere near the top of the trainers' table as we were very close in prize money to our colleague and rival Dick Hern. But it was only on 26 October that we realized how near the top we actually were.

I had shared a plane to Doncaster that day with Dick and Joe Mercer. We had run No Alimony in the Observer Gold Cup, and he had put in a good performance, although he could only finish third to the French champion Green Dancer, trained by Alec

Head. No Alimony had won two small races impressively since his second to Grundy, and according to Pat had run green at Doncaster, but basically was not good enough. (Not everyone agreed. Reading my papers the following morning I came across an article in the *Observer* by the brilliant journalist and very shrewd punter Richard Baerlein. He wrote: 'If No Alimony cannot beat Grundy over one and a half miles, I will go to work.' I immediately rang the post office and asked for Richard to be sent a telegram saying: 'Go to work, signed Grundy'. To his credit, Richard later told me that on that Sunday afternoon he had spied from his house near Haywards Heath an elderly post office worker toiling up the hill, pushing his bike, no doubt believing he was bearing a message containing news of life or death!

On the flight home, Dick and Joe suddenly produced a bottle of champagne, and shook me by the hand. When I asked what this was about, Dick said, 'I have very few more runners, I cannot beat you now. Well done; you are champion trainer!' I felt quite numb, and his generous words took a bit of time to sink in. We had indeed been having a rare tussle for the title, but I always thought we would only be second. But we did indeed finish up as leading stable with 97 winners (one in Ireland), 70 seconds, 56 thirds and 39 fourths: a winners-to-runners ratio of one in 4.5. We had amassed overall stakes of £337,425, of which £282,000 was winning stakes. Pat Eddery, aged twenty-two, in his second season for us, had ridden 148 winners, making him the youngest champion jockey since Charlie Elliott and Gordon Richards in the 1920s. And because of English Prince's win in the Irish Derby, I was leading trainer there as well. It was incredible, and I was so grateful for all those who had worked so hard to make it possible.

The winter passed very quickly, with all the enjoyment of a large helping of traditional country sport among friends and neighbours: as well as hunting, usually twice a week, with the Vale of the White Horse hounds, I was invited to shoot a lot. We had a short holiday in Hong Kong and Bali, but I hated being away from the horses for very long. As soon as we were back, I always went right round the stables with my head lads to find out their thoughts about how all the horses had done during my break. Happily, this year I came back to find the horses in great form. Before Christmas we always gave them a dose of 'physic' or laxative, after which they could have a few days in their boxes over the holiday. There is nothing worse than having sick horses (or sick staff!), and the physic clears out their systems.

After Christmas we always trotted the older horses on the roads and tracks for a month to settle them and harden them up. The steady trot right down the Blowing Stone hill – three miles there and back – on top of a trot in the covered ride first, meant they were doing a good hour and a quarter's exercise each day. We never trotted the two-year-olds on the roads, as I felt that it might be too hard on their immature legs. Instead, they would keep cantering every day with their chosen lead horses.

All went well in the early part of 1975, and we started doing sharp canters twice a week. Grundy did his first sharp work with No Alimony and Corby over six furlongs on 4 March. The weather was awful, though, with the rain pouring down day after day. On 14 March it was so dreadful I only worked my first two runners at Doncaster, Hilarious and Understudy; the others I left to canter in the covered ride, as they were far better off in there than being pulled about in the heavy going outside. But I did want to test the water with the horses I thought were the most forward, and this pair had both been showing me plenty. They both repaid me by winning easily at Doncaster.

Poor conditions in a wet winter are perhaps the most serious disadvantage of training in the otherwise near-perfect environment of the Berkshire downs. Noel Murless always said that although downland gallops are wonderful in summer, in winter the going becomes bottomless, and it is very difficult to repair, as the holes made by the horses' feet go several inches deep. Lambourn has always been a more backward place than Newmarket to train horses, as the gallops are in the most part privately owned and accordingly better respected; if trainers don't own the ground they are inclined to be more ruthless and not treat it with as much care. Early winners do come from Lambourn, but I never feel that the horses in our area really start to thrive until May. The Newmarket horses are usually a fortnight in front of ours, and even the hedges are always more advanced in Suffolk!

In April 1979 the racing world was treated to a demonstration of the perils of wet weather on the downs. A meeting was scheduled for Salisbury which had been transferred from Ascot. The reason the authorities gave for the switch was that the early racing at Ascot ruined the going for the rest of the year; consequently, it was decided to have the Ascot Guineas trials at Salisbury. At the meeting which was held to discuss the move I strongly voiced my misgivings, expressing the view held by both Noel Murless and myself, that the going might be far worse at Salisbury than at Ascot.

The Salisbury meeting took place as planned, but the heavens opened and the going was appalling. The course was virtually waterlogged, and the stewards' car got stuck on an inspection down the course. This was clearly shown on television, with Johnny Hislop still sitting in the car while others were endeavouring to free it. The crowd was nevertheless enormous and Steve Cauthen had his first English winner on his first day's riding in the country – but the experiment was not tried again. Many cars were stuck for hours and had to be towed out of the car parks before they could set off to return home.

Back in March 1975, we were to have other anxieties than the weather. One day I walked out of the house as usual at 7.30, on my way to the covered ride, only to see Grundy being led towards me with blood streaming down his face. Matty McCormack, Grundy's work rider, said, 'Guv'nor, he's been kicked.' We got the colt back in his box, and Matty explained that Grundy, being in his usual exuberant form, had bounded forward on entering the covered ride and lowered his head, landing right behind Corby's quarters. Great big horse that he was, Corby lashed out in self-defence, and caught Grundy right on the side of his face. It was a horrid kick, leaving the mark of the shoe only two inches below his near eye, and I felt that the horse's Classic prospects were now at risk. I immediately rang our vet, the highly experienced and unflappable Charles Frank. All he said, having seen the horse, was: 'You cannot hurry; you'll have to see how he gets on. If I were to operate, you could be in more trouble, as it might do no good. Let's hope it does not affect the sinuses.' He gave the horse the necessary antibiotics to prevent the wound getting infected; after that, we had to sit and wait.

I always found Charles very laid back and diplomatic – until recently, when I read Phil Bull's book, in which he is very rude about Charles, no doubt because the vet had told him some home truths. Bull was a brilliant man, but hated the Jockey Club, and it would appear from his book that George Wigg, who was head of the Levy Board, was his best friend. They were alike in many ways: both had chips on their shoulders and could be troublesome, but both loved racing – indeed, George Wigg may well have ensured the future of Epsom by persuading Stanley Wootton, who owned the downs, to give a long lease on the land to United Racecourses.

One of my main worries at this point was that the press would find out about this incident before I had managed to get in touch with Grundy's owner. This is a constant headache for trainers, especially with overseas owners who may be hard to contact quickly, for every stable has members of staff who are in touch with the press and bookmakers. I don't blame them; as long as there is no villainy involved, it is an understandable way of topping up their earnings. I tried Keith Freeman but he was in South Africa; Carlo Vittadini himself was unable to be contacted either at his home near Milan or at his chalet in St Moritz. Eventually I tracked them both down, and both were extremely understanding. In the meantime, the press had been on the phone every few minutes, but I was able to keep them at bay until I had talked to Bill Garland, the head of the Press Association racing team. I gave him full details and he was very helpful, taking on the entire job of briefing the press and freeing me for the crucial job of looking after the horse.

I have never been so depressed. I felt that Grundy had been an obvious winner of the Two Thousand Guineas, and yet a setback like the colt had just had could so easily jeopardise his chances. Charles Frank came over several times a day, and after Grundy had spent the prescribed two days in his box the main thing was to begin to exercise him again in order to clear the sinuses. Luckily the colt recovered very quickly, being so hardy; but the episode had obviously put him back. On 1 April he worked with Hard Day, who had won the Convivial Stakes at York the previous August, a very steady six furlongs. He was due to work again three days later but the weather was so bad, with sleet and snow, that I abandoned strong work and let him and No Alimony just do a swinging canter. On 9 April he was able to work again with Matt up, along with Corby ridden by Pat, Consol with Ron Thomas, and Patch with Tex Fahey. Grundy went very well, and we were pleased. On 12 April he galloped again, this time with Acquaint, Record Token and Charlie Bubbles, and worked well, but as Pat, who rode Grundy, said afterwards, 'Time is not on our side.'

Pat also rode Grundy on 15 April, when the colt did his final bit of work before the Greenham Stakes, which we had decided on as his preparation race before the Guineas – somewhat reluctantly, as it is a race that over the years has thrown up some rather odd results. Accompanied by Charlie Bubbles with a good work rider aboard, Acquaint (Ron Thomas), Red Regent (Frank Morby) and All Friends (Paul Cook) from Nicky Vigors' stable, he worked really well and seemed in very good form, and our hopes began to rise.

We had a great week at the Craven meeting at Newmarket. No Alimony won the Craven Stakes, and in the same race Patch, on his first run for us, ridden by Frank Morby, gave a respectable performance to finish fifth, although he was a stuffy horse and needed the race. Patch had been sent to us as a two-year-old by Carlo Vittadini, who had had him in training in Italy; as there were fewer horses there, and as a consequence fewer races for horses of his ability – good, but less than top-class – it had been decided to transfer him to England, where there would be more opportunities for him to win. A big, imposing chestnut colt with rather round fetlocks and a plain head, he had been taught to pull very hard, and always was hard to control. Record Token won the Wisbech Handicap over six furlongs and Giselle, owned by our old friend Dick Poole, won the Crawford Handicap over seven furlongs.

On Thursday evening Bonk drove me back home via Newbury racecourse. I walked down the course, and found a strip of new ground about five yards wide which had been opened on the stands side of the track. Taking into account the fact that there was sure to be a small field for the Greenham, I felt that Grundy should take his chance.

On the Friday night the heavens opened, and it became obvious that the going would be very heavy. Carlo called in to see the horses in the morning, and I put it to him that I did want to run Grundy before the Guineas, but did not want him subjected to a hard race, in view of the going and his recent injury. How did he feel about the possibility of his horse getting beaten? I did feel that Grundy needed the race. Carlo understood perfectly, and simply said, 'Carry on.'

The going was heavy, and there were nine runners. Grundy led two and a half furlongs out, but tired and eventually got beaten two lengths by Lester on Mark Anthony. Len Thomas of the *Sporting Life* asked me in the unsaddling enclosure if I was disappointed, and I replied, 'No, in the circumstances, I am delighted,' which startled him rather. But Grundy was blowing hard, and I knew he could only improve.

Everything went well after that until the Guineas meeting – except that there was a strike by Newmarket stable staff. A few militants were demanding higher wages and, encouraged by the Transport and General Workers' Union, were stirring things up and causing trouble. Johnny Winter, the chairman of the Newmarket Trainers' Association and a very decent man, tried to negotiate with them, but the ringleaders were a very nasty bunch, and refused to reach a settlement. This worried Johnny so much that I believe he was never the same man again. The lengths to which the hard-liners were prepared to go became evident when some of them tried to disrupt the One Thousand Guineas, even attempting to drag Willie Carson off his horse on the way to the start. They did themselves no good thereby: the strikers were driven off the track by a lot of very angry race-goers, incensed that the day's racing was at risk of being ruined. The One Thousand was run in normal fashion, but the security was increased, and Keith Freeman suggested that Grundy should be stabled overnight in a private stable, away from Newmarket, before his big race the next day. I vetoed that, arguing that he would be far better off in the racecourse stables with their own very competent security staff on duty.

On Two Thousand Guineas day the horses got down to the start, and were walking around behind the stalls, when the strikers suddenly appeared, and lay down right in front of the stalls. Immediately Alec Marsh, the starter, rang the stewards: Would they allow the race to be started by flag right in front of the stalls, thereby bypassing the protestors? Quite rightly the stewards agreed, much to the fury of the would-be trouble-makers. It was a level start, but trimmed about 70 yards off the normal eight-furlong distance of the race. Grundy led two and a half furlongs out, then got a bit tired, but ran on again when challenged by Bolkonski, to be beaten only half a length.

The week after the Guineas we ran Patch in the Lingfield Derby Trial on softish going, and to our delight he led virtually all the way and won, easing up, by ten lengths. This gave us another iron in the fire, as Patch was not only in the English Derby but, like Grundy, also in the French equivalent.

Grundy had stayed well at Newmarket, and just got beaten for speed over the unusually inadequate trip as a result of the start being moved. We felt he was sure to improve again and, as he could not now win the Triple Crown, decided to run him in the Irish Two Thousand Guineas as a possible consolation prize. We sent him over with Consol, a dour stayer who had won the Classic Trial at Sandown before finishing third in the Chester Vase, having failed to act round Chester's tight bends. Consol duly won the Royal Whip, a very old race started by King William IV, over a mile and a half, beating the top-class Irish mare Hurry Harriet by a length and a half, the evening before the Classic.

We nearly didn't get to Dublin in time for Grundy's race. The Aer Lingus Boeing 747 carrying Bonk, Pat and myself was taxiing down the runway that afternoon when there was a sudden jolt and crash and the aircraft came to a sudden halt. Another plane had taken off a great slice of our tail. So we had to change planes, and only got to The Curragh in the nick of time. (The Irish airline seemed to be in rather a chaotic state at the time. When June McCalmont came over a month later she noticed that the plane she was travelling in must have been the same one in which we nearly came to grief: it had some temporary sacking tied over the offending spot.)

In any event, all was well as far we were concerned, and I went down to the course in the morning to see Grundy do a nice canter. Afterwards I drove down to the mile start, and only then realised how tough the Irish Guineas course is: much stiffer than our Guineas course at Newmarket, and a very good trial for Epsom. It caused Grundy no anxiety: he was always handy and won easily, beating the French challenger Monsanto ridden by Yves Saint-Martin.

Suddenly we had a serious Derby horse on our hands. With just three weeks to play with, we felt that one nice spin round Moss Hill, the wonderful old Derby trial ground above Seven Barrows on the left of the Wantage road, would do. I have always used this gallop with the Epsom horses, as it has a left-hand bend early on, a distinct dip with a left-hand camber, and an uphill climb for the last two furlongs. Grundy galloped a mile and a quarter with his old sparring partner Corby (Frank Morby), Red Regent (Brian Taylor) and No Alimony (Joe Mercer). They did a lovely bit of work, quickening up together, with Grundy floating round the corners and down the hill. After that it was just a question of letting the horse tick over, and hoping there were no more setbacks.

We had had long debates about whether Patch should accompany Grundy to Epsom, but in the end decided that because Patch stayed so well, and because of his rather round fetlocks, which suited him to ground with more give in it, we would send him instead to France for their Derby, the Prix du Jockey-Club. Chantilly is much more of a galloping course than

Epsom, with a very stiff climb from the turn into the straight.

Grundy had a last spin on the Monday before the Derby, when he bowled up the Strip, a lovely little valley gallop where we used to try the two-year-olds: four furlongs on the bridle, along with Red Regent. This big colt was owned by Sir Douglas Clague from Hong Kong, who was very keen to run him in the Derby. Red Regent had won two handicaps very easily at Nottingham and Chester, after an unlucky defeat at Newmarket, where he had finished third in a four-horse race after getting himself shut in. This was one of jockey Frank Morby's rare lapses; although not a top-ranking jockey, he was tough and dependable, and a superb work rider, and we were glad to have him as second jockey to Pat. (On one of the occasions when we topped the trainers' table in terms of races won, the owners gave us a wonderful dinner during which Charles Smith-Bingham asked Frank where he was going for the winter. Frank replied that he was going to Kenya, where he was leading jockey, as he always did. Charles asked him about his family, and whether he could leave them for so long. Frank replied that he had got rid of his first wife, because, as he said, 'She was getting rather more rides than I was.') We also had Joe Mercer riding No Alimony, who had not only won the Craven Stakes but, after a mediocre run in the Guineas, had beaten Bruni in the Predominate Stakes at Goodwood, a recognised Derby trial which we had won the year before with English Prince, who went on to win the Irish Derby. We had already been placed twice in the Derby; but this was our great chance to win . . .

On our return to Seven Barrows after Grundy's famous victory, I found enormous banners up on the drive – and a host of people who had somehow found our cellar key and were now helping themselves to no mean tune. We did not complain; when things are going well, one must enjoy every minute of it, and there was plenty of celebratory spirit to go round. Then, all of a sudden, there was our owner Jim McAllister on the telephone, telling us that if we were in the car park on the Friday at Epsom, there would be a fresh Scottish salmon, in a creel, and a case of Dom Perignon champagne. I had told Jim before the race that I had confidence in Grundy, and he was a very generous winner.

Gradually the house filled up with more friends and family. Somehow, about midnight, dinner was conjured up by a bevy of helpers – accompanied by the sound of a car arriving.

It was a London taxi, containing a very refreshed Patrick Helmore, with a case of champagne. He had always been a terrific friend and for many years had been in charge of all my insurance. He was still in his morning coat, and though we were thrilled to see him, we couldn't resist asking why he had appeared; he replied simply, 'I couldn't miss this.' Patrick had a very good brain, but got in a terrible muddle over his love affairs. All his lady friends thought that they could reform him, but none of them ever could, and he enjoyed having them on the run, despite the inevitable complications. As he once said to me, 'Life is like a banana: one minute it's in your hand, the next it's up your arse.' He stayed with us for two nights, and I don't think he, or indeed any of us, had sobered up by the time he left. On that first night we eventually sank into bed at about 3 a.m., but I think the party went on much longer, with the tape of the race being endlessly played.

Despite the late night, I was up earlier than usual the next morning to catch the papers as soon as they arrived. This was probably the most exciting moment of all: when you read in black-and-white print that your horse has won the Derby, it really sinks in. There were plenty of hangovers, but it was lovely to see so many happy people working for us. I rode out as usual over the downs, and at the far side of the Faringdon road gallop met a fellow trainer, Hugh Williams, also out on a horse with his string. He rode across to where I was looking to see which one of my two-year-olds would make a Derby horse next year, and all he said was, 'Well done, boss – you've made it!'

On the Sunday after the Derby we ran Patch in the Prix du Jockey-Club, and he ran a wonderful race. We were perhaps fortunate to finish only a head behind the winner, Val De L'Orne, who had hit the front and looked like beating us decisively when he faltered, and Patch ran on again. Later it turned out that Val De L'Orne had broken down in the race. Corby, who had won the Horris Hill Stakes at Newbury in October and nearly put Grundy out of the Derby with that kick, won the Prix du Lys over a mile and a half; so all in all, we had a fantastic week.

It was coming home in the plane from France that I had the most extraordinary conversation with Keith Freeman. He told me that Grundy had been sold to the National Stud for the equivalent of a million pounds, with Carlo keeping a quarter share, and that the colt could only run four more times. I got hot under the collar, and asked who was stopping us, the Levy Board or him, Keith. At first he said it was the Levy Board (who controlled the finances of the National Stud), then he said it was him. I asked whose decision it was, and he told me 'the committee of the National Stud'. He told me that the horse was not allowed to run in the Arc de Triomphe, and should run in the Eclipse Stakes at Sandown. I asked why he could not run in the Irish Derby, and he said: 'the committee'. We sat at the airport arguing about the Eclipse and the Irish Derby, and he said, 'So many horses that have won the Derby have got beaten in the Irish Derby.' My reply was that you could not blame me for that as I had not trained them.

I could not believe all this, and over the next few days rang up every member of the committee, including Lord Porchester, as he was then, and Peter Willett. Their reply was, 'You can run where you like.' I did not mind not running in the Arc – it is a tough race for a horse who has had a Classic preparation, starting with the Guineas, and is very late in the year – but the Irish Derby was a different matter. I rang up Carlo Vittadini, and asked if I could run Grundy at The Curragh. He said, 'Yes, of course, if you want to run the horse, that is fine by me.' Having got my way so far, I thought, if all went well we could at least run in the Irish Derby, then hopefully in the King George VI and Queen Elizabeth Stakes, and possibly in the Benson and Hedges Stakes at York, though that was only a mile and a quarter. The other alternative would have been a final run in the Champion Stakes, in October, again over a mile and a quarter, but that would be very late in a busy year.

After Epsom, everything went according to plan. On 20 June, thanks to the kindness of the Candys, I worked Grundy on White Horse Hill: a round gallop a mile and a quarter long, undulating with a nice stiff finish. I felt that a change would be to his advantage; also, we were having a very hot summer, and the going everywhere was getting firm, yet the wonderful grass right on top of the hill is like a carpet. I used a dour old handicapper, Our Nicholas, to lead the gallop, along with Patch, Corby, and a very useful handicapper called Understudy. Frank Morby on Our Nicholas won the gallop, and I was a bit worried at breakfast, as Grundy finished about four lengths behind. It was not supposed to be a special bit of work, but I hadn't found Grundy's performance convincing. Pat, though, said the colt was fine and pronounced himself very happy with him; he thought that because it was a strange gallop the horse had been lobbing along at the back and enjoying himself. He did not blow at all, and after all we were only keeping him ticking over. I gave him one more bit of work up the valley on the Tuesday before the race, and he flew over to The Curragh on the Thursday.

In the meantime Charlie Bubbles, who had sprung back to

form after a heart problem in 1974 to win the Newbury Spring Cup, had a choice of engagements at Royal Ascot, having been entered in both the Royal Hunt Cup over a mile, with top weight, and the Hardwicke Stakes over one and a half miles. I debated the alternatives for hours with his owner Leonard Sainer, who adored Ascot as much as I did. I told him I did not think the Hardwicke entries made it a very hot race – unlike most years, as it was the big race for older horses at the meeting over a mile and a half; on the other hand, the horse was not certain to stay the distance. Leonard, in his usual relaxed way, left the final choice to me, and we plumped for the Hardwicke. We were rewarded by a most exhilarating race, with Pat at his very strongest, getting up to beat Lester on Arthurian by a short head. I don't think Pat has ever ridden a more powerful finish, and against Lester that was something special. Charlie had one more run at Longchamp, taking on Allez France, but was not quite up to it, and was sold to Spain as a stallion.

As for Grundy, the Irish Derby was one of his easiest races. He was always handy, and quickened up to lead at the distance and win by two and a half lengths, with the unbeaten King Pellinore, from Vincent O'Brien's yard, in second and Anne's Pretender, who had been fourth behind us at Epsom, in third place. I had known at the time that Pat had been disappointed in not being able to ride English Prince in the race the year before, and I had told him that there would be another chance; but I could not know then that it would be the following year! We were all thrilled, and fired up for the confrontation with Bustino in the big race at Ascot, the King George VI and Queen Elizabeth Stakes.

Bustino had been a rather unlucky fourth in the 1974 Derby, but had gone on to win the St Leger and then had taken the Coronation Cup in fine style on his re-appearance. Dick Hern felt that his only chance of beating Grundy in the King George was to put in two pacemakers, in case there was any weakness in our horse's stamina. Nor was Bustino the only top-quality competitor facing Grundy: the field of eleven at Ascot included Dahlia, who had won the race in both the last two years; Dibidale, who had won the previous year's Irish Oaks; and the good German horse Star Appeal, who was later to win the Arc de Triomphe.

On 18 July, six days before the race, I took Grundy back to White Horse Hill again with Spring Stone, a useful handicapper, No Alimony and Red Regent. He worked a lot better and quickened up well to the leader Spring Stone. A further bit of work up the Faringdon road on the 22nd, with a swinging canter up the bottom gallop, put him right.

When the stalls opened, Bustino's two pacemakers, Highest and Kinglet, went off at a furious pace. Four furlongs out Bustino hit the front, pursued by Grundy, and the battle was on. By the last furlong Pat was driving our horse for all he was worth, but Bustino would not give in. Slowly we edged forward, and though Bustino was coming back at us in the last hundred yards, Grundy held on to win by half a length. The others were well beaten, with Dahlia five lengths away in third place.

We came down in the lift feeling dazed. We had already won the opening ladies' race with Hard Day, ridden by Carlo Vittadini's daughter Franca, and to cap it all, later in the day we won the Virginia Water Stakes with the well-bred newcomer Inchmarlo. I don't remember much about watching the race; but I do remember Dick Hern in his usual wonderful way coming straight over to me and giving my hand an enormous shake with his bearlike grip. I also remember being presented to the Queen again, a very proud moment. Everyone said it was an even better race than the Gold Cup of 1936, when Quashed, who had won the Oaks the year before, just held on to beat the American challenger Omaha by a short head. I remember a splendid dinner in what was then the best restaurant in our area, the Noah's Arc at Frilford near Wantage, and another party by the pool at home that went on into the early hours.

I remember, too, that brilliant artist Peter Biegel, another great friend of ours, painting Grundy as the horse stood outside his box for a couple of hours on the Monday morning – the only day when he would have stood still for long. He could not be led out for a single day longer, so quickly did he recover from that struggle. It was obvious that we had to keep our eyes on Grundy now, as I did not want to run the horse again if he was showing any signs of being stale; but he appeared and worked in just as good form as ever.

The trainer and head lads know more than anyone about the horses in their care, but to know when a horse is over the top is the most difficult judgement a trainer has to make. Only when they run do you know for certain that the writing is on the wall, and history offers many examples of horses who showed on the racecourse that their best was over: Shergar, Troy, Nashwan. Everyone seemed so happy with Grundy that we decided to run him at York in the Benson & Hedges just over three weeks after Ascot. He was a long odds-on favourite, but never looked like winning and finished only fourth in a field of six, over ten lengths behind the victor, Dahlia.

This, obviously, left us all rather downcast. But training is the most extraordinary game; there is always a surprise around the corner, and just when you feel lower than a snake's navel, up comes a bit of good news. May Hill and Pasty, the only two fillies in training for their owner Percival Williams, relieved the gloom by winning the Yorkshire Oaks and Lowther Stakes. May Hill, who was a daughter of our good filly Mabel, had been second in the Fred Darling Stakes at Newbury and the Musidora Stakes at York, and fourth in the Oaks, failing to act down the hill. In the Yorkshire Oaks she beat Juliette Marny, who had won at Epsom;

she then went on to win the Park Hill Stakes at Doncaster and was third in her last race, the Prix Vermeille at Longchamp. Pasty also pleased us, as we had not initially known how good she was; she had won a small race at Wolverhampton, and followed it up with wins at Sandown and Goodwood, before showing her true class here at York. Her next and last race of the season was the Cheveley Park Stakes at Newmarket, where she again won readily.

After the Benson and Hedges we decided to retire Grundy, and off he went to the National Stud, having won seven of his ten races and set a new earnings record in prize money for an English-trained horse: £373,563. What a marvellous example of the English thoroughbred he was; tough, sound and genuine – and how proud we all were of being involved with him!

At the end of the year, at one of those very relaxed Lambourn parties, Jim Cramsie came up with another highly entertaining calypso. It went as follows:

> Keith is the Freeman we know and love
> He was sent down from heaven above
> . . .
>
> Not me, Richard Baerlein he say
> Grundy was a horse who couldn't stay
> But Richard, he got a kick in the face
> When Grundy went and won the very big race
>
> Pat is the man who rode Grundee
> Not to mention the young Nannie
> Grundy run like a bat out of hell
> But the Nannie, she pressed the panic bell
>
> Not me, Richard . . . [etc.]

Doctor Carlo from old Milan
Come up trumps every horse he ran
Never have a year when he's alive
Like Nineteen Hundred and Seventy Five.

Not me, Richard . . . [etc.]

Up in the stand as Grundy won
Was Big Pete shouting 'Come on my son!'
Now having won the great Derby
I'll go and train a century.

Not me, now Richard I've something to say
I'll do things in my own way
and you can write and you can scream
But at Seven Barrows we've the hellova team.

16. Lucyrowe (Frankie Durr) narrowly beating her stable companion Seventh Bride in the Nassau Stakes at Goodwood, 1 August 1969

17. & 18. Cartoon of Bonk by David Langdon, and of me by the American artist Peb

Facing page:

19. Humble Duty (Lester Piggott riding) after winning the One Thousand Guineas at Newmarket in 1970, led in by her owner, Jean, Lady Ashcombe

20. Bonk and me with Humble Duty at Seven Barrows the Sunday after the One Thousand Guineas, May 1970

21. *Above left:* Humble Duty wins the Sussex Stakes at Goodwood in 1970

22. *Left:* First lot: the string taken from the hill above Seven Barrows

23. *Above:* In the yard at Seven Barrows, early morning exercise

24. Planning the entries in the office at Seven Barrows; Lucy McDiarmid, my secretary, is on the left

25. Linden Tree (Duncan Keith, right) winning the Observer Gold Cup at Doncaster, beating Bill Williamson on Minsky at the rewarding odds of 25–1. As a three-year-old, Linden Tree won the Chester Vase and was only beaten by Mill Reef in the Derby

26. With Dave Dick at Newmarket October sales, looking out for yearlings for the stable

27. Lunchtime winning the Dewhurst Stakes at Newmarket, October 1972; he was a brilliant two-year-old, whose temperament unfortunately got the better of him

28. Polygamy (Pat Eddery) winning the Oaks, 8 June 1974. The saddle on Willie Carson's mount, Dibidale, has slipped right under the horse, forcing him to give an unwelcome demonstration of the art of bareback riding

29. Polygamy coming back to the winners' enclosure after the 1974 Oaks, with Tony Driscoll, our travelling head lad and Robert, her lad

10

Owners

To be a successful trainer, you have to find owners, and you
have to keep them. Today, this is harder than ever. So many
owners nowadays cannot or will not settle anywhere for very
long and are constantly moving their horses around. Trainers on
the receiving end of this approach feel that they are not being
trusted, and it is much harder to concentrate on training horses
if you are wondering whether they may be on their way at any
moment.

I was always very lucky with my patrons. The first person I
consulted when I was setting out on a training career was
Colonel Dick Poole. He had held the trainer's licence for my
cousin Helen after her husband's death, and was a great help to
me while I was working with her. It was he who advised Mrs
Peggy Chaplin, his cousin, to send me Golden Wedding, a
lovely-looking filly by the handicapper Sunny Brae; she won us
eight races and helped put us on the map, making people realise
that we meant business. He always kept an interest in the stable
– he bought Golden Wedding's foal Great Occasion, who bred
Lunchtime, which he shared with Peggy's daughter – and he
used to give us excellent advice, including the dictum: 'Choose
your owners, not your horses.'

The first people to offer us a horse were Percival Williams and
his wife Barbara, who sent us Be Hopeful – another horse who,
as I have told in an earlier chapter of this book, did so much to
get us launched at Windsor House. (When Geoffrey Freer, the
great handicapper, went round the Williamses' stud, he

remarked that there was a lot of barbed wire around the paddocks. Percival's reply was that there was a lot of barbed wire round Lambourn, and so if one of his horses got loose there it would always know what it was, and avoid it.)

The Williamses started their breeding operation at their farm in Herefordshire with just two mares, who between them produced a stream of winners. Both mares had legs like bars of iron, and Percival always said that he would never go to an unsound stallion. He had been master and huntsman of the Four Burrow foxhounds in Cornwall, breeding the hounds and hunting them for forty-two years since leaving the army after service at Gallipoli, so he knew a lot about soundness. Flat race horses, if respected, do not have the leg trouble that jumpers do, but one must always be vigilant.

To have two fillies in training from his two different mares, and to win two races, which would now be classed as Group One and Two, would be an achievement hard to match; yet this is just what Percival did with May Hill and Pasty, who, as recounted in the previous chapter, won the Yorkshire Oaks and Lowther Stakes in 1975. Sadly, after he died the two fillies went to stud, and suffered ill luck; they were not particularly well mated, and neither bred anything of much consequence.

A somewhat different figure was Evelyn de Rothschild, who had just inherited the Southcourt Stud at Leighton Buzzard on the death of his father. The family had bred a lot of winners here at the turn of the century; now Renee Robeson, Evelyn's sister and the stud manager, became a great friend of ours, and after training some fillies which won for them, we started training some home-bred colts, with some success; they included Town Crier, our first Royal Ascot winner, and Understudy, a very good handicapper.

My third major owner was of a very different type again. David Oldrey, a chartered accountant, had never owned a horse before he came to me at Newbury in the autumn of 1962. He had also been to see another trainer, John Sutcliffe at Epsom; luckily for us, he decided in our favour. Armed with an order from him to buy a jumper, I went over to Ireland and met up with that delightful and very successful bloodstock agent Tom Cooper. After visiting several yards, we ended up at the stud run by Mrs Kelly – the daughter of Joe McGrath, who had owned the Derby winner Arctic Prince, and founded the Irish Hospitals Sweepstake. From her we bought a good-looking gelding called Gail Greine who had scope and had been placed on the flat. David recalls that I sent him a bill for £2 for transport in a horsebox from Didcot station, where horses often used to arrive by train from Ireland. This was the first of a long series of purchases; thereafter I bought, and trained, most of David's horses – much assisted in virtually all the purchases by substantial help from that very good judge Robin Hastings of the British Bloodstock Agency.

Gail Greine won his third race for us, a novice hurdle on 4 May 1963 at the Bank Holiday meeting at Huntingdon, ridden by Josh Gifford, and the owner's prize money before deductions was £170. This was Josh's first winner at his home course; he had been born and brought up on his father's farm very near by.

How lucky we were that David came to us! By the time we retired, we had trained for David and his partners in the accountancy business, of whom he had several, thirty-one winners of eighty-three races. They included a John Porter Stakes, a Blue Riband Stakes at Epsom, two Jockey Club Stakes, two Doncaster Cups, the Guardian Classic Trial at Sandown, the Ormonde Stakes, the Royal Whip at The Curragh, the Geoffrey Freer Stakes, the Epsom Derby Trial, the Newbury Autumn Cup and the Grand Prix de Vichy – as well as a second in the King George VI and Queen Elizabeth Stakes at Ascot, and a third in the Derby. For a man who never spent large sums on his horses

– he loved stayers, which are in general cheaper to buy, as they take much more time to prepare – it was an impressive tally.

Training for David was one of those partnerships made in heaven. A patient owner makes things so much easier for the trainer; there is little pressure for quick results, which allows horses to come to hand in their own time. He has the best grasp and knowledge of racing of any man I know, and (outside the office!) he has devoted his whole life to it. The Jockey Club and British Horseracing Board are lucky to have had him in charge of race planning, for it is his inspirations which have invented so many races for the less good horses, with which, after all, most trainers and owners are blessed.

When Peter Hastings died in 1964, Johnny Henderson, who had been an ADC to General Montgomery in the Second World War, asked us to train for him and his great friend Herbert Ingram. They bred some good horses out of a wonderful mare called Acclio, and they all won – among them Acquaint, who loved soft ground and later won the Imperial Cup over hurdles ridden by Johnny's son Nicky. Johnny was the genius who started up Racecourse Holdings Trust, which now controls so many of our racecourses. Herbert too had a brilliant brain; among the horses I trained for him was the good-looking Record Token, winner of the Vernons Sprint and Victoria Cup.

In 1967 Charles Smith-Bingham and I were asked to find a filly for Christopher Spence and his stepmother Eileen. We went to the Houghton sales at Newmarket and found a filly by Crocket from the Kilcarn Stud in Meath in Ireland. She had been bred by Major Ned O'Kelly, who had been in the Veterinary Corps and was a friend of my father's in India just after the First World War. He was a terrific horsemaster, and produced a string of quality horses over the years. His stud is now run even more successfully by his daughter Pat, who has inherited all his expertise. Frontier Goddess was a good sort of rangy filly, and had a reserve on her of 4000 guineas. She did not make this, and was sold to Robin Hastings privately for 2,500 guineas. Then his client dropped out, and Robin offered her to us.

This was Christopher's first horse, but he was not at all impatient to see results, and quite happy for the filly to be given time to come to herself – which we thought she needed, as she looked a little backward. His patience was rewarded when Frontier Goddess won two of her four races as a two-year-old in 1968 and was placed second in the Oaks in 1969 before turning the tables on her conqueror at Epsom, Sleeping Partner, in the Yorkshire Oaks. She was sold privately in the autumn (for a large sum in those days) to Nelson Bunker Hunt, at that time one of the leading owner-breeders in America.

Christopher and his wife have become staunch friends since those days, and have shared several fillies and mares with us, but none quite in the same class as Frontier Goddess. She was the second foal of our Oaks runners-up, after Mabel, and she was a lovely ride. Bonk used to ride her a lot, and they were a great combination at home. Bonk was and still is an excellent and elegant rider, and would surely have made a name for herself if the opportunity had arisen, but in those days ladies' races had not been thought of. Christopher has a highly successful small stud near Newbury, and was clever and lucky enough to breed and own Celeric, one of the most popular winners of the Ascot Gold Cup when he took the race in 1998 – a timely achievement, as his trainer, Christopher's brother-in-law David Morley, was seriously ill, and died the following spring. In 1998 Christopher was made Senior Steward of the Jockey Club, and is doing a marvellous job coping with the many warring factions in the various parts of the racing industry.

Our relationship with Leonard Sainer began in rather odd circumstances. A well-known lawyer, in 1971 he was asked to monitor the Rock Roi case on behalf of the Hue-Williamses, and he was impressed enough with my behaviour during this episode to come to me straight after it was all over and ask me to train a horse for him. It was no good, and I told him so, whereupon he told me to buy another one.

I enlisted the help of a great character, brilliant judge of horseflesh and charming man Jack Doyle, and arranged to meet him at Dublin. On arrival at the airport, as I came through customs a man sprang at me and asked me if I was (as I thought) 'Mr Wa-Wa.' When I said 'yes', he said that he had been asked to pick me up and took me to his car. We turned left out of the airport gate and I had no idea where we were going. All of a sudden we pulled up at a Victorian mansion covered in ivy, with a stable yard behind. I was very puzzled – and then I saw the legendary trainer of jumpers Tom Dreaper coming down the steps to meet us. Realising that we were in the wrong place, I asked the driver what was going on, as we were certainly not trying to buy a jumper, and he in turn asked me whether I was David Barker, whom he had been asked to pick up. I explained that I thought Mr Doyle was going to meet me – whereupon he suddenly twigged that he had collected the wrong person . . . We drove back to the airport, and there was the well-known nagsman and judge of horses (and later famed huntsman of the Bicester and Meynell hounds) David Barker, on a mission to look at jumpers for Lord Bicester, sitting forlornly waiting for his driver; and there, too, was my guide Jack Doyle.

We eventually got on our way and had a hilarious day, visiting a lot of horses in different stables, accompanied by Johnnie Harrington. The first person we visited was Mick O'Toole, one of the most delightful men you could ever meet. We were shown about six two-year-olds of his cantering in a big field, and when we had seen them all canter slowly in one direction, Micko asked if I wanted to see them change course, whereupon he shouted, 'Let them go round on the other lock.'

This was impressively done, but I felt they were all a bit too expensive.

After a riotous lunch at the Hideout near Kilcullen, we eventually ended up at Paddy Mullins' stable near Gowran Park racecourse. Here we were shown a rather nice two-year-old by Wolver Hollow who was to be sold in a fortnight at Leopardstown racecourse at the dispersal sale following the death of his owner. Having reviewed all the horses we had seen, we decided to wait for the sale, and try to buy this colt.

I rang Leonard Sainer and related how we had got on; he told us to go ahead and try to buy the colt. The only snag was that he was already named, and Leonard felt that the name, Charlie Bubbles, would be embarrassing given that at this time he worked for Charlie Clore. The two had been brought up in the same street, and they had been close friends ever since; eventually they both rose to leading positions in the corporate world (Leonard became chairman of Sears Holdings, which eventually owned William Hill, the bookmakers). However, Leonard asked Clore's permission and all was well. Charlie Bubbles went on to win the Free Handicap, the Newbury Spring Cup and the Hardwicke Stakes, and afterwards stood as a stallion in Spain. Thereafter Leonard had horses with us for the rest of his life.

I have recounted earlier in this book how in the spring of 1967 we received a great vote of confidence when Major Dermot McCalmont decided to send his horses to us at Seven Barrows; sadly, he died in March 1968, before I ever trained a winner for him. His horses were split between his son Victor and his widow June. Victor's horses left me to be trained by Peter Nelson, as Victor and his step-mother did not get on. However, June was left the pick of eight animals from her husband's stud, and, taking the advice of Dick Warden, a little genius of a horse-master, these were added to her own small string of animals from the mares she owned herself.

June became a staunch and most generous ally, and her three sons, Hugh, Pat and Mikey, are still dear friends of ours. Pat told me recently that we trained a Royal Ascot winner for her for eight years running, with only that number of horses in training each year. From the earnings of just one horse – the volatile Linden Tree, who won the Observer Gold Cup and Chester Vase, as well as being second in the Derby to Mill Reef – she was able to buy and build up her stud farm at Martinstown in County Limerick. She was the most delightful woman; we telephoned her every Sunday to discuss results and plans, and never a cross word passed between us. She invariably came over to see her horses run, with a Balkan Sobranie cigarette always dangling from her lips.

Dr Carlo Vittadini and his wife Henriette sent us horses, having previously trained with Harvey Leader and Noel Murless. Grundy was obviously the star; but, along with Keith Freeman, we managed to find many other good horses for Carlo, and developed a very successful partnership that turned, as with many of our long-standing owners, into an enduring friendship. The first to come to us was a great big three-year-old called Ortis. He had won the Italian Derby that year, but it was thought that he needed a change of scenery. He took a fierce hold, and in fact I found that all the Italian horses we trained pulled very hard and had very bad mouths, suggesting that they had been badly broken in. One morning Ortis got loose, and ended up at Geoffrey Champneys' yard in Upper Lambourn, where Nick Gaselee now trains. He hadn't got a scratch on him when they caught him, and Geoffrey could not believe that he was only a four-year-old, he had such strong and well-developed legs. I think that he was rather envious and would like to have popped him over a few hurdles! Champneys was a very good jumping trainer, but never had much luck. He had come close to winning the Grand National in 1948, but Eddie

Reavey on Zahia went the wrong way two fences from home and ran out when disputing the lead with Sheila's Cottage.

One morning I thought I would ride out another hard puller of Carlo's, Patch, and asked Bonk to follow me up the short gallop by the Faringdon road as I wanted him to do a sharp canter. By about halfway up Patch was pulling my arms out and I was going faster than I wanted; but I was just able to pull him up before we got to the white railing at the top of the gallop. Bonk was not fooled, and said to me as we pulled up, 'That was a funny sharp canter.'

Owners can turn up in the most unexpected places. I once went to speak to the Eton Equestrian Society, and one of the boys asked how a colt I trained called Royal Boxer had run in the Horris Hill Stakes at Newbury that day. I said, 'He is a typical son of Royal Palace (like Patch); they all sweat a lot, and pull like hell. Why did you ask that?' and he replied, 'I am the owner Mr Joel's nephew,' which was a bit embarrassing.

Another owner of whom I was very fond was Lord Howard de Walden – who, for reasons entirely unconnected with racing, earned himself a curious footnote in modern history. Driving in Munich as a young student, he had to brake hard to avoid a man with a moustache crossing a street. He did not know until later that he had nearly mown down Adolf Hitler. Had he been a less conscientious motorist, history might have turned out quite differently.

The Howard colours, among the most famous on the race-course, had an artistic inspiration. When his father had started racing, he went to his friend Augustus John, the painter, and asked what colour would go well with the green of the turf. Augustus John replied 'apricot'; and thus the celebrated colours were born. Lord Howard had trained with Noel Murless and bred some lovely horses at his well-established studs at Newmarket, Thornton (near Thirsk) and Avington, near his beautiful house at Hungerford. We did not train the best of his horses, but we did train one of his nicest fillies, Sancta, who won three races, and became one of his best broodmares. Beautifully bred herself, she produced several nice winners. Lord Howard's knowledge of racing was immense, as was his enjoyment of life. He was ably supported by his second wife Gilly, who made him so happy until his death aged 87 in 1999.

The last big owner for whom I trained was Sheikh Hamdan Al-Maktoum. When he first asked me to buy some horses in America in 1982 I had never met him, but I knew he was expanding his interest in bloodstock. Tom Jones, who already trained for him, is a great friend of ours, and I asked him as a courtesy if it was all right by him to train for the Sheikh. He said, 'You'll never meet a better owner; carry on.' I soon came to realise that Sheikh Hamdan is a most remarkable man. I have never had an owner who knew his horses better, and even taking into account that he has a very efficient staff, how he kept tabs on his enormous operation was a revelation to me.

In 1985 Bobby Dalby and Hubie de Burgh, both of whom worked for Sheikh Hamdan, were asked to go with his stud manager Angus Gold and myself to the yearling sales in Canada to look at possible fillies, as there was a partial dispersal sale of yearlings from E. P. Taylor's stud at the big sales at Woodbine in September. All three were excellent company, and we had a hilarious time. The sales looked impressive, but it appeared to all of us, and to me in particular, that there was only one yearling worth buying, a filly by Vice Regent. She was only small, but I have never minded small fillies, and we bought her for the astronomical figure in those high-flying days of $1 million. She was called Thaidah and did quite well at two, winning round Chester, and finishing a close fourth in the Moyglare Stakes at The Curragh.

As a three-year-old, her first run was in the Fred Darling

Stakes at Newbury, and after this, thinking that she was not quite good enough for the Guineas, we decided to run her in the Italian Guineas in Rome. We were not sure that she liked soft ground, as she had very small feet, and inevitably, when we arrived at the racecourse, the heavens opened. Needless to say, the going was much too heavy for Thaidah, but she did win a Listed race at York in August.

Although I felt I probably got only the second division of Sheikh Hamdan's horses, it was a pleasure to train for such a generous man.

Not all our owners were an unmitigated joy to deal with, however – though sometimes the problems lay not with the owners themselves so much as with their associates and advisers. I have related in an earlier chapter how the owners of Rock Roi, Colonel and Mrs Roger Hue-Williams, sent some horses to us on the retirement of Sir Gordon Richards. Their main stud was in Ireland, at Rathasker near Naas in County Kildare, where all their big winners were bred. They also had a stud at their home at Woolton Hill near Newbury, which is a wonderful area for breeding good horses. Just adjacent is the stud owned by Johnny Hislop, while over the hill Sheikh Maktoum Al-Maktoum has his Gainsborough Stud, formerly owned by Herbert Blagrave.

Vera Hue-Williams was reputed to be of Russian extraction, and certainly had a very strange accent. The Colonel was her third husband; she had previously been married to a Mr Berger of the paint firm, and Tom Lilley of the footwear chain Lilley & Skinner, who had owned Supreme Court, trained by Evan Williams to win the first King George VI and Queen Elizabeth Stakes at Ascot in 1951. Evan was an all-round genius. Born in Wales, he had arrived with Ivor Anthony at Wroughton as a light boy of no consequence. Ivor was a wonderful trainer of jumpers and soon realised the potential of his new recruit, who went on to be a leading jockey, winning the Grand National on Royal Mail and the Cheltenham Gold Cup on Golden Miller. After the war Evan bought Kingsclere, and trained very successfully there. After retiring from training he was master and huntsman of the Tipperary foxhounds for eighteen seasons from 1953, and not only gave wonderful sport but, along with his delightful wife Jill, was extremely kind to all the young people like me who came over for the most glorious hunting in beautiful wild country.

Evan had trained for Mrs Hue-Williams, and said that in those days when she first had horses it was always 'Yes, Mr Williams,' and 'No, Mr Williams,' and 'Do what you zink is best for ze 'orse, Mr Williams.' But she learnt a lot very quickly, and was not so docile when we started to train for her. She may not have known much about the look of a horse, but she was very clever; and she and her husband had very good stud managers when I first trained for them. Their adviser at that time was Johnny Hislop, a cunning little man who caused trouble at times, and with whom I had several rows. He had been a very stylish amateur rider, and rode Kami into third place in the 1948 Grand National. By complete luck he bred and owned Brigadier Gerard, a smashing horse who was beaten only once in his entire racing career. Johnny had been fortunate to have been given a nomination by Lord Carnarvon to his stallion Queen's Hussar, who stood just down the road from Johnny's stud, because he helped Lord Carnarvon with his matings. The mare he sent was a useless bitch, and it says much for the ability of Dick Hern and Joe Mercer, who trained and rode Brigadier Gerard, that the colt did so well, although Johnny always announced to the world that he had planned the mating to bring together the bloodlines of some famous stallions. He also stated that he had trained the horse himself. One day at Salisbury, Henry Candy, who was then training for him, asked Hislop, who often moved his horses about from trainer to trainer, why he did not want Philip Waldron, who was stable jockey to Henry and a decent rider, riding his horses. His reply was, 'I have decided to go freelance with my jockeys.' Henry's reply was, 'You appear to be doing the same with your trainers!'

Roger Hue-Williams could be troublesome at times. One Sunday morning, when he had asked if he could come round to see their horses, he was very late arriving. We left the horses tied up but put their lunchtime feeds in their mangers, so that they would be happier. Roger, being rather nosey, looked in their mangers but did not say anything at the time. However, on his return home he wrote me a furious letter asking why the horses had not eaten up. He got a fairly sharp reply to the effect that the only reason the feeds had been in the mangers was that he had been so late turning up.

For all the ups and downs we had with the Hue-Williamses, though, they were entirely supportive over the Rock Roi case and could be very generous. As soon as English Prince won the Irish Derby, they were enquiring what we would like as a present; the swimming pool we asked for was installed and running by September.

We had a lot of fun with another couple: Bobby and Helen Kennard, who now live in Lambourn, having previously been based in Salisbury. They suddenly rang me and said 'Would you train for us?' They had been friendly for a long time, but had their horses with Bill Wightman at Winchester, and I was surprised and worried that they wanted to move, as it has never been my wish to take horses from other trainers. I told them this, and also rang up Bill, who had been a friend for many years. He told me to carry on, as they said that they were going to move anyway as they believed he was about to retire, which indeed he did shortly afterwards. So we took the horses, and they nearly all won. The Kennards had bred Cadeaux Genereux, winner of the July Cup and the Nunthorpe Stakes, and other good horses, and always got good prices at the sales.

I trained the occasional horse for Charles St George – a very clever man, one of the shrewdest judges of racing and form, and best friend of Lester Piggott. My first involvement with Charles came through William Pigott-Brown, whom I had known since he was a small boy in Gloucestershire. William, in those days a top-flight and very stylish amateur rider, had a stud near Didcot in Oxfordshire, and shared a nice filly trained by us, called Jakomima, who won the Musidora Stakes at York in 1972. He had also bred a good horse called Virginia Gentleman, who won the Queen Anne Stakes at Royal Ascot; he had dressed in rather exuberant fashion on this occasion, with a very loud purple morning suit and hat, and as I was walking just behind him to get a saddle from the weighing room, I saw the two very smart gatemen in their green velvet suits try to stop him. When he protested, saying, 'Let me through, I bred the last winner!', they let him past, after which one turned to the other and said, 'I hope he doesn't breed anything else!' William has a heart of gold, and now lives in Cape Town, where his hospitality is legendary.

The one mistake I made was getting too heavily involved with the Wildenstein family. In 1973 I was asked to train a three-year-old filly called Pixie Tower for them, because there were very few sprint races in France; we won two races with her that year, and three in 1976 with a three-year-old called Indian Warrior, again sent to us as there were so few suitable races in France. The owners seemed very pleased, and when Angel Penna, their brilliant but volatile trainer in France, decided to move to America, I was asked if I would take more of their horses to be trained in England.

I went over to Chantilly to see Alec Wildenstein, Daniel's son, and Penna, and we discussed what should be sent. The horses were a motley collection of well-bred animals, with their tails down to the floor, and obviously just ticking over while their whereabouts was decided. Crow, the St Leger winner of 1976, was among them, looking very miserable and lean, after an unsuccessful four-year-old season in New York. Buckskin, that dour but good stayer, was also there, but his flat feet were a nightmare, and the blacksmith's handiwork had to be seen to be believed. We agreed to take ten of them in the first instance; but only a little later, I was asked to take another twenty-five. This posed a dilemma; I longed to train good horses and was tempted to be greedy and take what was offered, but at that time had a full yard of 100 occupied boxes. I told Alec Wildenstein I could find room for ten more, though it would mean leasing another yard, and would find somewhere for the others. I found that Charlie Nelson, at Kingsdown in Upper Lambourn, had an empty bottom yard, and I was able to rent it temporarily and put in separate staff. It was an effort, but not knowing how long the Wildensteins would last, because of their reputation for rapidly firing their employees, we felt it was worth it. I found a young trainer, Gavin Hunter, at East Ilsley to take the others, thinking it might be a help to him.

The horses arrived by plane at Gatwick and some from New York in February 1978. We checked them all over thoroughly straight away, and sent reports on them to the Wildensteins. One problem I mentioned to them was that Crow had a slight blemish on a tendon, and although our vets passed it, before the days of scanners we were always conscious of a possible latent problem.

We started off the season very well in 1978, with a Wildenstein winner at the Craven Meeting in Leonardo da Vinci, who cantered home in the Wood Ditton Stakes for unraced three-year-olds. This colt, a great big rangy creature with legs that went everywhere, was by Brigadier Gerard, out of Lupe, the filly that had beaten our State Pension in the Oaks. He did not show a lot at home, and always looked like a bit of a camel to us; but in the race he amazed us, cantering home on a tight rein. Pat got off him, and said, 'This is the best horse I have ever ridden,' which I thought was a bit premature; I also thought at the time that Pat had had a very short memory, as only a year or two before he had ridden horses like Grundy and Vitiges, a very good horse on his day. These remarks, made by trainers and jockeys in the heat of the moment, often come back to haunt them, and are best avoided. Seraphina won the Nell Gwyn Stakes at the same meeting before finishing third in the Guineas, so things were going along nicely.

We gave Crow his first outing of the season in a conditions race at Longchamp. Having appeared to lose his form the previous year, the horse had put on a lot of weight since he joined us and was showing plenty of sparkle. The bloodstock agent Gilles Forien, one of our great friends in France, said he had never seen him looking better. In the race – ridden by Yves Saint-Martin, who at the Wildensteins' insistence rode their horses in France – he cruised up to the leader, Rex Magna, the winner of the French St Leger the previous year, but then came off a straight line; inevitably, he was disqualified for crossing the other horse and was placed second.

We had had terrible trouble with the feet of Buckskin, the best French stayer of 1977. I have never seen flatter front feet on any horse I have ever trained. The French blacksmith's policy had been to let his toes grow longer and longer, but our blacksmith, Barry Payne, disagreed. He had had a very good grounding from an excellent farrier, and on his advice we decided to pull his feet right back. Buckskin ran well in the Sagaro Stakes at Ascot, where the going was very testing and the horse was possibly a bit short of work because of his foot problems. We then ran him at Longchamp, where he was very impressive in winning the Prix du Cadran, the French equivalent of our Ascot

Gold Cup, by three lengths. All was now set for the Ascot Gold Cup, but in the meantime the horse's feet were causing us merry hell. We decided to try and let his feet grow again by exercising in rubber shoes, but he was such an extravagant mover that he used to shed them as if he were throwing plates in a Greek restaurant. In those days we did not have the benefit of the modern glue to hold shoes on, since perfected by the Lambourn farrier Gary Pickford, who now employs ten people at his shop in Upper Lambourn.

As for Crow, we ran him next in the Ormonde Stakes at Chester, where he got upsides in the last furlong to beat Hot Grove by a head. Hot Grove had been second to The Minstrel in the 1977 Derby, and so the form looked rock solid; moreover, Pat said that Crow, having won the St Leger two years before, over a mile and seven furlongs, had not really appreciated the tight track at Chester. The horse's next outing was in the Coronation Cup at Epsom. Alleged, the Arc de Triomphe winner, and Dunfermline, who had been expected to take part, declined the invitation to run, so the race did not turn out to be as good as billed; we needed something to make a good gallop for Crow, and fortunately had a useful pacemaker in Paico, a nice colt who had just won the Aston Park Stakes at Newbury. Our main opponent was Balmerino, a prolific winner in New Zealand and Australia, and now trained by John Dunlop. He had been unconvincing in his second race at Goodwood, winning narrowly, but that was only over one and a quarter miles, and it was felt that the mile and a half at Epsom would suit him better.

After Paico had made the running at a good pace, with Frank Morby on, Smuggler, winner of the Yorkshire Cup and Henry II Stakes at Sandown, took over; then, after hitting the front two furlongs out, Crow drew away to win by four lengths, a very easy and impressive performance. It was a great thrill to get this dear little horse back to his very best, and even Daniel

Wildenstein, who I felt seldom showed much emotion, seemed pleased.

Despite our continuous worries with his feet, we let Buckskin run in the Ascot Gold Cup, as the going was firm and, although the feet were growing slowly, time was not on our side. In the race he was always struggling, and finished a well-beaten fourth to Shangamuzo. He was as brave as a lion, but there is no gainsaying the racing adage: no foot, no horse. I went to saddle up for the next race, only to be met on my way back to the stands by Charles Benson who told me that Daniel Wildenstein, in the usual family style, has been screaming blue murder at Pat's riding. He apparently announced that either Lester or Yves Saint-Martin would have won on the horse, and that he did not want boys riding his horses again. I ignored this outburst, and counted to at least twenty. My only reply was that if they did not want Pat they could take their horses away; we were doing well for them, but they were known to be difficult people and poor losers.

We continued to try to train Crow for the King George VI and Queen Elizabeth Stakes, but suddenly the suspect leg started to show signs of warmth and filling. He was completely sound, but had done a lot of mileage in several countries, and we knew the writing was on the wall. This news, predictably, did not go down well with the horse's owners. I got back from the Keeneland sales to take a furious telephone call from Alec Wildenstein, who in my view was the worst troublemaker of the lot, to say that the horses were leaving the next Monday.

I was sad to lose the horses, but relieved that I would no longer have to train for such unpleasant and ungrateful people. I worked out that we had had forty-six runners for them and thirteen winners, including two Group One races.

The Wildensteins sent their horses to Henry Cecil, and although he got Buckskin back to his best form, because of the remedial work we had done on his feet, they did not stay very long there either. They also sacked the best young trainer in France, the Englishman John Hammond.

In general we have been very lucky with our owners, and many of them have become real friends; but I found that as time went on there were fewer and fewer of the old school of owner–breeder, and more owners who tended to look over their shoulders at the bright new man coming along, and to change trainers at the drop of a hat. The new trainer probably does not do any better, but they feel that a change is as good as a rest. I felt that it was little use trying constantly to please and placate owners who had their own fixed opinions. If you have a dentist who says you ought to have some teeth out, and you disagree, he might want to tell you that you would be far better off tying a bit of string round the door handle, and the other end to the offending tooth, and kicking the door shut to get rid of it. You give advice, as a so-called expert, and if they don't heed it they are better off elsewhere.

Nor can you expect all owners to share your own priorities where horses are concerned – not without persuasion, anyway. I had one owner early on, who owned a garage, and for whom we won a race at Bath with a rather nice potential stayer. He then rang me up and said that he must sell the horse. I asked why, and his answer was that he wanted to do his drive up. I bounced back with the reply that the horse was a lovely big staying horse with a future, and he would make far more money later on. I apparently said to him that if he kept him, he 'would be able to tarmac the whole house'. Despite my efforts, he sold the horse to some cowboy who then broke him down.

The trouble is that if owners keep moving, they obviously don't trust their trainer, and therefore the trainer does not trust them, and the whole system breaks down. Since I grew up I have had only one lawyer, one accountant, and one stockbroking firm; trust and loyalty have always been extremely important to me. Unfortunately, the average racehorse owner today is probably a self-made businessman who wants a quick return and has not grasped the basics of horse management. You can buy the most forward-looking yearling, but suddenly it will start to grow and look backward, and if the owner is always ringing up and asking when his horse is ready to run, you are inclined to rush it and give it work too soon, before it is ready. Some horses are just not ready to race seriously at two, and it is often a good idea just to give them their three runs that season, in order to get them handicapped, so that they can start off as three-year-olds on a reasonable handicap mark. Sadly, in many cases, if a horse does not win on his first or second outing, the owner takes it away and sends it to another trainer – as happened, for example, with Oath, winner of the 1999 Derby for Henry Cecil, who had been trained by Roger Charlton as a two-year-old.

Another aspect of the problem is the purchasing power of the Godolphin operation. Watching as they constantly do for any horse with promise, they are inclined to offer such a sum that the owner cannot refuse it; and so again the horse leaves its trainer. Those who train for the Sheikhs from Dubai are particularly vulnerable to losing horses in this way. The Arabs, too, tend to be very chary about running their two-year-olds in case they don't train on, and often don't allow their trainers to run against other horses of theirs in other yards, when they think they have a certainty with another trainer. This reluctance to engage in proper competition has distorted a lot of our two-year-old form, with colts and fillies fully capable of winning or being placed in Group or Listed races often not being properly tested at two years old, and this in turn risks lowering the prestige of the Epsom Derby.

11

MANAGERS AND AGENTS

When I started training racing managers were a rare breed. In those days the owner and trainer worked together, and built up a relationship of trust and friendship over the years. Nowadays a lot of big owners have a manager to monitor the progress of their horses in training – an individual who probably knows less about horses than the trainer and is unlikely ever to have worked in a racing stable or learned how such an operation works, owned a racehorse, or looked at entries from a trainer's point of view.

This is not to say that all racing managers are either uninformed or unhelpful. Certainly the most helpful one I have dealt with has been Angus Gold, manager for Sheikh Hamdan Al Maktoum, who has an enormous number of horses worldwide, and I also found Michael Goodbody, who managed for Sheikh Maktoum Al Maktoum, very understanding, and receptive to my suggestions, when I trained for his employer. Another excellent manager is Leslie Harrison, who we have known for a long time since he worked for the Hue-Williamses in the Rock Roi days. Others, however, have been less than co-operative, some even downright obstructive. I often felt they would report to the owners things that suited them and not the horse.

A case in point was that of Spike Kirby, manager and veterinary surgeon to the Hue-Williamses after Leslie. We had a colt called Illustrious Prince that they wanted to run in the 1976 Derby. He had been third in the Wood Ditton Stakes at

Newmarket for unraced horses, before winning a good class race for maidens at closing, the Glasgow Stakes at the York spring meeting. The race was run in slower time than the Dante Stakes, a well-known Derby trial at the same meeting, and I felt that while Illustrious Prince was a useful sort, he would not be ready for the hurly-burly of Epsom, especially given his rather straight forelegs. Horses with this kind of conformation are standing on a stilt-like undercarriage, and are unlikely to act around the undulations of Epsom. A typical case was Henbit, who had won the Chester Vase on Chester's level track; while he did go on to win the Derby, he broke down in the process, because his conformation was not suited to the track.

Epsom has its fair share of critics, and some have even suggested that the Derby should be run elsewhere; but that would destroy the point of the race. Some horses are not athletes, and don't act at Epsom, but the course is so fair now, with a superb covering of grass, that most come home as sound as a bell. Some connections excuse a horse's running on the configuration of the track, but quite often their horses have gone lame going *up* the hill in the first half mile, so that theory does not hold water either.

Given my doubts about Illustrious Prince, I decided to work him on the Moss Hill gallop – which, as I have already explained, is an excellent trial ground for potential Epsom horses, with its camber and gradients – with Oats and others, before making a decision about the Derby. Oats, who had been second in the Craven Stakes before winning the Blue Riband Trial at Epsom, acted well, but Illustrious Prince virtually fell down the hill, and showed himself clearly unable to cope with Epsom's gradients. At evening stables, moreover, I found that while Oats had a slight sore shin, which we were able to treat, Illustrious Prince was extremely sore on both front legs, with bony enlargements also emerging – clear signs of physical stress. I rang both Spike Kirby, whom the Hue-Williamses called 'the *professeur*', and the owners themselves. Mrs Hue-Williams's response to my news was that the horse must run, as I had stopped them running English Prince two years before. Spike Kirby said that he would take the colt's sore shins away by treating him with an ultrasound machine, and told the owners that it would be fine to run him. He said that he had used the same machine on a horse of Jeremy Tree's called Gulf Pearl a few years before, and that as a result the colt had been able to run in the Derby – to which I responded that he never ran again after the Derby. Illustrious Prince was certainly less sore after the treatment, but I hardly dared canter him on grass until the day of the race, although we only had primitive plough gallops in those days, very unlike the sophisticated all-weather gallops of today.

Pat Eddery decided that Oats had the better chance and decided to ride him. His decision was justified, as Oats finished a good third to Empery. However, the Hue-Williamses were determined to run their colt, and booked Yves Saint-Martin, the best jockey of his day in France, to ride. It was a complete waste of time. Illustrious Prince was handy at the top of the hill, but fell down it much as he had on Moss Hill, and was beaten by a long way. After the race the Hue-Williamses came up and asked me what had happened to the horse; he 'must have been interfered with at Tattenham Corner'. I replied that that was not the case, and it was now my job to cure the trouble they had caused.

I was seething with rage at the unnecessary harm inflicted on the horse, and next day summoned Kirby to the yard. I asked him who was he working for, himself, the owners, me, or in the horse's interest? When he mumbled some excuse, I resolved never to employ him again, although he had been doing our work after the much-lamented retirement of Charles Frank. He never appeared in the stables again.

It took several months to repair the damage to Illustrious

Prince, so sore was he. He did eventually come sound and won two more races, as well as taking third in the St Simon Stakes at Newbury, before being sent to John Cunnington in France; but I don't think he was ever the same horse again after his ill-advised trip to Epsom.

Another manager I had words with was Johnny Hislop, who appointed himself adviser to the Hue-Williamses at the time we took over Rock Roi from Gordon Richards in 1969. Johnny Hislop was a very stylish amateur rider and wrote good articles on racing each week in the *Observer*, as well as a fine auto-biography, *Far from a Gentleman*; but as a racing manager he was a liability. At York that year Rock Roi, ridden by Duncan Keith, ran very well in the Great Voltigeur Stakes, a race run at a muddling pace, to finish third to Meadowville – showing in the process that he was a little short of top-class speed. After the race, in the unsaddling enclosure, Colonel Hue-Williams asked why Keith had made so much use of the horse, while Mrs Hue-Williams asked why he had been held up. I asked them if they could make their minds up as to how the horse wanted to be ridden, and swept off with Bonk to have a drink – whereupon I suddenly found them trotting along behind us, to try and calm me down. It transpired that Johnny Hislop had told them that Duncan Keith was only a 'handicap' jockey, and not good enough to ride their horses.

I was furious, but contained myself until the Newmarket December sales, when I saw Hislop oiling up to Mr Jim Joel. I walked across to him, and asked him if he would desist from interfering with my riding arrangements. I told him that as far as I could remember he was the only man who had learned about training for nine years and never had the guts to start himself. It was not surprising that he never spoke to me for several years after that. 'Owners' friends' can be a nightmare to professional and conscientious trainers.

My efforts to maintain a professional relationship with the Wildensteins while I was training for them were not helped by a portly journalist called Jim Stanford, who without my knowing had been appointed a Wildenstein mole to supervise our horses. He was a journalist who arrived on a stable visit one spring, greeting me with, 'Hello Peter, nice to see you again, Jim Stanford here.' As far as I knew, I had never met him before. He certainly had a knack for getting hold of information: he announced that Michael Dickinson was being sacked by Robert Sangster, when it was being hotly denied by Robert (though it was quite true), and was also able to extract information from Portman Square which was officially known only to the Stewards of the Jockey Club. He apparently used to report back regularly to the Wildensteins, but as his knowledge of horses was rudimentary, he was probably not much help.

Nor was Charlie Dingwall, a less than successful trainer who, when the profession gave him up, got a job as racing manager – as do many failed trainers – to Prince Fahd Salman of the Saudi royal family. We were training a great big colt called Physical, and on the way home from the gallops one morning the horse occasioned a very nasty accident for one of my best riders and head lads, Ron Thomas, rearing up and coming over backwards on top of him while being led up the drive. Just after this incident Dingwall came to breakfast, and seemed quite charming, looking around the horses and saying how pleased he was with their condition. At lunchtime that day we got a call saying that the horses were being removed that afternoon. Needless to say, that was the end of much communication with him.

Another controversial group of people in racing are blood-stock agents. They are a funny bunch, though I would not go so far as the friend who once described them to me as 'parasites'. I have always found them very helpful when you are trying to buy horses, and they have the time, which trainers away from sales districts don't have, to go round yearlings and mark your card. What one wants is an agent who can tell you what horses not to bother with, as a quick glance at most animals will tell you their qualities and imperfections, bar its eye and heart; not an agent who, when the horse they have suggested to you wins, is first in the unsaddling enclosure, shaking the owner by the hand, and announcing to the world that the horse's success is entirely their responsibility. When an agent comes to you trying to buy a horse, he always asks, 'What will you take for it?' My reply is always, 'What will you give us?' This puts them on the spot, as although horses are nearly impossible to value nowadays, they often have a big mark-up, and to work out what they are going to get out of the deal themselves (and it is often more than 5 or 10 per cent) involves a fair bit of time-consuming arithmetic.

Having said all this, I have found a lot of agents completely fair. I would number among these Robin Hastings and Christo Phillipson of the British Bloodstock Agency, and I always think that John Ferguson, James Delahooke and Joss Collins are very professional – as is the hard-riding Charlie Gordon-Watson, who became a master of the famous Cottesmore hounds in 1999. One of the hardest workers is Johnny Lewis, again of the BBA, who had just two rides for me in amateur races on the flat and won them both. I also used to deal with Julian Lewis, a most amusing man who had been based in France and spoke perfect French. One day he told me that Phil Solomons, an important figure in the music industry, wanted to buy a filly of ours by Riverman called Huahinee, who was for sale. He came to see me and the filly, looking very well; I remarked on his looking so brown and he said he had been on holiday in Tel Aviv. I asked what it was like and he said, 'I'm not going back there again; there's too much competition!'

Certainly agents have a job to do; but they very seldom employ anyone, and do not understand the economics of running a large and underfunded operation like a racing stable, and so for the most part fail to see things from a trainer's point of view. The worst scenario is when you introduce a new client to an agent, and then suddenly find them going off to buy horses to send to another trainer, behind your back. This has happened to me on several occasions, and you then feel that the agent is not entirely on your side.

1 2

GLORY YEARS

The mid-1970s were wonderful years, when hardly anything went wrong.

In the summer of 1973 we were having fun with a sweet little two-year-old filly of Louis Freedman's called Polygamy. She was brilliantly named, as were all Louis's horses, being by Reform out of Seventh Bride. Polygamy came from a grand old-fashioned family, descending in direct female line from the great Hungarian mare Kincsem, who raced for four seasons and won all her fifty-four races, including the Goodwood Cup. Polygamy was only tiny, but won three of her six races as a two-year-old, and in her last race finished fourth, just two short heads off second place (though admittedly over six lengths behind the winner) in the Criterium des Pouliches, the top French race for two-year-old fillies at Longchamp.

She did not grow at all over the winter, but romped home on her first race as a three-year-old, winning the One Thousand Guineas trial at Ascot by four lengths. This made us think that she would have a good chance in the Guineas – and indeed, she ran a wonderful race, and was catching Highclere, ridden by Joe Mercer, when she got nudged off a straight line by Mrs Tiggywinkle, who finished third. We thought she was unlucky not to have won, as she was only a short head behind on the line.

We drove home from Newmarket in deep gloom, as I could not believe that with bigger, and possibly better, fillies coming on, we would have a chance in the Oaks. I felt that we had had our Classic chance with her. But the filly thrived between

Newmarket and Epsom, and we began to feel that all might not be lost. She was so fit that I only kept her ticking over. Then, all of a sudden, ten days before the race, we found one morning that she had got cast in her box overnight, and had a haematoma on her near quarter. There was nothing we could do; we dared not lance it, or treat it with any medication. Charles Frank, our vet, was as usual wonderful, and the condition did not get any worse; so, as the filly was in no way lame, we decided to let her take her chance.

Two furlongs out Dibidale, ridden by Willie Carson, and Polygamy, ridden by Pat, were in front, when there was suddenly a gasp from the crowd, as Willie Carson's weight cloth flew off, and Willie was left balancing like a tightrope walker on a loose girth. Polygamy, having the hardest race of her career, proceeded just to get the better of Furioso, while Dibidale finished third, but had to be disqualified, as Carson would not have weighed in correctly. I never liked the broad, white elastic girths which both Lester and Willie favoured at that time; the elastic used to fray, and lose its grip with time. I never used them myself, and after such incidents as these they were speedily given up, because of the risk of slipping.

Polygamy's final race was the Irish Oaks, where she produced only an ordinary performance to finish third behind Dibidale. The experts all said that this meant that Dibidale was certain to have won the Oaks had it not been for the mishap with the weight cloth; but she had been carrying a stone less weight from two furlongs out – and in any case, surely it was our turn after being so unlucky in the Guineas!

We sent Polygamy straight off to stud after that, hoping she would breed us a good horse, but sadly she died when having her first foal.

Meanwhile we had another good horse going from strength to strength. English Prince had come to us as a great big backward yearling in the autumn of 1972. He had a marvellous temperament, but was terribly weak, and every time we tried to make progress with him in the summer and autumn, he kept going lame. The vets could find nothing wrong, and I felt the whole problem was caused by the colt being so backward; his owners, the Hue-Williamses, insisted on the horse being sent up to Newmarket for tests by the Animal Health Trust, but they found nothing wrong, and we just kept him going through the winter with lots of trotting, and steady cantering, in order to get him right.

In his first race, over a mile at Newbury, he was second to a very good gelding of Dick Hern's called Final Chord. Final Chord afterwards won the Britannia Stakes, a top-class handicap, over a mile at Royal Ascot, and not long after that Keith Freeman rang up Dick Hern and asked if the horse was for sale. Dick asked what price was being offered, and when told accepted rapidly on behalf of his owner Tom Egerton. The deal was done. Later, Dick Hern asked Keith whether he knew that Final Chord was a gelding, and obviously not worth half as much as the price mentioned. There was a slight pause; obviously Keith had not done his homework. However, to give him full credit, the deal still went ahead – though how he explained it all to the purchaser, from Saudi Arabia, history does not relate.

We took English Prince next to Ascot in May, for the White Rose Stakes (now sadly discontinued), which he won very nicely, and then aimed him for the Predominate Stakes at Goodwood, again over a mile and a quarter. Here he was very impressive, and won by six lengths. At this point the question of the Derby inevitably arose, and I was glad that the Hue-Williamses had another good colt in Imperial Prince, who had won the Wood Ditton Stakes at Newmarket and then been second in the Chester Vase, as their first choice to run at Epsom;

for I felt that English Prince, with all his soundness problems as a two-year-old, would not cope with the undulations of the Derby course.

The next problem we had was that Pat Eddery was suspended for Royal Ascot, but luckily Lester was available. I deliberately left English Prince short of work for the King Edward VII Stakes, as I felt we had a chance, if he impressed, of running him in the Irish Derby – on the Saturday of the next week, only nine days afterwards. English Prince won very well at Ascot and blew hard afterwards, achieving a record time for the one-and-a-half-mile trip. Lester Piggott nevertheless decided not to ride him in Ireland, as he said he was not good enough.

The Hue-Williamses allowed our horse to accompany Imperial Prince to The Curragh. We had no jockey, as Pat was still suspended, but were fortunate to find that Yves Saint-Martin was available. The race went according to plan, and was run at a good gallop. I told Saint-Martin, in my best 'franglais', to have the horse handy and hit the front in the straight, but Yves, feeling the horse to be going very well, let him stride along a long way out, and he ran on strongly to beat Imperial Prince by a length and a half.

We were delighted; the horse seemed to be improving with every race. We felt the St Leger was in our sights and ran him in the Great Voltigeur Stakes at York, taking on Bustino, who was improving fast, and had been fourth in the Derby and second to Sagaro in the Grand Prix de Paris. Bustino quickened up to win by four lengths, but Pat eased English Prince when he was beaten.

On our return home, we found heat and filling in one of the colt's tendons. This put an end to his racecourse career, and he was retired to the McCalmonts' stud, Mount Juliet in County Kilkenny. He bred a few winners but was not a great success at stud; nevertheless, he was a pretty good horse, and bar his leg trouble would have made an even better four-year-old.

In the autumn of 1975 we were asked to train a horse called Orange Bay for the Vittadinis; he had won that year's Italian Derby, but then lost his form. He was the first Italian horse that had come to us who had a good temperament and did not pull, and after he won his first race for us, a nice conditions race at Windsor on 1 September, with ridiculous ease, we decided that we had a very good horse on our hands. At the end of that year we had won 124 races in England and Ireland and one in France, for a total of nearly £488,000, and had established records in both number of races won and prize money. The good horses seemed so easy to train and the whole team was swinging away in unison; we felt that 1976 could be just as good.

We started off nicely with Oats, who had won a maiden very nicely at Newmarket the previous season, running second in the Craven Stakes at the same course. He had been looked after by John Warren, a very nice-mannered boy, who was to leave us for a job in Germany; little did we think then that he would gradually work his way up the ranks to the point where he is now a very well-respected bloodstock agent and manager of Lord Hartington's Side Hill Stud, but I hope the time he spent with us gave him a solid grounding in high standards.

Another useful colt had emerged in June McCalmont's good-looking Free State. Home bred by Hotfoot, who stood at her son Pat's stud at Gazeley near Newmarket, and going back to one of her husband's old families of mares, he had won his maiden, the second of two races, at Lingfield in the autumn of 1975. Having won but not run three times, he was allotted a reasonable handicap mark, and we started him off at three in the Stroud Green Handicap at Newbury; he won very easily, but he was rather a stuffy sort and we knew that he was sure to come on after the race. So we stepped him up in class for a better

151

handicap eight days later at Sandown; again he won very easily, and we decided to look at the Irish Guineas, which in 1976 was not looking like a very hot contest. We sent him over two days beforehand and were all set to run him, until on the Friday morning my travelling head lad over there, Eddie Towell, rang me up to say that Free State had kicked the window out of his box in the so-called security block and cut his hind fetlock very badly. We got Ned Goring, a wonderful Irish vet, in to look at him, and he said that there was no chance of the colt running: he would have to have several stitches in the wound, and although it was not very serious, it would take time to heal.

I flew straight over, and we arranged for the horse to be transferred to Ned's clinic. At the stables I found that, although there were grilles on the inside of the windows, the bars were held in place only by a simple and not very effective catch. Free State had, in a fit of exuberance, jumped and kicked, dislodged the mesh of bars and then, with a second swipe, put his foot through the glass. When I arrived, unannounced, after lunch, I found the stable manager staggering down the stairs from his flat, smelling strongly of drink. I told him that I wanted compensation for the owners over his negligence, and after a good deal of haggling the racecourse agreed to refund all the expenses of the colt's abortive journey. When I went over later in the year I found that the bars had still not been put right on the windows, so once again The Curragh got a rocket.

Oats, meanwhile, had pleased me by winning a rather substandard Blue Riband Trial at Epsom nine days after the Craven Stakes. This proved to us that he would act at Epsom, and he was showing us that he really needed more than a mile to show off his talent. He had only had four races and was still immature, but we did not run him again before the Derby, feeling that he knew his job now and could go to Epsom nice and fresh. Despite getting sore shins in the meantime, which did not help his preparation, he pleased us by finishing a good third.

Orange Bay, too, was coming on well. After a promising run in the Earl of Sefton Stakes at Newmarket over a barely adequate nine furlongs, finishing third, he won the Jockey Club Stakes, also at Newmarket, giving weight away and running on well in a slowly run race which did not really suit him. After this we laid him out for the Hardwicke Stakes at Royal Ascot, where we could have a pacemaker, Loud. As the build-up for the race took shape, it appeared that our main danger was Bruni, trained by Ryan Price, a tough stayer who had won the St Leger in 1975 and the Yorkshire Cup this May, and obviously needed a strong gallop. I suddenly had a suspicion that a pacemaker would help Bruni more than Orange Bay and, after consulting with the owners, decided not to play into our opponent's hands. At the last minute I took Loud out.

By this time Tony Murray, Ryan Price's stable jockey, had been replaced aboard Bruni by Lester. There were only five runners, and the gallop was set by a useful horse, Libra's Rib. Bruni was slowly away, and although he got to Orange Bay, who had taken up the running four furlongs out, our horse held on to win by a short head. It was one of those satisfying moments when tactics come right. Not satisfying for everyone, of course: I did hear Ryan Price call Lester a c**t as he came in to dismount. It wasn't really Lester's fault, of course, as Bruni was by this point in his career showing signs of reluctance to start, and the mile and a half of the Hardwicke Stakes was barely adequate for him. The trouble is that these days the winning of the Ascot Gold Cup, admirable race though it is, does depreciate a horse's stud value, so that genuine stayers are hard put to show themselves at their best over the shorter distances.

Orange Bay and Bruni next met in the King George VI and Queen Elizabeth Stakes at Ascot, where our horse ran a wonderful race at a very good pace to finish a close third to Pawnese and his old rival Bruni. By then our old friend Free State, who had returned from his recovery in Ireland looking magnificent but with a very large tummy on him, had run a good race to finish third in the Britannia Handicap, following up with a second at the July meeting at Newmarket, where he gave the winner Trusted 18lb. We were winning lots of races.

After the Derby we rested Oats until Goodwood, where in the Gordon Stakes he failed by just a short head to catch Smuggler, a good, tough stayer trained by Dick Hern. Free State excelled himself by running second, beaten only a length, to Wollow in the Sussex Stakes, to give him a place in the top flight of milers. We thought he would have a very good chance in the Wills Mile at Goodwood at the end of August: conditions were ideal, as he was getting weight off all five of his opponents, including the very tough Boldboy, who was giving him 18lb. After a tremendous battle our horse got up in the last stride to win by a short head. It was the hardest race he had had, and we felt he had done enough for 1976, so we put him away for the year.

Oats had his warm-up race for the St Leger in the Geoffrey Freer Stakes at Newbury, with four opponents. It was a hard race for him, run at a slow pace, and he was beaten by a head by Swell Fellow. In the final Classic, his last race of the season, he was fourth to Crow, who showed blinding speed to leave the others standing. He too had now done enough for the year, and we thought he might be an even better horse in 1977. Orange Bay had one more run, in the Grosser Preis von Baden Baden, but he ran deplorably in bottomless ground. At this stage he was still in the Arc, but the going at Longchamp turned very heavy and there was no point in running him.

It was in the autumn of 1976 that I was suddenly telephoned from France and asked if I would like to train a leading three-year-old colt called Vitiges. The caller was Monsieur Marc Laloum, owner of a toy factory in Paris; he did not speak very good English, but I gathered that he felt his horse needed a change of scene, as he had rather lost his form. He had won the Prix Robert Papin at Maisons-Laffitte and the Prix Morny at Deauville over five and a half and six furlongs respectively, before being second to Manado in the Prix de la Salamandre and fifth to the same horse in the Grand Criterium, over longer distances. As a three-year-old he had blown up in the Prix Greffulhe over a mile and a quarter before winning the Prix Djebel, a recognised trial for the French Two Thousand Guineas. In the English Guineas he had blazed away in front until collared by Wollow, finishing a very good second. He had then finished sixth to Crow in the Prix Eugene Adam before running a respectable sixth of twenty-three in the Derby. He next ran a wonderful race in the Prix Jacques le Marois at Deauville, beaten just a head, before returning to six furlongs for his last race in France, in which he finished fourth, only a length behind the winner Kala Shikari.

Considering he was by the out-and-out stayer Phaeton, these were pretty good performances and I took up the offer with alacrity. Finding his ideal distance was obviously a problem, but the way he had been trained did not give us much idea, though clearly he had seldom been ridden with restraint. He came to us in September, and one of my best lads (also a head lad), Alec Nicoll, asked to look after him. We found that he had a lovely temperament; he also had a very light mouth, and several bad cuts inside his mouth, so we put a rubber bit on his bridle, and this seemed to settle him. He was a fine, big, tall horse, with a high action, and, like so many French horses, a bit light of bone and a bit upright. M. Laloum seemed very happy for us to set about training him in whatever way we thought best, and with our good friend Julian Lewis acting as interpreter, we were getting on well.

I felt that, ridden with restraint, the horse should surely stay a mile and a quarter, and so we aimed him for the Champion Stakes at Newmarket. There was not much time to prepare him before the race in October, but we worked him once up the Faringdon road gallop and Pat, who rode him, said he gave him the best feel since Grundy.

Stupidly, I did not have a bet on the race, as he started at 22–1; but we did not really know enough about him to be very confident. The colt went steadily to post, and the race went according to plan. The field split into two groups straight away, as it often does. On this occasion the stands side had no chance, but went a good gallop, led by Frank Morby on our Red Regent. Rose Bowl, who had won the Champion Stakes the year before, hit the front, but Vitiges, brilliantly settled by Pat, came in the last furlong to win by a neck, with Crow, the St Leger winner, Northern Treasure and fifteen others left trailing. Admittedly the draw made a difference, but Rose Bowl too was drawn on the far side, and it was a very strong field.

On the strength of this result, the handicappers put Vitiges top of the free handicap for three-year-olds, 5lb in front of Wollow. The horse stayed in training, but was syndicated after the race for around £23,000 a share. He did well over the winter and we thought he had thrived, but he did not show any form in three suitable races, so we sent him off to the Someries Stud, owned by the charming Nicky Phillips. Possibly the change of scenery had helped him regain his very best form, but I always felt that with no plan in his previous training, and no real idea of his preferred distance, he had got himself in a muddle.

Soon after the Champion Stakes, the Laloums flew over and took a small party of family and friends out to the Bell Hotel at Sutton Benger, near Devizes. This was about the very best restaurant in the area, and gave us probably the most superb dinner we have ever eaten. During the meal, Marc Laloum kept calling me Monsieur Walwyn, and eventually I turned to him and said in my very best Franglais, 'Je m'appelle Grand Pet,' meaning 'They call me Big Pete.' He and all the other French-speakers present burst out laughing: in French, 'grand pet' means 'big fart'. So much for my linguistic skills!

At the end of the 1976 season we were narrowly pipped for the trainers' title by Henry Cecil, just £1,189 ahead of us in prize money. Even this margin was attributable solely to one race: the Eclipse Stakes, handed to Wollow on the disqualification of Trepan, the French horse trained by François Boutin, after traces of theobromine were found in his system. (Trepan had already been disqualified from the Prince of Wales Stakes at Royal Ascot, after testing positive for caffeine and theobromine.) This disqualification deprived us of a third title in a row: but how lucky we were to have been top of the table once, let alone twice.

In 1977 we had two good older horses still in training, Orange Bay and Free State. Always a stuffy horse, Free State needed a fair bit of racing to get him really fit. He was fourth in the Lockinge Stakes, then third to Jellaby in the Queen Anne Stakes at Royal Ascot, and each time we felt that he would improve. At the Newmarket July Meeting he ran in the Bunbury Cup and finished second to Kintore, giving him 28lb; after that it was another crack at the Sussex Stakes, where we had the misfortune to take on Artaius, a top-class three-year-old who duly beat us a comfortable one and a half lengths. After that Free State, one of the best-looking horses I ever trained, was sent to stand at David Gibson's stud at Barleythorpe in Rutland, before being exported to South Africa. There he stood at Pat O'Neill's amazing stud, Broadlands, at Newcastle West near Cape Town. Pat is very hospitable, and when we visited her among her menagerie of monkeys, birds and dogs we saw on a wall a poem about the horse, which I copied and have put up at Windsor House:

Thou shalt be for man a source of happiness and health.
Thy back shall be a seat of honour, and thy belly of riches.
Every grain of barley given thee shall purchase indulgence
   for the sinner.

Orange Bay, after a poor showing in the John Porter Stakes at Newbury, struggled home to beat Laomedonte in the Aston Park Stakes at the same course. A moody run in the Hardwicke Stakes at Royal Ascot gave me the impression that he needed blinkers; we tried him in them at home and they really galvanised him. We thought he would have his best chance in another go at the King George VI and Queen Elizabeth Stakes at Ascot, where the two outstanding horses would be the four-year-old Crow and The Minstrel, a tough winner of both the English and the Irish Derbies. Starting at 20–1, we thought we had an outside chance.

The race was strongly run, and Orange Bay hit the front over a furlong out, but The Minstrel held him off to win by a short head. We were not allowed in those days to use a visor – an American innovation, with a small hole in the blinker shield which allows the horse a small amount of sideways vision – and only when The Minstrel passed Orange Bay 100 yards from home did our horse see him, running on again to be beaten by a whisker. With a visor instead of blinkers, he might have seen the danger looming and held on. Still, it was an impressive performance, even better than the previous year's; he beat the third horse Exceller, winner of the Coronation Cup and Grand Prix de Paris, by a length and a half, while Crystal Palace, winner of the French Derby, was fourth, three lengths further back.

Orange Bay went on to take third place in the Benson and Hedges Gold Cup at York before winning the Cumberland Lodge Stakes at Ascot in September in very easy style. His last run was in the Arc de Triomphe; sadly he was never in the race and finished seventeenth. He then retired to the Vittadinis' Beech House Stud at Newmarket. He may have been just below top class, but he was a serious racehorse.

At the end of 1977 we had again won over 100 races – 111 in all, including one in France – and were third in the table, with over £316,000 in winning prize money. Another glory year.

13

MORE JOCKEYS – AFTER PAT

When Pat got a remarkable offer from the team then known as 'Sangster's Gangsters' of a job riding the best horses in Europe, we knew we would have to find ourselves another jockey. As soon as Stavros Niarchos heard about it, he immediately offered to increase substantially the retainer for riding his horses, but to no avail; Pat had made up his mind, and indeed it was an offer he could hardly refuse.

In all the controversy over the whip, I cannot remember that, in all the winners Pat Eddery rode for me, he ever marked a horse so that the weals showed next day. Surely this must be one of the criteria for judging whether a jockey is guilty or not. He rode us a total of 689 winners in England, Ireland, France, Germany and the United States and has equalled Lester Piggott's record of eleven championships. He is riding as well as ever and must have a great chance of being champion again.

His first ride for us was on 31 October 1970 at Newmarket, and his first winner, 13 September 1971. His full record is:

1971	1	1978	48
1972	14	1979	36
1973	76	1980	62
1974	86	1981	1
1975	109	1982	—
1976	95	1984	4
1977	96	1985	3

1986	2	1993	2
1987	2	1994	5
1988	16	1995	4
1989	11	1996	2
1990	5	1997	4
1991	2	1998	1
1992	2		

Pat would be a hard person to replace; but, as it turned out, we had a great stroke of luck.

That August we held our annual lurcher show at Seven Barrows. We ran this event for about ten years, until the local landowners got fed up with the unauthorised coursing and poaching on their land that came with some of the visitors. One year we had an archery competition, in which we all took part. At about three o'clock, the organiser came to me and asked me if he could pack up, as it was raining. I said that I thought this rather feeble, and that I was sure that the English or Welsh archers who had served under King Edward III and King Henry V would not have downed their bows at Crécy or Agincourt because of a spot of rain. His reply was, 'Guv'nor, if you had been at Crécy or Agincourt, we would all be speaking French.'

At this year's show, Joe Mercer came up to me and straightforwardly asked me what my plans were for a jockey, having obviously heard of Pat's good fortune. He was riding as well as ever, but had just been eased out by Henry Cecil, who had grabbed Steve Cauthen from Barry Hills. It really was musical chairs that year. Joe said he would go on riding as long as he felt like it, and give me good warning when he was intending to retire. During our years spent battling against the virus we had lost some good horses, but we were still a pretty strong stable, and I immediately accepted his offer to come to us.

We had a big, lovely-looking three-year-old by Exbury in the stable in 1981, called Halsbury. He had won his first two races in good style and was gradually improving, with the look of a genuine stayer. He was unplaced in the Queen's Vase at Royal Ascot, but after that won a conditions race at Chepstow very nicely, and followed up in July with a very respectable second in the Tennent Trophy, an all-aged handicap at Ayr. We then ran him in the Goodwood Cup, where three-year-olds get a very big allowance. I have always hated running three-year-olds in all-aged handicaps until about July, as the older horses are so much more mature, but it is fine to run them in conditions races, as they meet older horses on very advantageous terms. He ran a very respectable race at Goodwood, finishing a close-up third.

His owner David Oldrey then concocted a plan to win the Cesarewitch with him. The first job was to wait for the handicapper to compile his weights. When these came out, and we saw that the handicapper had given Halsbury 8st 3lb – a fair weight for a three-year-old – David, being a genius on racing in general, and having spent all his spare time on studying it, decided with his partners to have a substantial bet. I have never dared to ask him what it was, but I believe it was a huge amount by their standards, as they felt that everything was in their favour. All I remember is David ringing me up and saying, 'Whatever you do, do let me know if anything goes wrong with the horse straight away,' so that he could lay the bet off in time. Our main job was to find a race about a month before the Cesarewitch to give the horse a good run, and hopefully a win, without getting a weight penalty. We found a conditions race at Ayr, with only three runners, and Joe was able to ride him.

Halsbury was in great form, having had a break after Goodwood – so great, in fact, that he nearly dropped Joe going to the start. However, he won nicely and all was well; there was no penalty attached to this win, and he still looked like carrying 8st 3lb. This was one pound below Joe's minimum, but that did not bother me, as Joe was such a superb jockey. In the run-up to the race the horse did everything right, and on the morning of the race we were in our bungalow at Newmarket watching a preview of the day's racing on television. Suddenly, to our horror, Peter Bromley announced that there was one non-runner in the Cesarewitch: Halsbury. The news was flashed up on the screen from the number board on the course. I rang up the racecourse stables immediately, and asked to speak to Tony Driscoll, my travelling head lad. I asked him whether everything was all right with Halsbury, and he replied, 'Fine,' he had travelled up well, and had a nice lead out that morning. It turned out that some horse was wearing blinkers, and the announcement had been put against the wrong number on the board. Panic over, we were able to relax, while David, who was on his way to the course from his home near Bedford, did not know anything about the drama until he got to Newmarket and we explained what had happened.

The race itself went very smoothly, being run at a good pace, and Halsbury appeared out of the autumn haze to win very tidily from that doughty old campaigner Heighlin, prepared by a very clever trainer who at that time was just getting started, David Elsworth, a man whom I now like and admire very much.

We felt that Halsbury had done enough for the year, and hoped he might improve and be nearly up to Listed or Group class as a four-year-old. He wintered very well, and probably was better as an older horse, being rated 4lb higher by Timeform. However, he did not win again, finishing third, two lengths behind the winner, in both the Prix du Cadran and the Goodwood Cup, and second to Little Wolf in the Jockey Club Cup over two miles, before being sold to India as a stallion. He was a very good-looking horse and had given his owners a great deal of pleasure.

David had another useful horse in Wagoner, who won the

Doncaster Cup in 1984. Sired by the Arc de Triomphe winner Rheingold, he had been a backward colt, running only once as a two-year-old. David Oldrey loved this sort of horse, and allowed me all the time in the world to let them develop. One of the most important reasons for his success with his horses was that he never got me flustered or in a hurry. If a trainer is being pressurised by impatient owners, he is under strain, and likely to make mistakes in the placing and training of his horses. The two parties must have complete confidence in each other, just as jockey and trainer should, and as indeed happened more often in the days when jockeys were employed by trainers rather than retained by owners.

Wagoner won at Kempton on his first run as a three-year-old and ran only twice more that year, including in the Queen's Vase at Royal Ascot, where he was unplaced. He came into his own at four, winning at Chester, where he led all the way, scorching round that difficult course, and at Newmarket. We then decided to run him in the Doncaster Cup, where he was a 10–1 chance to beat the hot favourite Gildoran, trained by Barry Hills, who had won the Ascot Gold Cup and Doncaster Cup. We did not really think he could win, but there were only four runners, including Harly, who had won the Henry II Stakes at Sandown in May. Joe Mercer had several rides for us that day at Salisbury, where I went to saddle them, so I booked a very good, tough jockey called Tony Ives, and as usual gave him the orders myself on the telephone. If someone else passes on your instructions, they are sure to get it slightly wrong. It is rather like being in a long line, and passing a message on from one end to the other; the message eventually delivered bears no relation to the one sent out at the start. I told Tony that Wagoner was a rather funny character, and did not really like passing horses. When Gildoran and Harly surprisingly dropped out, Petrizzo went on about two furlongs out, and Wagoner gave chase. As he came up to Petrizzo, the leader flashed his tail and Wagoner's head went up, as the two horses were very close together.

When Tony Ives came in, Tim Thomson Jones, my very able assistant at the time, asked Ives whether he should object, and I felt that it was his suggestion that prompted Tony to make a move. Tony immediately put in his objection, and there was then a furious discussion as to whether the objection should be sustained. Eventually, by two stewards to one, Petrizzo was thrown out. We were able to study the Channel Four video tape at our leisure at home; this tape showed the race from a very different angle from the official film, and it did show Wagoner in a much more favourable light. The connections of Petrizzo had appealed, and a final decision was deferred to the Jockey Club stewards.

When the inquiry took place in Portman Square, a week or so later, I asked if I could bring the copy of the Channel Four tape which I had managed to obtain, and show it to the stewards. To my amazement, the stewards allowed this, and after further lengthy deliberations, the appeal was dismissed. I felt justified, as it was my job to keep the race for my owners, if I could, and I myself had not objected to the winner. I have seldom admired a man more than I did when, directly afterwards, Clive Brittain, Petrizzo's trainer, came up to me and shook me warmly by the hand. I wonder how many other trainers would have done the same?

Wagoner did not win again; he was tried over hurdles at Ascot, but jumped poorly to finish second, before running well in the big race at Cagnes sur Mer, the Grand Prix des Alpes Maritimes, and being sold profitably to a French trainer.

In 1985 we were lucky enough to have some good two-year-olds. The sharpest of them was Sperry, a sweet little colt whom we tried to buy in September at the Doncaster sales, where he had been sent by Robin Knipe and his wife Scarlet. Scarlet was the daughter of the great National Hunt jockey and trainer Fred

Rimell, who sent out four Grand National winners, and his wife Mercy. When Fred sadly died, Mercy continued training, and is still a keen racegoer. Sperry looked far too fat at Doncaster and did not make his reserve, but at the December sales was a different cup of tea, and Tim Bulwer-Long and I bought him for a new owner from the Lebanon. That owner did not last very long, and we bought the colt from him for 10,000 guineas. He rewarded us by winning his first race at Salisbury in good style, enabling his connections to collect on a nice bet. He went on running well, and won a nursery at Newmarket.

We also had two small, sharp youngsters, Luqman and Stalker. Luqman was a typical potential two-year-old whom I had bought at Newmarket October sales; he won five of his ten races, including the Mill Reef Stakes at Newbury, and was second in the Middle Park Stakes. We knew Stalker and his family very well, as Charles Smith-Bingham and I had bought her grand-dam cheaply for his father and stepmother. We had won five races with her, and then I had bought her daughter Tarvie for 5,000 guineas, who for Bridget Fetherston-Godley won at two and three years. Stalker set off by winning at Lingfield and Newbury, but had to miss Royal Ascot because of sore shins. He then gradually came back to form, finishing a good third in the Richmond Stakes at Goodwood. He was only fourth in the Seaton Delaval Stakes at Newcastle, not quite getting the seven furlongs; we decided to run him in the Gimcrack Stakes at York and, starting only fourth favourite, he ran on well to win by four lengths. The owner has to make a speech at the Gimcrack dinner; in this case Paddy Fetherston-Godley was asked to do the honours, as his wife Bridget had sadly died of cancer in the summer. Stalker went on to finish second to his stablemate Luqman in the Mill Reef Stakes, before beating his old rival in the Middle Park Stakes at Newbury to take his tally to four wins out of eight races.

The following season neither Luqman nor Stalker trained on or won a race, but that can often happen with neat, precocious two-year-olds – and they had done us proud the previous year. Sperry, however, was second in the Free Handicap to Green Desert, who afterwards was runner-up to Dancing Brave in the Two Thousand Guineas. After another second at Haydock, we let him take his chance in the Cork and Orrery Stakes at Royal Ascot, where Paul Eddery rode a race reminiscent of his brother Pat, getting up in the last stride to beat an over-confident Willie Carson on Cyrano de Bergerac by a short head.

Sperry was sold later to race in America. Several bloodstock agents came to look at him before he was sold privately, one of whom was a well-known Newmarket agent called Peter Wragg – brother to Geoff Wragg, a very successful and thorough trainer. Peter had Sperry led out for his inspection, and, as the horse walked away, shook his head and said, 'I could not possibly buy him, he turns his feet out so much.' This has always made me laugh: you certainly would not buy Peter Wragg as a yearling, as he certainly does turn his feet out.

In the autumn of 1985 Joe Mercer said that he had decided to retire. True to his word, he gave us plenty of warning, and after a lot of discussion I felt that the obvious choice as his successor was Pat Eddery's brother Paul. He was very much in the same mould as Pat, and was at the time second jockey to Henry Cecil. He took quite a lot of persuading to move, as he was very much a Newmarket jockey, but he did come – and he started off well. He rode a big three-year-old colt called Mubaris quite beautifully to win a maiden at Newmarket, and a maiden at closing at York. He also rode Sperry to win at Royal Ascot. However, he is a rather complex character, with little of Pat's charm, and I always found him a bit chippy. At the end of the season he decided to go back to Newmarket, and has been riding abroad for some years.

I chose in his place Brent Thomson, who had done brilliantly well in Australia before being retained by Robert Sangster at Manton. He was a happy person, and we started off in good style, with Turfah being given a fine ride to win the Rosebery Handicap at Kempton, and all was going well until Brent had a fall pulling up in a race at Goodwood, breaking his wrist in the process. This meant that he was sidelined for nearly a month, just when the season was getting into gear. During this period I was very lucky to be able to have Pat Eddery back for some important races at Epsom, and I also used Steve Cauthen. Having developed quickly from youthful prodigy to leading rider in his native America, Cauthen had then fallen somewhat out of fashion there and had been tempted over by a retainer from Barry Hills. He was an instant success; a brilliant judge of pace, with a lovely long length of rein and beautiful hands, he could really get horses running for him. One of his most superb rides was on Reference Point in the 1987 Derby. The previous year's top two-year-old, having closed his season by winning the William Hill Futurity at Doncaster, Reference Point had thereafter been held up in his work, but Henry Cecil did a brilliant job of getting the horse ready after the setback, always the most difficult thing to do; the horse won the Dante Stakes at York in workmanlike style, although still short of work. In the Derby Steve took him to the front from the start, and kept enough up his sleeve to win by half a length, balancing the big and rather heavy horse beautifully to hold on. Now I used Cauthen whenever I could, because not only was he a very high-class jockey, but he had impeccable manners too.

Brent Thomson was back in the saddle in June, but in my opinion wasn't the same man; he seemed to have lost his panache. The end for me came on the horse on which he rode his first winner for me, Turfah. The horse was improving, and I had found a suitable Listed race for him at Deauville. I love

Deauville, but it is a course that takes a lot of riding, and on the round course the turns are quite sharp. I rarely gave explicit instructions, but did so on this occasion, and they were to lie handy and come with a nice long run in the straight. There were about twenty runners, and what did I see to my amazement but Turfah nearly last all the way round, finishing with a real burst of speed to end up fifth, beaten about three lengths. I was speechless with rage, but perhaps not long enough for Brent, who unfortunately for him had to come back on the same plane as us. There is a story told by Angus Gold, who had just taken over as racing manager for Sheikh Hamdan Al-Maktoum, that he rounded the corner to the saddling boxes that afternoon to be confronted by a strange sight. He saw me bashing my head continually against a box door, and when he asked me what it was all about, I am supposed to have said, 'It is all my fault, I am the f*****g idiot that employed this imbecile . . .' I don't deny the gist of the story, and no doubt must have looked very like my nickname Basil Fawlty.

All of a sudden, at the end of September, I had a call from Brent to tell me that he was going back to Australia, as he had a new contract there. After that Pat Eddery came to our rescue on many occasions, and apart from him we used freelance jockeys. One very stylish jockey who has ridden consistently well over the years, and whom I admire, is John Reid. In 1999 he was suddenly sacked from his position as retained jockey to the Manton stable – an astonishing decision, as John is very experienced and I for one would be very happy to have him as stable jockey. There are also several northern jockeys for whom I have considerable regard, including John Carroll, Mark Birch (now retired) and the very able Kevin Darley; we always knew that they would give our horses a proper ride. One of the nicest of the letters I received on my retirement was from Mark, which gave me a great deal of pleasure.

Another jockey I have been very fond of is Ray Cochrane. He started off as an apprentice to Barry Hills, and rode a lot of winners on a two-year-old filly of Barry's called Nagwa, who for a time held the record for the number of two-year-old races won with her tally of thirteen. He then put on too much weight, and, having also become rather unfashionable, started riding over hurdles. Then suddenly he hit form again, riding Chief Singer, a fine big black horse with curious forelegs, to win the Coventry Stakes at Ascot on his first outing, and was again in demand. Ray has terrible problems with his weight, which he has conquered with complete discipline and a rigorous routine of running, but is utterly sound and dependable, and has ridden a lot of winners for me over the years. He rode Kahyasi to win the Derby for Luca Cumani, who retained him, until Luca decided to promote another Italian in Frankie Dettori.

Frankie is undoubtedly a very good jockey, and indeed I gave him his very first ride in England, in a handicap at Kempton. The colt he rode was very good-looking, and always carried a lot of condition. He ran very well, and finished third on his first outing of the season. When he got off, Frankie beamed at me, and said, 'He run well, he fet.' I did not at first understand what he meant, but suddenly deciphered his Italian accent and realised that he meant that the horse was *fat*. I retorted, 'You cheeky little blighter, just go and weigh in.' He is now, of course, a world-class jockey, and earning a lot of money, but I do wish he would desist from his ridiculous habit of throwing himself off a winning horse at a big meeting in the unsaddling enclosure. It is completely unnecessary and could easily scare a horse, to say nothing of the risk of breaking an ankle. In fact, of course, Dettori *did* break his ankle in that awful aeroplane crash in June 2000, when the very brave pilot was killed, and Frankie and Ray Cochrane were very lucky to survive. Perhaps after that, with a suspect ankle, he will stop these antics. They are, after all, only gimmicks for the benefit of the public, and I feel that such behaviour should be prohibited officially, before other jockeys take up the idea. The same applies to standing up in the stirrups and waving the whip as you pass the winning post.

I do not approve either of jockeys who are continually looking round in a race. It is inclined to get horses unbalanced, and what good it does I have yet to discover: a jockey can look one way while a horse comes up on the other side. Greville Starkey did it all the time – but he was a very good jockey, even if he did ride an overconfident race at Epsom on Dancing Brave to throw away the Derby.

The revelation among jockeys in the last few years has been Kieren Fallon. Coming over from Ireland as apprentice to Jimmy FitzGerald, he gradually rose up the ranks to a position riding for the astute Ramsden family – at which point Henry Cecil, out of the blue, suddenly chose him as stable jockey, amazing us along with most other people in racing. It was thought that the partnership would not last beyond the Craven meeting, but on the contrary it was a tremendous success. He lost the plot in the Eclipse Stakes on Bosra Sham when going the wrong way up the straight, but otherwise has shown time after time what a brilliant jockey he is. His style is very effective: he sits very low in the saddle, and really punches horses along. He would have been with Henry a long time but for a controversial sacking over a matter not connected with the racecourse. He now has a retainer from Michael Stoute, the trainer with about the strongest string in the country, and is fairly sure to be champion jockey or runner-up for several years to come.

When Sheikh Hamdan's racing manager, Angus Gold, approached me in the autumn of 1989 about Willie Carson riding all the Sheikh's horses as his retained jockey, I felt fairly happy about it. Carson, rising inexorably from very humble beginnings in Stirling, Scotland, had been stable jockey to several trainers before getting the job with Dick Hern – apparently because Joe Mercer, who had ridden for the West Ilsley stable for so many years, had suddenly got the push for supposedly telling Lord Weinstock that the horse he had just ridden was no good. Carson had already ridden some winners for me, including a good-looking handicapper Royal Dancer, who had won the King George V Handicap at Royal Ascot in 1971. He was extremely strong and very light, and knowing what a success he had been with Dick, with a highly impressive big-race record, I thought the arrangement would work very well. He also appealed to me in that, like so many old-time jockeys, he loved slipping away to hunt in Leicestershire, and I felt we were probably on the same network.

He was, however, known to be very tight with his money, and lads in the stables where he worked had little time for him. Even as an apprentice with Gerald Armstrong at Middleham, he used to come across to the apprentices at Spigot Lodge close by to ask for boot polish, soap and toothpaste, as Colonel Wilfred Lyde, their employer, used to provide these items for them, while Gerald Armstrong did not.

It is only when a retained jockey is riding for you on a regular basis that you really get to know them and their foibles. In the old days the stable jockey was retained by the trainer on behalf of the owners; Pat Eddery, for example, when he was our jockey, would ring me up every evening to discuss the stable prospects, and what had happened that day, whether I had been there or not; it was like a successful marriage, where every confidence is disclosed. There is no point in the jockey getting off a horse and delivering an immediate verdict on the spot – especially not to the owners – as there are so many other factors to consider, which may only reveal themselves that evening or the next day. It is also, in cases where the horse has not won or done as well as expected, inclined to upset the owners, who think that their pride and joy which they have bought or bred can do no wrong, when it may well be ungenuine or have some bad habit or temperamental trait.

In contrast to Eddery, Carson seldom if ever rang up after a race because his retainer was paid directly by Sheikh Hamdan, and so he felt his main duty was to the owner and his manager; as a consequence I felt that probably even Sheikh Hamdan's butler, if he had one, would know more about the jockey's verdict than I did. Willie certainly rode some winners for us, but he also lost some big races which I felt he should have won. He rode a pretty good horse called Rami in the Queen Anne Stakes at Royal Ascot, came to win the race, thought he *had* won, and dropped his hands, being beaten a whisker. On another occasion he got in a terrible tangle up the straight at Ascot on an old horse called Hateel, a very good handicapper on the fringe of Group class, in the two-mile Sagaro Stakes. Ascot's straight is very difficult to ride, as it is very short from the turn on the round course. After having the horse nicely placed all the way, Willie elected to come up the rail through a wall of horses. Frequently impeded, he suddenly lost the plot, finishing a close-up fourth, but in the process flattening the horse on his outside, when trying desperately to get through. Hateel was disqualified and placed last, so that everyone lost out, including the struggling stable staff who rely on their percentages of winning prize money to boost their earnings.

Another horse over which Carson annoyed me was a fine big colt by the dual Arc winner Alleged, called Husyan. He won two of his first three races as a three-year-year old, and at four led virtually all the way to win the Brigadier Gerard Stakes at Sandown over a mile and a quarter in May. His next target was the Hardwicke Stakes at Royal Ascot. Carson elected to set him off in front and dispute the lead at a furious pace with Old Vic. Joe Mercer had told me not to let Husyan make the running with

Old Vic, who had won the French and Irish Derbies the year before, because although it was Old Vic's first race of the season, he was going like a train at home. Not only did Carson make the running, but he decided to race right round the outside of Swinley Bottom, going a furlong further than any other runner. I was asked after the race for my opinion, and all I said was that I thought the little man was going to drop in for a cup of tea at Windsor Castle on the way round, after the very strange route he had taken. In fact both horses ran themselves into the ground and finished well beaten, Old Vic third and Husyan fifth.

I am not saying that going around the outside at Ascot is a bad idea; but it only works on the Old Mile, as Carson showed when he used this tactic to good effect on Bahri when winning the Queen Elizabeth II Stakes a few years later. In that race the going was far better under the trees.

Husyan came back to form in the Scottish Classic at Ayr, leading from a long way out to win readily. He was sent to America afterwards, but as I feared would be the case he did not do very well, as the tracks there were too tight for him.

Carson is very opinionated, and thought that he was never wrong. After his retirement in 1996 he was appointed a new commentator for the BBC, where he was something of a contrast to his new colleague Clare Balding. I did, however, hear him on the radio in April 2000, with Peter Bromley, and thought he was far better to listen to than to look at. Clare, Richard Pitman, Jimmy Lindley and Peter Bromley are an excellent team; and I remember well the halcyon days of Clive Graham and Peter O'Sullevan, who captured the whole racing scene on television with their knowledge and flair. At one point, when things were going really well, I was rung by Claude Duval, a long-serving writer on the *Sun* with a very dry sense of humour. He asked me whether a certain horse was going to run in a big race. All I said was, 'I have just had someone else on asking the same question.'

When Claude asked me who that was, I replied, 'Peter O'Sullevan, who I call Pedro the Fisherman: like St Peter, he is always angling for something!'

On Carson's retirement I was asked for my comments on possible successors. I suggested Pat Eddery, who had done so well for the stable in the past, and with whom we got on like a house on fire, but in the event Sheikh Hamdan decided to promote Richard Hills, who had been riding for Tom Jones. Hitherto he had hardly ridden for us, but had had a good grounding, being the son of Barry, one of the most successful trainers Lambourn has ever had. I thought Richard a much nicer character than his brother Michael, but he lacked confidence, and my first experience of him in a big race was not very encouraging.

We had a fine big two-year-old by Storm Bird called Mukaddamah, who won his maiden at Nottingham and the Group Three Champagne Stakes at Goodwood in exemplary fashion. He was due to run in another Champagne Stakes at Doncaster in September, but then he coughed a few times, and when he was scoped we found that he had some blood and muck down his windpipe. We therefore postponed his next appearance, and once the problem had cleared up with treatment we decided to run him in the Racing Post Trophy at Doncaster at the end of October. We had won the race three times in the past, and always felt it was a good race for a backward colt, though not up to the standard of the Dewhurst Stakes, the recognised two-year-old championship.

Willie Carson chose to ride Dayjur in the Breeders' Cup Sprint at Belmont Park (of which I have a photograph showing my father riding in a race before the First World War), and I wanted to go over there too: we were running Relief Pitcher, a very good four-year-old, in a stakes race the same day. In Willie's absence Richard, at this stage his understudy, came in for the ride. There were only four runners and I talked about the race endlessly with Richard, discussing how he should ride Mukaddamah. I remember saying that I thought Doncaster had the longest, stariest straight in the world, a tremendous test for a two-year-old, and he should not make his run too soon. I told him not to be in a hurry, but to keep Mukaddamah balanced and come with plenty of speed, remembering that this was an immature colt.

After seeing our horse win very easily in America with Pat Eddery, it was with astonishment that I heard that Mukaddamah had been beaten a short head at Doncaster by the ordinary Peter Davies, trained by Henry Cecil and ridden by that artist from America, Steve Cauthen. When I rang up Bonk, who had had a long and frustrating drive home from the races, she said that she was very glad I was not there as I would probably have had a coronary and throttled Hills. Apparently, after I had gone to America, he had been given different orders to let him stride along from a long way out. Mukaddamah had faltered with a furlong to go, and Peter Davies, given a peach of a ride by Steve, got up in the last stride. I do wish that owners would leave the instructions to the trainers, who live and work with their horses every day and so must inevitably know them better.

Notwithstanding this uncertain start, Richard Hills was duly ensconced as Sheikh Hamdan's jockey and, although he seldom came to ride work, he did take a full interest in the stable and staff. He may not be a Pat Eddery, but they are few and far between.

I think that the American jockeys who have come over here have improved our jockeys' riding styles, as they are brilliant judges of pace, but I dislike their habit of putting only their toe in the stirrup iron. My father always said that unless you were riding a show hack at a horse show, there was only one place for the foot, and that was right in the iron. The other thing that has improved the style of our jockeys is the tightening up of the rules on use of the whip; this has made them open their shoulders and use their hands more, instead of reaching for the whip when either they or the horse get tired. I hate to see horses hit down the flank, as this hurts them; the South African jockey John Gorton, who came over here and rode some winners for us was a very pleasant man, but in a tight finish he always looked as though he was hitting the horse with his handbag.

We have also had great fun and success with our lady jockeys. They will never be able to compete on the same terms as men – even in tennis, women are not allowed to take on men in singles tournaments – but they are such an important part of racing that they must be encouraged. So many girls now work in racing stables, and many have become very proficient work riders. And when you see neat girls crossing the country superbly while out hunting, there is no reason why they should not excel against their own sex in races.

The first girl who rode for us was Franca Vittadini, Carlo's daughter: she won on Hard Day in 1975 in the De Beers ladies' race at Ascot, then the opening race on the card, and followed up this achievement by winning the same race twice more, on Stavros Niarchos' Cracking Form, in 1980 and 1981. She was very strong and determined, and horses really ran for her. After her, there was a long gap before two more good lady riders came into our lives. The first was Becky Blandford, the wife of the heir to the Duke of Marlborough. She was mentioned to us by Judy Gaselee, whose niece was a friend of hers and who told us that she wanted to ride out racehorses. In March 1993 she had had a terrible fall off a hunter on the road while out with the Heythrop hounds, and fractured her skull; she had not been wearing a crash helmet. I believe that nowadays it should be compulsory for everyone riding horses to wear a proper helmet, even hunt servants. They may be uncomfortable, but riding produces the second greatest number of head injuries of all sports after skiing – and after all, the skull is only an eggshell protecting what little brain most of us have.

In any event, the brilliant surgeons in Oxford helped Becky to a miraculous recovery, and when she came to me in the spring of 1994 I could see that she had ability, albeit of the hunting variety, and though I promised her nothing in the way of rides in races she was soon riding out for us and took to it well. Over the summer, with regular work riding, she improved greatly, so that when Rose Nugent, who had leased a horse of ours called Stalled, decided to give up race riding and return to Vietnam, where she had a boyfriend, we decided to let Becky take her chance in a ladies' race at Newbury that September. After unprecedented scenes in the paddock – Becky was quite a celebrity – Stalled really pulled out all the stops and ran on strongly to finish third. Becky won three more races on him, and became very much a part of our life – as well as a great inspiration to people who suffer severe head injuries, proving that, with luck and good treatment, one can recover to live a full life again. As for Stalled, on his retirement he went on loan to the apprentice school at Newmarket, where I see him on my periodic visits, very happily teaching the young aspirants to ride.

The sad sequel to this story is that in 1998 Rose Nugent was driving a cart through Great Shefford when it overturned and she was thrown out and killed. It was a tragedy; Rose was so pretty, such fun, and loved Lambourn and everything to do with racing and its way of life.

The other girl who rode for us was Susie Samworth, who came to us through Bruce Hobbs, to whom she was distantly related. Bruce had been friendly with us for a long time; since riding the Grand National winner Battleship as a seventeen-year-old in 1938 he had turned his attention to the flat and trained a lot of top-class horses in Newmarket. Susie's parents were masters of the Quorn and Cottesmore at different times, and great supporters of countryside sports; like Becky, she had a lot of hunting experience, though she had never ridden in a race. She came on in leaps and bounds with regular riding out, and we managed to buy her a four-year-old filly called Marjaana that Sheikh Hamdan wanted to sell. Marjaana had won as a two-year-old at Newbury, but had rather lost her form since, and was now well handicapped. In her first race with Susie she finished second, and the pair never looked back thereafter; they were a formidable combination. Susie rode nine winners for us, of which the best was probably on Righty Ho, a little horse by Reprimand. Susie was the only jockey to win on him, which she did twice, notably at Epsom in a ladies' amateur race, where she took a handy position and came with a long run on the outside up the straight, keeping the horse balanced to win cosily – no mean feat at Epsom, given the camber of the course. It was a ride of which Lester Piggott could have been proud.

14

TRAINERS

I don't believe there is a more fascinating profession than training racehorses. From the moment I got involved in this industry, I have never got bored with any facet of it. I first started riding out for our neighbour, Fred Heath, a mile away from where my parents lived at Chastleton in Gloucestershire. He had probably as bad a collection of slow horses as you could not ever wish for, but he kept them running, and winning in their own class. He was a dear man, and worked very hard – as did his stable jockey Malcolm Smith, not a very stylish rider, but quite adequate on Fred's horses. The main owner was George Hackling, a very astute businessman with a beaming toothy smile who seemed to dabble in all sorts of concerns and would no doubt today be described as a minor entrepreneur.

I used to be driven up the hill in my father's car, with a bicycle in the boot, and then pedalled my way home, nearly all downhill, after work in the mornings. We used to trot for miles, and since those days I have always believed in steady trotting as a way of hardening and strengthening horses' legs, especially the older ones. On the way back we used to do a canter on Adlestrop common, then a lovely expanse of old turf, and twist our way among the gorse bushes and rabbit burrows. The horses were kept happy, and their frail old legs, much blistered and fired, thrived, as they were seldom under pressure at home; many bad-legged racehorses are kept sound with such sensible handling. Fred had one dear old selling plater called Teetotal who used to win a lot of selling steeplechases but was never claimed, as his legs were never a pretty picture; no doubt Fred made sure – as so many of us would in a similar situation – that there were enough obvious potions on the legs to put anyone off bidding. When I started training I asked him to come in as my head lad, but he said he was too set in his ways, and I think his judgement was right: I don't believe that he would have been well suited to life at a large training centre.

What a contrast, when I went to Newmarket! The yards were run with military precision, and everything went like clockwork. The trainers were like gods, and their head lads were much respected as masters of their trade. Next door to Geoffrey Brooke, with whom I started out in Newmarket, was Joe Lawson, who trained Never Say Die to win the Derby in 1954, the first summer I was there. Never Say Die was a lovely little liver chestnut horse ridden by Paddy Newson in all his work. Paddy was the best work rider I ever had; his daughter Maureen married Barry Hills.

Two stables away there was the 'Captain': Cecil Boyd-Rochfort, a brilliant artist in his profession. In those days his jockey was Harry Carr, who drove him everywhere, as the Captain either could not or did not want to drive. Harry Carr's daughter, the extremely pretty Anne, who rode hacks beautifully across the Heath, married Joe Mercer, and they both became great friends of ours. The Captain had the most glorious lot of horses, and in the spring of the year they used to come past our string, with a swagger about them, as though they would conquer the world.

Another great man of the old school still training then was Reg Day, who used to wear box-cloth gaiters and rode a splendid old hack who looked completely square. He trained Sweet Solera, ridden by Bill Rickaby, to win the One Thousand Guineas and Oaks of 1961, and was so unhappy with her last piece of work before the Oaks that he sent the filly and several of

30. Newbury, April 1975; my owners gave me a beautiful silver salver for being Champion Trainer for the first time in 1974. At the front is Carolyn Sheffield, Charles Smith Bingham is on my left and Percival Williams is second from the left

31. Carrying the tack in the unsaddling enclosure at Royal Ascot, where I enjoyed great success over many years, with twenty-one winners in all. As George Lambton wrote, a trainer should have a serious expression

32. With two of my outstanding owners, Lord Howard de Walden (left) and Louis Freedman

33. Be Hopeful in the yard at Windsor House, painted by Lionel Edwards, a gift from Percival Williams

34. Bonk and me on the gallops at Seven Barrows, painted by John King; a gift from all the winning owners in 1975

35. The highs and lows of a trainer's life: Duncan Keith on Rock Roi at Seven Barrows in 1971; Rock Roi won two Ascot Gold Cups for us and was disqualified from both of them but won the Prix du Cadran, Goodwood and Doncaster Cups, John Porter Stakes and Jockey Club Stakes

36. Returning home from exercise at Seven Barrows, October 1974

37. Grundy ridden by Matty McCormack and Charlie Johnson on Red Regent, in their final work on the Valley gallop two days before the Derby in 1975

38. Matty McCormack taking a turn at the top of the Faringdon road on Grundy in the spring of 1975

39. Grundy, ridden by Pat Eddery, wins the 1975 Derby on 4 June by 2½ lengths from Nobiliary. One of the best days of my life

40. Giving Bonk a kiss after Grundy's Derby triumph; we hadn't watched the race together

41. With the Vittadini family (the owners) and Pat Eddery after Grundy's Derby win

42. Grundy winning his epic duel with Bustino in the King George & Queen Elizabeth Stakes, July 1975 – it is often referred to as 'the race of the century' (*photo: Gerry Cranham*)

43. Charlie Bubbles (right) winning a titanic battle for the Hardwicke Stakes at Royal Ascot, June 1975. Lester Piggott's and Pat Eddery's vigorous whip action would probably fall foul of the stewards nowadays!

44. Bonk and Pat Eddery exercising on the covered ride at Seven Barrows in 1975

45. Supervising the horses coming back from the Faringdon road gallops, near Seven Barrows, in March 1978

her workmates back down again on Racecourse Side to do the same gallop of one and a quarter miles all over again. That brilliant writer and great wit Roger Mortimer once described Sweet Solera's owner, Mrs Costello, to me as looking as if she was the sergeant major of a regiment of lesbians.

We did not see a lot of Noel Murless's horses as they were up the hill at Warren Place. His methods were very quiet, and he built his horses up in a very slow and well-planned manner. At the Craven meeting in the spring of 1966 John Sutton, who was very friendly with us and also with Noel, was going round stables at Warren Place. When they came to a fine big two-year-old colt of Mr Jim Joel's by Ballymoss, Noel just turned to John and said, 'That's my Derby horse *next* year.' How many trainers nowadays would be able to say that, especially as the colt, named Royal Palace, had not at that time even been out of a canter? As a testament to Noel's judgement, Royal Palace won the Two Thousand Guineas narrowly, before winning the Derby in handsome fashion. Sadly, he broke down before the St Leger, but I'm sure that John Sutton, who was a very keen punter, had taken good notice of the advance warning given to him. Indeed, Noel's words of wisdom on all aspects of racing were well worth listening to. He was also a generous and supportive colleague; later on, he got some of his owners, like Lady Sassoon, to send us horses he felt would be better suited to downland gallops, which unlike Newmarket do not dry out so readily in the summer.

We used to see a lot of Jack Jarvis's horses. They used to come out in the winter looking miserable, with poverty lines on their quarters, and their heads down, without a buck or a kick in the lot of them. We laughed about the Jack Jarvis 'swinging canters', with the horses nose to tail, going faster than most of ours could go at full speed, up Long Hill. But gradually, as the summer went on, they looked better and better – and they never stopped improving. Apart from the Classics, one of Jack's great fascinations was raiding the September meeting at Ayr, where he used to lay horses out for the owners, many of whom were grouse shooting close by.

He had been a very successful light apprentice, and was booked by the Druid's Lodge stable for the Cambridgeshire after riding Hackler's Pride in the Stewards' Cup in 1903, on a rotten day with pouring wet weather. The filly finished unplaced, and when he dismounted, there was only an Irish lad with her. All the lad said was, 'If I were you, I would ride her again, as she has not done a canter for a month.' He hardly rode for the stable again until he was booked for the same filly in the Cambridgeshire, where she had been laid out to win a fortune for the Druid's Lodge Confederacy, as it was called – probably £1 million, a vast amount in those days. She went down to the start early, as she pulled very hard, in a pair of ankle boots, and the lad was told to run down to take them off at the start. On the way down she was tearing little Jack's arms out, but a hundred yards from the start the lad, who had got down there, started calling 'Whoa, old girl, steady up,' and she heard his voice and pulled up. In the race itself, Jack recalled that after a hundred yards he never saw another horse, and the filly cantered home.

I was very fond of Norman Bertie, a grand little man, who had been travelling head lad to Joe Lawson at Manton. He trained Pinza, a big heavy horse, to win the 1953 Derby. Pinza had bad forelegs, and eventually broke down, but to everyone's amazement acted well on the Epsom course, and won comfortably for Gordon Richards, who had been knighted that morning. I used to quiz Norman about training methods, and ask him all sorts of questions. Was it best to keep chatting up, and possibly boring, owners or prospective owners, or to concentrate on the galloping side of it? Norman, who I remember used to keep saying 'Yep, yep,' replied: 'Forget all these things, just watch the droppings,' in other words, keep your eye on the horses' well-being above all.

In those days there were far fewer trainers, and many fewer horses, but I remember that among the best turned out were the strings of Fred (Sam) Armstrong, and Harry (Tom) Thomson Jones. Tom, who retired just before me, has a brilliant brain (unlike me) and a great sense of humour, and, apart from being able to do the *Times* crossword in about ten minutes, writes the most superb racing poems. One which we used to laugh about with Tim Forster was entitled 'Ode to an Amateur Rider' and ran as follows:

His legs were long, his seat was loose
His knees were knocking from self-abuse
But he rode through his field like shit from a goose
And won by the length of his doo-dah.

Among the other people who gave me a lot of help and support in Newmarket were Fergie Sutherland, who had had a leg blown off while serving in Korea, and his wife Judy. Far from being deterred by his disability, he came to Geoffrey Brooke as a pupil while I was there, and then bought Carlburg, next door to Clarehaven, from Joe Lawson, and started training there. Fergie did very well, winning the Queen Mary Stakes at Royal Ascot with A1. He loved his hunting, and rode very bravely in point-to-points with a wooden leg. He eventually retired to Ireland, and we all had a great thrill when he showed he had not lost his skill by training Imperial Call to win the Cheltenham Gold Cup of 1996.

When I moved to Blewbury from Newmarket I saw training from a different angle. No longer did one see the long strings of competing trainers passing and the friendly rivalry between the staff. At Blewbury we hardly saw another horse, bar Michael

Pope's which were trained down in the village. In an environment like this, you only start to know whose horses are the most forward when they start to run, although I always feel that, with a few exceptions, Newmarket horses are always a fortnight or so ahead of the downs horses.

On moving to Berkshire, I met a whole new lot of people and a different bunch of trainers. John Goldsmith became a great friend, as did Jack and Sue Colling, and we always seemed to be in each other's houses. John had started training before the Second World War, and then went into the army, being recruited into security services straight away. He spoke fluent French, and had a most eventful war, being flown on several missions to join the Resistance in occupied France. He was captured by the Germans, but escaped through a loo window on to a balcony outside the Metropole Hotel in the middle of Paris – he climbed down the drainpipe and walked back in through the front door to sign the visitors' book. Understandably, given his experiences, he hated the Germans, but he was a very brave and attractive man, and great fun, with a fund of wonderful stories. He had trained some very good steeplechase horses including the brilliant two-miler Le Jakobin.

Jack and Sue Colling became two of our closest friends. Their hospitality at their very comfortable house, Hodcott, at West Ilsley, was legendary, and Jack was my *beau ideal* of a real professional trainer. A genuine countryman, he loved his hunting, and was a fine shot. He loved having a day's grouse shooting on the Monday before the big meeting at York, when he liked having a tilt at the bookmakers – usually with great success. He was always immaculately turned out, and his horses looked hard and fit. I remember some of his expressions. One was: 'Horses are all different; some are born lean, like Pharaoh's "lean kine", and whatever you do, you can't put meat on them; they will always need a breastplate.' Another was: 'A trainer should be mending his nets [like a fisherman] when he is not training his horses.'

When I was first in Blewbury, Dick Hern was assistant to Michael Pope, a very amusing and skilful trainer of ordinary horses; then Dick was tempted away to train for Major Holliday in Newmarket – which he did very successfully, for a notoriously difficult owner. When he accepted the offer of training for Jakie Astor at West Ilsley, in place of Jack Colling, it was a bonus for us to have him and his wife Sheilagh close by again. Dick took to West Ilsley like a duck to water, and broke record after record with strings of Classic winners, until two very sad things happened. The first one was his bad fall while hunting with the Quorn. He had just taken an ordinary hedge when his horse shied at a china water trough about twenty yards out on the landing side. Dick was thrown heavily, and badly damaged his spine. Having partially recovered from that, entirely due to guts and determination, he was able to train many more winners, including the brilliant Nashwan, who was champion three-year-old in 1989. Having gone through a heart by-pass operation, just to add to his troubles he was then suddenly told that his lease of the West Ilsley stables was going to be terminated. The lease was eventually extended for a year, but the business was very badly handled and left a nasty taste in the mouth. A lot of people were incensed, and it is hard to imagine that Her Majesty the Queen was responsible, although she was the owner of the yard. The problem could have been eased if Dick Hern had been offered a few horses each year to train for Her Majesty, from wherever he was based. Fortunately, there was a benefactor around in the shape of Sheikh Hamdan Al-Maktoum, who, in a typically bold and generous gesture, bought and built up a stable called Kingwood House at Lambourn specifically for Dick. Here Dick continued to train winners, including the winner of the 1995 One Thousand Guineas, until he retired in 1998.

Another man we got to know very well – and another who had had a busy war in the secret service – was Colonel Dick Warden. He too had trained briefly for Major Holliday in Newmarket, and for Lord Fitzwilliam, until the latter's death in a plane crash. He then encouraged Jeremy Tree to go to him before starting training at Beckhampton. We had not been in Lambourn long when Brian Marshall's wife Mary said, 'You ought to go hunting with the Vale of the White Horse hounds, just down the road around Swindon and Cirencester.' We had hardly met Dick then, but he had just become master of the hunt, having previously been master of the Ledbury hounds. What fun he gave us, riding a little cob with a docked tail, and wearing a thick set of spectacles; he went like a bomb, and was very hard to keep up with.

Dick was arguably responsible for the whole of the Arabs' initial investment in British racing. When he gave up the mastership of the VWH in 1964, he joined the Curragh Bloodstock Agency and met up with Sheikh Mohammed from Dubai, for whom he bought a filly called Hatta who won the Molecomb Stakes at Goodwood, trained by John Dunlop.

Dick often used to drop in, and then suddenly ask if he could use the telephone. It was usually a call to Japan or New York; but he was such good value that we could never be cross with him. He was a brilliant judge of a horse, with a remarkable memory, and would roar with laughter at any gossip.

Henry Cecil is probably the best Classic trainer I know. He is also an extraordinary man, his private and professional lives alike are no strangers to turmoil – as witness the departures of his heavenly first wife, Julie, and a top-class head lad like Paddy Rudkin. However, he always bounces back and produces good horses year after year. One fault he has is that he is entirely self-centred as regards himself and his horses. The format of racing has now been altered to give smaller trainers a chance, but he opposed the abolition of the graduated races because they favoured the kind of horses he trains, being usually uncompetitive events, in which his runners started long odds-on. He has hardly ever run horses in the new rated stakes, a series of limited handicaps of around a stone weight range. If only he would serve on the odd committee, like so many other responsible trainers do, he would be able to add his voice to collective thoughts from those committees, and perhaps gain an insight into the concerns of other trainers. A good example of his somewhat blinkered thinking came in his announcement that in his view the Epsom Derby should be run three weeks later. This is entirely impracticable. It would mean its being run after Royal Ascot and would destroy the whole international racing programme, including the Irish Derby. However, to do him credit, I believe that he has since seen sense and withdrawn the suggestion.

A trainer whom I admire very much and like immensely is John Dunlop. He was in the right place at the right time, when he was suddenly promoted from assistant at Arundel, that powerful stable owned by the Norfolk family, to trainer in 1966. He hardly uses the grass gallops, which may not be on the best soil, but instead relies on woodchip all-weather gallops. He appears the most relaxed of trainers, but with upwards of 200 horses cannot afford to let his attention drift for a second. He has an office manager, but his travelling head lad, Robert Hamilton, must know more about the world than any travel agent, and is a delightful man. John is a brilliant trainer of every sort of horse; he is adept at placing his horses, and a master of the art of getting the lesser ones handicapped well as two-year-olds. Once that is done – and there is no need to cheat, it is simply a question of intelligent choice of races – the world is at your feet. Some horses are just not two-year-old racehorses, and will just improve naturally, given time. John's list of winners in every sphere is mind-boggling; and yet he still finds time to devote to the broader good of those involved in racing, both people and horses. Not only is he on the council of Racing Welfare and a trustee of the British Racing School, the main apprentice school in the country, he is also a director of the National Stud. If ever there is fund-raising to be done for any kind of good cause in the industry, you can be sure that John is up there in the forefront of the action.

Among the Newmarket trainers, one for whom I have great regard is Sir Mark Prescott, another genius at placing horses and the most assiduous student of the form book and race conditions I have ever met. I sometimes think he is apt to go for small races a bit too often, and as a result his big-race successes do not reflect his skill brightly enough. The turn-out of his horses is always immaculate, and he is often quoted as saying, 'I've had many girlfriends, but never changed my jockey.' Certainly in George Duffield he has an excellent partner. He loves to remind me of an occasion many years ago when he saw a horse of his turned over by one of mine at Carlisle – after I had forgotten to let him know, as I had promised I would, if I was going to run my horse in the race. He rang me from a petrol station to point out that my negligence had cost him a race, as he thought I was the only danger, and we had beaten him easily.

At least I got off more lightly than Ben Hanbury. Ben is very much like his father Tom. If we ever went to dinner with Tom, after a very good meal he would ask us up to see his collection of suits and shoes. Most people would have a glass of port or brandy after dinner, but Tom just loved showing people his clothes. We never considered him a Brain of Britain, but he was good company. Ben takes after his father in the way he dresses and did much the same thing to Mark Prescott at Edinburgh as I did at Carlisle. Mark never said a word. Ben asked for a lift home after racing. Mark replied, 'That's fine, be in the car park five minutes after the last race, and I'll give you a lift.' Ben put his smart bag into the boot, and as he was about to get into the car, Mark said to George Duffield, who was at the wheel, 'Drive on, George,' and left Ben to make his own way home. I don't expect Ben ever made the same mistake again.

Newmarket is lucky to have a lot of very intelligent trainers. One who has stood out over the years is Geoff Wragg. He took over from his father Harry, one of the few flat race jockeys who has made the grade in the highest class as both rider and trainer, and in turn has shown his skill with the training of Teenoso, who won the Derby in 1983, and also has done so well for the trustees of the Moller family.

Some, though, might on occasion be considered *too* clever. In 1987, when Luca Cumani was training for the Aga Khan, he had run a three-year-old called Raykour in the seven-furlong Ladbroke Handicap at the Craven meeting at Newmarket. This had finished an eye-catching fifth, swallowing up his rivals in the last furlong without getting to the leaders. Luca is a very good trainer, but he could be described as being so cunning that he does not let his left hand know what his right hand is doing. Raykour had also run in the Esher Cup, the big handicap at Sandown, and had fulfilled the promise of his run at Newmarket by winning very easily. The two races had not escaped the notice of the stewards at both meetings, or indeed that of the general public. The Esher Cup had been run the day before I was on my way to Rome with Angus Gold to run our filly Thaidah, and there had been a lot of discussion about the incident in the plane. As Angus and I got out of the taxi into pouring rain and hid under an awning at the racecourse entrance, we saw a wizened Italian attempting to brush the torrent of water uphill, to no avail. Angus turned to me and said, 'By Jove, that looks just like the Wop,' the name Luca was always known by. My tongue-in-cheek reply was that it could not be Luca, as he would surely be pulling the broom, not pushing it!

There are also several very bright young trainers in Newmarket. William Haggas, who kept a dynasty going by marrying Lester's daughter Maureen, has renovated Claude Halsey's old stable and has already trained a Derby winner in Shaamit. Michael Bell, too, has wasted no time in showing his expertise by training lots of winners, and is clearly on the way up. Mark Tompkins, who started off as assistant in several stables, including those of Walter Wharton and Ryan Jarvis, before setting up on his own, has likewise amassed an impressive record, including a St Leger winner in Bob Back. He has, moreover, been a great help with his positive comments on the Apprentice School at Newmarket, of which I appointed him a member of the Trainers' Committee, which I am honoured to chair.

James Fanshawe, known as 'The Skeleton' because of his tall, lean frame, had a wonderful grounding, being the son of a great huntsman in Brian Fanshawe, huntsman of the Cottesmore hounds. Brian, like Tim Forster, had followed me as pupil assistant to Geoffrey Brooke, and James had been first with David Nicholson and then Michael Stoute before setting up his own operation at Pegasus stables, built by Fred Archer. An extremely hard worker, he now trains for some very successful owner-breeders.

Barry Hills is another remarkable man. The son of Tom Rimell's head lad at Kinnersley, he started off as an ordinary lad himself, looking after an attractive colt called Acropolis at George Colling's yard in Newmarket. When I first knew him he was travelling head lad, and was already sure to go places. His great break came when he backed Frankincense to win the Lincoln; he and Greville Starkey had laid the horse out to win, and Barry made enough money on the punt to buy Southbank, Keith Piggott's then small yard in Lambourn. Barry is extremely shrewd; when, after a brief stay at Manton, where he was invited to go by Robert Sangster, he was suddenly asked to move when the lease came up, he was able to return to Southbank, which he had cannily kept on. He then made a very bold move. Feeling that his yard in Lambourn was too far from his main gallops up the Faringdon road, he decided to sell some land round his house, and develop a brand new site at Mile End on the Wantage road. Here he has built a state-of-the-art complex, with three separate barns, and a covered barn for winter exercise. The whole set-up is magnificent, and the results are proving it.

Our first training base at Windsor House was bought later, from the Spicers, by Roger Charlton. He started out working in the City, but hated it, and decided to move into the training world. At Windsor House he built the equine swimming pool – and I have never seen one better built – and lived in the cottage at the end of the yard. He became friendly with Jeremy Tree, then training at Beckhampton, and was offered the job as his assistant. Notwithstanding his laid-back demeanour, Jeremy was a very astute trainer and won a stream of big races for some of the most delightful owners. He was also great fun, with high standards of life and behaviour; however, he suffered ill-health and eventually retired as a result. Sadly, Jeremy never trained a Derby winner; but Roger, in his first season, succeeded in winning not only the Epsom Derby but also the French equivalent, with respectively Quest for Fame and Sanglamore. He and his wife have done wonders at Beckhampton, and with the patronage of the Queen and other influential owners have every chance of following in the footsteps of Jeremy, or even Fred Darling, who also trained there.

Of the northern trainers, the Easterbys stand out. Peter and Mick are brothers; Mick is perhaps the greater character of the two, but both have a great sense of humour (and some wonderful but unprintable stories) and both send out horses which are extremely fit and very hard to beat. Both have also been very astute, building up their farming interests alongside their increasing success in racing. Peter had great times under both codes, winning most of the big jumping races and lots of handicaps on the flat. The family interest looks like being continued for some time, for while Peter recently retired, he handed over to his son Tim, while his son-in-law Richard Fahey has also launched forth in this risky business. Both younger men have grasped Peter's baton with enthusiasm, and I was fortunate to get Richard on to the Trainers' Committee of the Newmarket Apprentice School; just after being appointed he made a trip down to Suffolk specifically to look round the whole place. What a contrast to some other trainers I know, who are only too happy to moan about the school, but have never bothered to visit it.

There are up and down the country many other hard-working trainers, all struggling to make a living in this very competitive industry. I feel it wrong that the government will not allow trainers to have a minimum training fee, when they insist on their paying a minimum wage to their employees. Before the Second World War, I believe trainers were charging £5 per week, and staff getting £2 per week, and trainers were able to make £1 per week on keep alone. The ratio is very different now. It is ridiculous to see some trainers advertising their fees at around £100 per week all in, when any trainer who does not charge at least the same as he is paying his staff either is cutting corners to the detriment of his horses, or is a wealthy man subsidising his business to no mean tune.

Like so many others, I have often been unlucky enough to have found myself training some pretty ordinary horses. We once had a very light-framed filly belonging to the Rothschilds, and we had a debate in the yard over whether she would ever win a race. Her lad said it would be impossible, to which I replied: 'I'll find and win one with her, and we will have a bet for fifty pence.' Sure enough when Monemvasia, ridden by Frank Morby, won at Salisbury, there was a buzz around the stable. At 7.45 the next morning, after the string had had their preliminary trot, I pulled them all over and held out my hand, to roars of applause, for the ceremony of collecting my fifty pence. That is the pleasure of training: to win with every possible horse, however modest its abilities may be.

15

VIRUSES, VETS AND VACCINES

There are so many problems nowadays with the health of horses in racing stables that it is very tempting to think that 'the virus' and all its associated problems are modern phenomena – until you read George Lambton's *Men and Horses I Have Known*. In 1906, in a brand new yard at Stanley House, his horses went down with something called 'pink eye', an illness practically unknown among racehorses, which was obviously some sort of anaemia. The horses ran badly and were off colour; with one or two exceptions, they did not recover their form for a long time, and he won no races between Royal Ascot and the Houghton meeting in Newmarket at the end of October.

We always had pretty healthy horses, bar the routine coughing epidemic, during which one left them alone until they cleared up. In my earlier years as a trainer there were no endoscopes to see whether there was muck or blood down the horses' windpipes or in their lungs, so one had to go by observation and knowledge of the horses alone.

What really exacerbated the problem of infection was the onset of rapid international horse travel. It was rather similar to what happened when Chinese seamen came with their ships into Liverpool, bringing strains of disease that the locals had not come up against before, and the whole population went down with Hong Kong flu. In just the same way, a population of horses builds up resistance to common bugs in its everyday environment; but when they come into contact with foreign diseases, they will catch anything that is going. When the only means of transport was by boat the problem was less acute, the journeys being slow enough and long enough to give the horses in transit time to get anything they were carrying out of their system before landing and mixing with other horses; once the trip could be made quickly by air, this useful delay vanished. I was also unconvinced that the aircraft were disinfected efficiently enough between one set of horses disembarking and the next boarding; they were making three, four or five trips a day, and the divisions between the stalls were padded with coir matting, which takes a deal of cleaning to disinfect thoroughly. They carried both horses in training and broodmares; every time an animal comes into a racing yard or leaves it to return to a stud there is the risk of infection.

Our first major attack of the virus appeared in the summer of 1978. I had been to the Keeneland sales in Kentucky in July, and on my first morning back home walked out into the covered ride and asked the lads to trot on. As soon as they did, the horses started sneezing – and carried on sneezing. Something was obviously wrong. There was no discharge from their nostrils, and they had no temperature; nor was there any coughing. We called in the vets, and they took endless blood tests, but could find nothing. In despair we called in Jenny Mumford, the respiratory expert from Newmarket's Animal Health Trust; and within a few days she was able to tell us that we had EHV1, the most virulent of the equine viruses, and that the stable had some sick horses in it. There was no real cure, just rest and even more attention to detail in stable hygiene. As far as the origin of the infection was concerned, my own suspicions lay with the Wildenstein horses, which had arrived from France that February, in a less than wonderful condition.

We had had fifty-four winners up to 18 July and had been on course for another good season; now we were stopped in our tracks. We had no winners between 5 August and 9 October.

Gradually our horses recovered, and as they seemed to regain their health we checked them very carefully before beginning to run a few. At the end of that season we had had no more than about seventy winners, a big drop from the previous year's total of 111.

We set about examining all our procedures and routines. For advice we called in Professor David Sainsbury, head of the Cambridge Veterinary School and a most helpful and sensible man. He looked at our ventilation system and advised some changes. We had two barns at that time, with forty horses in each. On the recommendation of the manufacturers, Colt, we had set the fans in the roof to come on when the temperature reached 60 degrees Fahrenheit, which we thought a comfortable level. Professor Sainsbury suggested that we alter the settings and install timers so that the fans came on every fifteen minutes, whatever the temperature, to ensure a sufficient number of changes of air throughout the day, the roofs being high enough to ensure adequate ventilation.

Another improvement that we made, this time on the suggestion of Johnny Harrington, who had in turn been advised by Michael Osborne, director of the Irish National Stud, was to leave the top doors of the boxes open as much as possible, and to paint the boxes with aluminium paint – in Osborne's view the cheapest, most hard-wearing and most antiseptic paint you can buy.

I was annoyed that our local vets had neither the equipment nor the expertise to find a solution to the problem, and was far from happy with the advice that they were giving us. The average local vet has no idea about the virus; they hardly stay long enough in the yard to gain an impression of the general well-being of the horses, and are always in such a hurry to get to their next appointment that they barely have time to exchange words with the trainer. I decided to buy our own endoscopes, as

I felt that if we had our own equipment this would minimise the risk of infection spreading into our yard from outside, or indeed on from us to anywhere else. This infuriated one of our vets, who accused me of disloyalty; he thought that we would scope our horses ourselves, thus depriving his firm of lucrative business. In fact this would have been both illegal and dangerous, and I would not have contemplated it. I replied that my whole future, and the future of all my horses, was at stake, and that I was going to consult vets on a freelance basis. He asked what would happen if I had a sick horse; I replied that if a vet refused to treat it, I would immediately report him to the Royal Veterinary College. This stopped him dead in his tracks. I felt that, just as if one had a bad heart, one did not want to go to a doctor who specialised in treating piles, so I would not want my horses to be examined by a leg vet when suffering from respiratory infection.

I stopped giving the horses blood tests, which are unnecessary. This, again, is something the vets recommended, but they are a complete waste of time. They only show you have had a disease in your yard, not what is happening at the present time. I believe that really to determine the health of a racehorse you have to have it scoped. If there is no muck or blood in the horse's respiratory system, and he is otherwise in good shape, then you are perfectly entitled to run him. If there is any muck there, then he is not at his best and is not going to run well. If you scope twenty horses at the beginning of the season, and fifteen show cause for concern, then there is a very good chance that you have a serious infection in the establishment.

I am also convinced that injections against the cough and virus are helpful. I flew out to Kentucky to consult Dr John Chandler, a qualified vet and stud manager, for his advice, and he recommended the most effective vaccines. Apart from the statutory injections, which should be given annually (though some trainers, who do not approve of the statutory injections, make their vets sign the horses' passports without actually giving the injections), they should be given whenever a horse comes into the yard and when it leaves. While the horse is doing light exercise, an inoculation will do no harm; even if it has worked on a Friday morning, it can be given the injection on the Friday evening and have an easy time over the weekend.

I believe, too, that every vet should wear a smock, to be provided by the trainer, as soon as he comes into the yard, so that he does not carry infection around with him from one establishment to another. We bought a steam cleaner early on, to make sure that every box was thoroughly washed out as soon as its occupant left and before the new resident arrived, but even so I am sure that the virus are carried by the horse and not by the stable – as is indeed proven by the fact that it attacks brand new yards, despite the buildings and everything in them being completely pristine.

It seems that better horses suffer the virus less often, and less seriously, than the more moderate animals, probably because they are under less pressure. But while we have so much racing, and so much rapid travel of horses, not only around the country but around the world, we are never going to beat the problem. We can only contain it with ever higher stable standards and ever greater vigilance.

16

STABLE STAFF AND STABLE CRAFT

When anyone decides to start training, the first thing to consider is a head man. In the army the second-in-command of a regiment is the adjutant; in a racing yard the trainer's right-hand man is his head lad. He must be more than an employee; he should be a friend as well. There must be complete mutual trust and loyalty, so that the trainer feels that all the many things that inevitably come up in a training stable can be talked over in confidence, and the head lad knows that he can rely on his 'Guv'nor' for support in difficult times, when the staff are moaning, or when the stable is not firing. It is hard to keep a stable together when things are not quite right, and any suspicion that the head lad does not believe in his boss starts a chain reaction of disaffection.

I always felt that when Michael Dickinson was asked to train at Manton, he did not have an experienced flat racing head lad. Michael is a very hard worker and a nice guy, but he was also very secretive. We were asked to go round stables when he was there, and I remember walking round with him and coming to the work board, which had a list of the riders and horses on it; to my amazement, it had a canvas cover over it to stop anyone looking at it. I had never seen this before.

Michael did not use the main old yard at all. This yard was where all the Classic winners of old were trained, with very good ventilators and marvellous cage boxes. Instead, he had had a brand new yard built, with enormous boxes, and great big draughty high ceilings. The racing stable office could well have been suitable for the company secretary of ICI, and the travelling head lad's room had a table and an armchair in it. All a travelling head lad really needs is a hook in the ceiling to hang his tack from while he is cleaning it, lots of hangers for the colours, travelling sheets and rugs, and some big wardrobes for his bandages and other necessaries. Michael did not last at Manton very long; but he has since moved successfully to the United States, where he trained Da Hoss to win the Breeders' Cup Mile twice – no mean feat.

The yard need not be military in the way it is run, but there must be a system. The staff should have a definite time to start, and the morning's work should finish ideally at around 12.30 p.m., certainly before 1 p.m.; if they go on later than this, especially in a training centre, they will see staff from other stables bicycling or driving home when they are still riding out, and may become disgruntled that they are working longer hours than other yards. Similarly, at evening stables there should be a routine, with the trainer going around all the horses at a certain time, so that he can spot any problems; in a big yard the trainer should go a different way each evening, so that the same lads are not always last to finish. I always loved going round stables every night; and just by having a few moments in each box, and feeling all the legs, you can usually catch anything that is wrong, especially if your head lad has, as he should have, felt all the legs earlier and primed you for anything he has noticed. If he has, he can start feeding the horses after you have looked at the first few horses. In that way each horse is being fed nearly as soon as you walk out of the box. Even when we had 100 horses at Seven Barrows, and I was going round each box in the evening, always starting at 5.30, I was back in the house by about 6.15 with time to spare to give the head lad a drink and talk things over. On an evening before a work morning, we always went through the work list, so that as soon the lads got in the next day, they knew exactly what they were riding.

The head lad must have a routine, feeling all the legs when he is going round feeding the horses first thing in the morning. He must be able to report to his trainer afterwards that they have all eaten up or otherwise; if he hides or is unaware of any horse's lack of enthusiasm to clean the manger out, the trainer may well overwork the horse in error. The only way to keep horses eating is to give them very slightly less than they need, and always take out stale food. I hate haynets; they are unnecessary and dangerous (like rack chains), and horses get tied up in them. I find that the best way to feed hay to a horse is on the ground, as then there is no dust going into his eyes.

I was lucky in all my head lads. My first was Ray Laing, whom I inherited from Syd Mercer when I bought Windsor House. He was brilliant at feeding horses to bring them to their best, and we have always fed in the same way since his day. I am not a believer in buying hay in bags; you do not know at what time your hay has been cut, or whether it is the first or second cut, and if the plastic bag gets punctured, the hay can go off overnight. We have always tried to feed the best English hay, normally a mixture of timothy and ryegrass, with a bit of clover thrown in and also a little lucerne added to it, but only sparingly. A nice change is a comfrey bed, which is simple to lay down; comfrey is full of trace elements and a useful contribution to the feed. Many trainers now import hay, but if the enormous load that comes over is not up to standard, it is a laborious and expensive operation to remove it.

As for oats, which remain the principal energy source, I am a firm believer in English or Scottish produce, because of the high price of cereals from outside the EU. I did try nuts for a short time, but found that with so much salt in them, to bind them, they were inclined to make young horses purge on their way to the downs. The trouble with nuts is that you cannot tell what they are made of. Even with a balancer, which we always got from the Kettering firm of Dodson and Horrell, you cannot see what is in the mixture. One well-known firm of racehorse cube manufacturers ceased trading when it became known that they were using straw as the fibre element of their feed. I am also a firm believer in giving the horses a linseed mash twice a week after work; it is very good for their digestion, and with the modern linseed boilers very easy to prepare.

When I first started training at Windsor House, we rigged up a primitive oat crusher in the feed-house below the oat loft. I have always liked to feed oats slightly bruised, but it was a slow and laborious exercise. The oats arrived in a lorry, in sacks, and had to be manhandled up into the loft, with a pulley, from where gravity would send them down through the crusher into the feed bins. When we got to Seven Barrows we rigged up a more sophisticated system, by which the oats were blown into the loft we built, which was capable of holding up to ten tons, before being fed through the crusher and then into a dust extractor, to try to eliminate the dust which can have such harmful effects on horses' lungs. We did away with the corn bins, relying instead on big galvanised barrows, so that we could keep at bay the mice and rats that were inevitably attracted by the corn.

However carefully you feed your horses, you are at the mercy of what they breathe when they are out at exercise, and in this respect the scourge of the countryside at the moment is oilseed rape. This crop is very profitable to farmers, and clears the ground, but I am sure it has harmful effects on horses – unlike the equally attractive, but harmless, swathes of flax and linseed also to be seen across farmland in the summer. I brought the subject up at a meeting of the council of the Animal Health Trust, on which I sit, but got a pretty negative response. According to the National Farmers' Union and the Ministry of Agriculture, there was no indication of any loss of form in racehorses trained with oilseed rape in the vicinity; but I would like to argue to the contrary. How many people do we all know who are affected by it? I have heard of schools having to close down because the pupils were so sick during the flowering season of this crop; in some years we have deliberately avoided exercising our horses anywhere near it. It is very pretty, but I hate to see it; and yet unless farmers can be persuaded to avoid growing it near stables, we have no control over its effects. The only consolation is that the subsidies that encourage so many farmers to grow it are being withdrawn, making it less profitable.

Another pest that is worryingly prevalent today is the virulently poisonous ragwort; although it does not affect stabled horses, even a small amount eaten in a field can be fatal. Thankfully, there is now a strong campaign to eradicate this dangerous weed from neglected pastures and waste land.

When Ray left me, he felt that the responsibility of a large string had become too much for him; but by this time he did have the back-up of three other head lads at home, so that at a weekend there were always two at home to supervise the yard. We also had at least two travelling head lads at any one time, to share the duties with runners all over the country and abroad. After leaving Windsor House, Ray decided to sell insurance for a bit, but got bored with that, and eventually was set up to train for Tony Stratton Smith and some friends at Eastbury Cottage, where Bill Payne had trained a small string so successfully. He did quite well, winning the Cherry Hinton Stakes and a few other big races before finally retiring.

Ray was responsible for a lot of our big winners during the seventeen years he was with us, for which we have always been grateful. One of many simple but shrewd ideas he had was to move the work mornings from Wednesday and Saturday to Tuesday and Friday. This change of routine enabled us to canter the horses on Monday, work on Tuesday, do a gentle canter on

Wednesday and canter again on Thursday, with a further work morning on Friday. By doing it this way, we were more likely to get our jockeys to ride work on both days, because they were usually very busy at the weekend. Friday work also gave me the chance to see the horses ridden out the following day, to check straight away that they were sound.

Maintaining the horses' soundness is one of every good trainer's chief preoccupations. Whatever Martin Pipe has done – and make no mistake, he has been very successful; horses everywhere are a great deal fitter, because of his regime – I often feel that his horses only last one or perhaps two seasons, whereas those trained by the likes of Ryan Price, Fred Winter, Fred Rimell and Fulke Walwyn went on for year after year, probably fired and patched up, but still maintaining most of their form. Unlike Pipe, who places great emphasis on interval training at canter and gallop, I am a firm believer in trotting horses. With very few exceptions, if a horse does not trot sound, it should not be allowed to canter, as there is something wrong with it; if it canters sound and so you don't notice anything amiss, you are simply allowing the problem to go unaddressed. A horse can be walked out without the least sign of anything wrong; only in its faster paces can the trainer and head lad see there is a problem. This is not to say that trotting suits all horses: a very good miler called Town Crier whom we had early on was the worst trotter I've ever seen, and the whole string nearly had to pull up to a walk in the covered ride when he was in front of them.

Covered rides are of course a luxury, and many top trainers (Roger Charlton, for example) do not have one, but I do think they are a help. They won't make a horse go faster, but they do give the opportunity of exercising in safety when the weather is miserable and there is snow or ice on the ground. The old straw bed was always a bit dangerous – and never popular, because it took a lot of laying down and keeping level, and even more clearing up when the weather improved.

Ray Laing's opposite number on the travelling side was Tony Driscoll. He had been in the King's Troop, and afterwards with Keith Piggott. As travelling head lad he was meticulous, and the horses were always very well turned out. As I have mentioned earlier in this book, I have never believed that plaiting horses has any beneficial effect at all – indeed, it worried quite a lot of them, and a well-pulled mane and tail look just as good. Another practice which is sadly widespread nowadays is to put a patterned plastic template, with something like a chess-board pattern, on the horse's quarters and brush over it, to pretend that the lad has groomed the horse with great care, which is quite ridiculous. There should be just one half-moon quarter-mark on each side of the horse's quarters to make it look smart.

Travelling tack must be chosen and maintained with great care. My lead reins were always of leather – webbing lead reins can break – and I never allowed spring clips on them, because they are dangerous and can get jammed, or cause the horse an injury. In the travelling head lad's bag which he brought to the saddling boxes there was always a spare racing bridle, in case one broke while it was being put on the horse. This was used very effectively on several occasions by other trainers, whose horses might not otherwise have been able to run, especially when the racecourse stables were a long way from the saddling boxes and so there was no time for anyone to run back for a replacement. These are all simple ideas, but the only object in mind is safety, and getting your horse to the race intact.

The other essential, to my mind, is the right kind of elastic girths. In my early days in racing there was a fashion for wide, full elastic girths. These are deceptive, and it was often difficult to tell how firm they were. Most horses will blow themselves out when being girthed up, so that the girth needs tightening considerably thereafter; horses would often 'gallop through' these girths even after they had been tightened at the start, and as a result the saddle would end up too far forward or back for the jockey to ride a finish at all. This happened to Lester Piggott on a horse of Sam Armstrong's, Meadow Mint, at York; and certainly Durtal would have had a good chance in the Oaks, again ridden by Lester Piggott, if she had not bolted going to the start, and the saddle slipped. More recently, as I have already described, Dibidale's saddle slipped in Polygamy's Oaks, when challenging for the lead two furlongs out – on which occasion Willie Carson was again using one of the wide white elastic girths. The best elastic girths come from Australia, but even these require regular careful checking as they are inclined to fray, and lose their spring.

As far as tack at home goes, I always insisted on a surcingle and rug or sheet over the saddle, for several reasons. First, it means that there is air circulating around the stable rubber, saddle and covering; and secondly, if a horse starts to sweat excessively, you can get the sheet pulled off quickly with a flick of the buckle on the surcingle. Very few stables now do this. Another regrettable recent practice is the use of ghastly floppy saddles made of synthetic materials. They may be simple to keep, as the staff cannot break the saddle trees if they are thrown down; but our horse and human chiropractor, the brilliant Mary Bromiley, disapproves of them because she says that they give the horse's back no support, and actually cause a lot of back problems. I have always used a solid race exercise saddle; recently, in collaboration with an excellent saddler called Andy Huggins, Mary Bromiley has invented an even better and more horse-friendly one, called Savaback. Certainly, it is more expensive; however, in my tack sale on retiring in November 1999, we found that her saddles made nearly as much second-hand as when they were new.

Of course, even in the most efficient and carefully managed yard, a proper standard of care depends on having sufficient staff to take time over the essential tasks. In our heyday, as I have said, we had four head men at home, and three travelling head men, to supervise operations. I dread to think what is going to happen from now on, with racing on so many Sundays in a row. Stables, especially those that don't look after their staff, are already short enough of labour, and with the lads having every other Sunday off, frequent Sunday racing will put great strain on everyone. A lot of lads do not like leaving their families on a Sunday anyway. One top yard, according to the travelling head man, whom I know well, recently had only eight lads at home to look after 100 horses. One suggestion I have is that the racecourses, who seem to want Sunday racing more than anyone, should pay into a pool a sum, say £25, for each stable that has a runner at the meeting. This should only be for those actually at work at home on that day, as those who go racing are now getting good rewards in expenses and overtime. And it should not be paid by the owners! A measure of this kind would at least quell the resentment now often felt by those who have to stay behind and look after the yard.

When Ray Laing left I promoted Matty McCormack, a rather fiery little Irishman who had been one of my assistant head lads, and another in Red Groves to take over from him. Both did a good job. Matty in particular was a very good rider, but, like so many who had been used to the flat gallops at Newmarket, was inclined to go too fast when riding work. Horses at Newmarket appear to do much more work than downland horses, because of the lack of hills. He had, however, been with Noel Murless, a master of his craft, and rode Grundy in all his work when Pat was not around. When he in turn left me, he started training at Sparsholt, near Wantage. He did particularly well with his sprinters, training Horage to win two years in succession at Royal Ascot, before retiring to the West Country.

Over the years I had gradually been promoting a very sharp lad called Ron Thomas, who had come to me in 1970 from Tim Forster. He had arrived as an ordinary lad, but it quickly became clear that he really knew the time of day, and he soon found himself with some high-quality horses in his care, including the Norfolk Stakes winner Habat and Orange Bay. He was a top-class work rider, and completely transformed Crow, whom he started riding out as soon as the horse joined us from France in 1978. A sullen character when he arrived, with his ears back all the time, within weeks Crow was thriving and starting to bounce about. We let him enjoy himself with nice little canters and no stress, and because he was not under pressure, he became happy again. Ron, by his efforts and ability, rose to be head lad, and I could not have chosen better. Then he had that horrible accident involving Physical, which I have already described, when on the way home from the gallops one day. It was a horrendous fall, and he was taken to the Princess Margaret Hospital in Swindon and X-rayed; but although he was still in agony, they could find little wrong. He was put into traction and then sent home. When he failed to improve and was still in great pain, I rang his doctor for his advice. Luckily I had put Ron, along with several other senior members of staff, on to BUPA, and he was whisked immediately into the Acland nursing home at Oxford, where the specialists put him straight into the very expensive bone scanner. This showed that he had fractured several vertebrae, and over the following years he had to have a series of grave operations to remove a disc and then to keep the back right. He was not able to ride a horse again; but he remained the most wonderful and conscientious head lad, and probably spotted even more on his feet than he would have riding out. Indeed, as long as the trainer rides out, there is a possible advantage in having a head lad on the ground, as one should always have someone in a vehicle to help catch loose horses; and he can be back in the yard earlier than the riders, to start preparing feeds.

How much Ron saved me in vets' fees I will never know; he was clever enough to deal with all the minor ailments and cuts without calling in the vet. Don't get me wrong – vets have a big part to play in dealing with colic, operations and other serious problems; but most of them have no idea about spotting why a horse might be off colour, and some of them can be an expensive luxury. Many are inclined to gallop into a yard with a stop-watch, mobile telephone, calculator and needle so that they can do as many jobs as possible in the shortest time possible. Their usual final remark is 'Leave it in the box,' which is the worst thing for any athlete, racehorses included. Some trainers have the vet in the yard every day, but I always feel this is because either they or their head men don't know enough about basic stable management.

When Tony Driscoll decided to retire after thirty-five years with us, Jimmy McCrory, another excellent and skilful man, took over as travelling head lad, and held the job until we retired. He, like many of my very good staff, has since got an excellent job with Jamie Osborne, who retired from a very successful career as a National Hunt rider to begin training at Kingsdown, Peter Nelson's old yard in Lambourn. Travelling head lads are an extraordinary breed; they seem to know everything that is going on, and, like most hunt servants, have the most remarkable manners, able to converse with kings and commoners alike. One such is Michael Stoute's travelling head lad, Jimmy Scott; another in the same category is Robert Hamilton from John Dunlop's yard.

Another person who is an asset in a yard is an assistant trainer. Some trainers won't have them, and certainly most head lads hate them. In some cases maybe they don't get on with the head man, and think they are a bit superior. This is ridiculous; it is the assistant's job to muck in with everyone. It is an odd job being an assistant – neither trainer nor head lad – but there are now so many different tasks to be done, which the head man is probably too busy to do, that it can be a key role, and a good assistant trainer can learn a great deal, while taking care of a lot of essential, if perhaps sometimes boring, jobs. Checking passports, weighing the horses, liaising with the secretary, head men and trainer are all important facets of a training stable.

I've had some brilliant assistant trainers, many of whom went on to train on their own account. I always felt that I could not teach them anything; it was up to them to watch what went on, and learn from any mistakes we made. Peter Bailey, my first assistant at Windsor House, came out of the army; he was a quick learner, and after two years with me started training on his own account at Sparsholt. He had Jeff King as his jockey, and they had considerable success for a time; then, under the twin burdens of the virus and a few very slow-paying owners, the business foundered and eventually he gave it up. He now owns a lovely estate near Stonehenge.

Later I had two young men in succession who stand out: Mark Smyly and Jamie Douglas-Home. They were very similar: both worked very hard, had the knack of getting on with everyone, and seemed to know the way my mind was working. I remember that Jamie arrived on the same day that Christine Stephenson started as secretary. Five years later, they also left on the same day – to get married to each other! We were delighted to see them go in such happy circumstances.

Jamie is fond of recounting the story of how he drove me to Leicester one day, when Bonk went to Goodwood with a winner. On the way back the car started overheating, and we just managed to limp into the Watford Gap service station, where we sought help. I had just lifted the bonnet and was about to put my

46. Vitiges beating Rose Bowl in the Champion Stakes at Newmarket, October 1976

47. Crow before winning the Ormonde Stakes at Chester in 1978 – a year in which the stable was stricken by the virus

48.Crow beating Hot Grove in the Ormonde Stakes at Chester, May 1978

49. Ron Thomas, who later became our head lad, on the gallops with Habat, winner of the Norfolk Stakes, Mill Reef Stakes and Middle Park as a two-year-old and the Guineas Trial at Ascot as a three-year-old. A good horse, but a softie

50. *Right:* Bonk on Koko, out with the Vine and Craven Hunt in 1985

51. Willie Carson wins the July Cup at Newmarket on Hamas at the remarkable odds of 33–1 in 1993

52. With Munwar in 1995, after he had won the Lingfield Derby Trial, becoming a leading fancy for the Derby – in which he ran unplaced

53. With our dog, Robert the Bruce, back at our original base of Windsor House in 1998

54. With trainers Barry Hills (left) and Nicky Henderson (right) supporting Lambourn at a charity show-jumping event at Ascot

55. Cabaret time on Corfu!

56. Enjoying the flowers in the garden of Windsor House with Bonk in the summer following my retirement

57. The famous bus presented to me in December 1999 to mark my retirement

58. Selling the tack from the stables on my retirement, November 1999. The so-called 'tinkers' are in fact our friends Jim Cramsie (on the left) and the trainer Mark Smyly

59. With our son Edward and daughter-in-law Katie at their wedding in August 2000

60. My daughter Kate with Edward's best man, Ed James

hand on the radiator cap when a gentleman wearing a turban came across and shouted, 'Don't touch that! You will get burnt!' I said to him, 'Can I borrow your head cover to unscrew the cap?' – and all hell broke loose. Luckily it all calmed down again; but I never felt, even before this, that I would ever have a role in the United Nations.

I don't think that I ever had a cross word with either Jamie or Mark – or with Patrick Macewan, who came into much the same category. They all seemed to get on with the head men, and all had that gift of saying, 'Is there anything else I can do?', which seems to be sadly scarce today. Patrick was also a very good rider, and rode a beautiful race on the lovely Hateel at Ascot, outriding a leading amateur. He is now well settled as assistant to Marcus Tregoning at Kingwood stables.

Another key role in a trainer's yard is that of the secretary. We started out in 1960 with a dear if rather highly strung lady who had recently got divorced, but this was never going to be other than a temporary arrangement, and it was obvious that we needed someone permanent. We put an advertisement in the *Sporting Life* and *Horse and Hound* and received one reply that stood out. This was from Moira Briscoe, who had been working as secretary for a well-known farmer and permit-holder in Norfolk called Rex Carter. She was, and remains, the most wonderful person, and we took her on straight away. One of the things she began to do soon after joining us was to ride out hunters for Ian Lomax, master of the Vine and Craven hounds. One morning his head lad asked, 'Is that there Miss Frisky riding out this morning?' and the nickname stuck; she has it to this day. She was with us for thirteen years, towards the end of which we shared her with Tim Forster, and has remained very much part of our lives ever since, always at our side in all our triumphs and disasters. She has been married to another great friend of ours, Nick Nutting, for over twenty years, and we spend most of our holidays together.

After Moira left, we were lucky enough to have a succession of splendid girls: Rose Adams, afterwards Rose Baring; Christine Stephenson, daughter of that versatile trainer Willie Stephenson; and Sandra Bentinck (now Nolan), whose father was a leading saddler. We formed enduring friendships with all of them.

The one disaster we had was a man. I had never felt very happy about having a male secretary, but I did interview a couple, thinking a change might be a good idea. On one occasion I rang up Chris Harper, a leading breeder and farmer and a good friend, to ask about one applicant who had been working for him. He said, 'He is very good at his job, but I don't think he is quite your cup of tea.' When I asked why, Chris replied that this chap had a beard, wore 'Jesus Christ' sandals, voted Social Democrat, read the *Guardian* newspaper and was anti-fox-hunting. As usual, Chris was quite right; the interview was as far as it went. But 'Frisky' suggested that we should try one more man, and she and I interviewed the new candidate. We both thought he might do. His references were impeccable, and he swept into the office with a large briefcase, as though embarking on a takeover bid in the City. We appointed him, and although his deadpan and rather bureaucratic approach prompted us to nickname him 'the system', everything went along quite well – until we came to an important weekend in September 1973.

We had in the yard at that time a horse called Habat, who had been a very good two-year-old but had not really trained on at three, although he had been second in a sub-standard Sussex Stakes. He was entered in the Queen Elizabeth II Stakes at Ascot on the Saturday, and as a precaution in the Prix du Moulin, also over a mile, on the Sunday at Longchamp. On the Friday we had had both Pat Eddery and Frank Morby riding work, and it had been a very satisfactory morning, with horses and riders alike doing what they were told. As we tucked into our usual delicious breakfast, cooked by Bonk and Sharon Brace, the wife of another good head lad of mine (Sharon's official job was to look after the children, but she was a great racing fan and helped us in innumerable ways), we suddenly heard on the news that racing that Saturday at Ascot was abandoned, as the course was waterlogged with so much rain. I left the dining room immediately, walked into the office, and said to 'the system': 'Right, we will send Habat over to France by plane tomorrow and he can run in the Moulin on Sunday.'

Our friend's mouth dropped open, and he said, 'I took him out of the Moulin last night.'

There was no need to have done this; there was not a further forfeit stage until that morning, Friday.

By this time everyone had made themselves scarce, having discovered what the assiduous secretary had done earlier; so my lifelike imitation of Basil Fawlty lacked much of an audience. 'The system' was on his way very soon after this.

The nickname 'Basil Fawlty' was bestowed on me long ago by one of our lads, Alan Bailey, and I am afraid it has stuck ever since. Alan, who came to us from Bill Wightman, was a good and knowledgeable horseman, and looked after Be Hopeful, Lunchtime and Rock Roi. He was one of those lads who always had an answer for everything, but one couldn't help liking him; he was also a keen punter and was very friendly with the bookmaker John Banks. Alan loved his horses, and the ones he looked after always did well, which may have been due to his character as well as his care of them. It was one of the saddest days of his life when Polygamy got beaten a short head in the One Thousand Guineas; not only had he ridden her in all her work, but he had backed her at very long odds, and had she got her nose in front it would have been a big day for him. She did make amends by winning the Oaks, but I don't think the price was quite as good. Alan was very heavy for a flat rider, and when, each spring, the weighing morning came around – when every lad was weighed, to see if he was light enough to ride work – Alan would prepare for the trial by starving himself until the day of doom. He always just scraped by; and in fact I have never minded about a rider being slightly too heavy, as long as he rode well, and led the animal he was riding home from the gallops.

After Alan left me, with all my good wishes, he started training at Newmarket for Terry Ramsden, who had a roller-coaster career in the City on the Japanese money markets. All this investment went up the spout when he went to prison, but Alan always said that Terry was very good to him. From Newmarket he moved to Tarporley in Cheshire, where Eric Cousins had done so well; he now has a full string and is winning a lot of races.

It was not really surprising that I lost my cool at 'the system's' excess of zeal in the case of Habat, for timing counts for so much in training racehorses, especially the really good ones, and when you have your horse ready to run you do not want to be baulked at the last moment. I have always found that when preparing a potentially top-class horse for a big race, any interruption in his schedule will inevitably stop him winning. The stages of the build-up are so finely tuned that whether he is cantering, galloping, or merely trotting or being led out, one slight hold-up is enough to put your plans in disarray. You can get away with it in minor races, but the top ones will inevitably elude you; and a horse that has had a setback, even for a day, will almost always drift in the betting market.

Closely related to timing, of course, is the business of entries: a constant problem, as well as a constant fascination, for trainers. When I first started training, the entries for ordinary races closed eight weeks before the event, with a forfeit stage two weeks before; this meant that you could see how competitive or high-quality a race was likely to be, and how other horses' programmes were taking shape, some way in advance, which in turn gave trainers time to plan, especially for the better horses. Nowadays, for all ordinary races, entries do not need to be in until four days ahead, and this is a great saving for owners, as you do not have to enter horses that have any sort of problem way in advance in the hope that they will be able to run, only to lose that entry fee if they are withdrawn at the forfeit stage. You can keep horses ticking over more, waiting for races whose entries appear suitable, rather than planning a horse's programme a long way in advance. Also, we now have a centralised handicapping system, so that horses are all uniformly handicapped, whereas in the old days one had the additional problem of individual handicappers who were lenient to certain horses. The trouble with the new system is that they go up in the handicap quickly, but seem to come down more slowly.

My last secretary was Lucy McDiarmid, and she was a star: an excellent rider and keen follower of hounds as well as a tremendously hard worker. She married our vet, Stuart; but though he was at one time a very good vet, he turned out to be a rather less than good husband, and the marriage went awry. We count her among our dear friends, and are delighted that she remains close by, working with Oliver Sherwood.

17

HAMAS AND HOME

Hamas arrived with me in the autumn of 1990. He was superbly bred, by the Northern Dancer stallion Danzig, whom I remember seeing at Claiborne Farm on one of my visits to Kentucky. Danzig only won two conditions races before getting leg trouble, but having started out on his stud career with a very low covering fee, suddenly blossomed into a leading stallion. Rick Nicholls, Sheikh Hamdan's astute manager in America, had bought Hamas as a foal for only $90,000, and he was a good-looking colt; he turned his feet out a bit, but in my view that is not too serious a fault. In fact, if you examined the average home-bred and retained winner after a race, you would in most cases be appalled at its conformation. Some defects, of course, are more serious in a racehorse than others; the Americans, for example, are much more concerned than we are at very straight pasterns, because they have so high a rate of breakdowns on their tracks; but, as I have mentioned earlier, that has a lot to do with the nature of American tracks and the drug regime in the United States.

Hamas always had something about him which I liked, though he was the most laid-back colt I have ever trained. As a two-year-old he was beset by a sequence of minor ailments, and I was unable to run him; but he showed enough promise to make us decide to give him his first outing in a maiden race at the 1992 Craven meeting at Newmarket. He started favourite and ran really well, to be beaten a neck. His second and third races were at Sandown, where he won nicely over the stiff mile and then finished a very respectable second to Ezzoud (now a stallion at the National Stud). He had an easy race at Chepstow over the May Bank Holiday – and then ran a stinker in the Jersey Stakes at Royal Ascot. This up-and-down pattern was to be typical of Hamas; he was a bit of a moody individual, and just to make things more difficult he never gave us a clue to how he felt; unlike most racehorses of character, he would never give a squeal, or buck at home, to show his well-being.

Our own home life was changing this year: by the beginning of June we had made our move back to Windsor House. After twenty-seven years at Seven Barrows, it was a wrench, but inevitable; owing to the dreaded virus, and declining numbers of horses, the financial figures did not add up any more. By the spring of 1991 we were down to sixty-seven horses; by the end of that season we had had only twenty-seven winners, and though Hateel had won twice in Ireland, and Mukaddamah had won a Group Two race on Irish Derby day, the writing was on the wall. Big training establishments need filling up with good horses, preferably Group winners; we were locked in endless discussions with our advisers and accountants, but whatever one does, when a decline starts it is hard to halt, and eventually we decided to bite the bullet. I did not want to give up training for the time being, but felt a smaller property might suit us better. I rang up Micky Wiggin from Lane Fox, and he summed the whole thing up with a simple but inspired suggestion: was there someone about who would like to train at Seven Barrows, and possibly do a partial swap with us?

The obvious candidate was Nicky Henderson at Windsor House, bursting at the seams with his successful jumping string; so Micky agreed to approach him and his family to see if a deal could be done. The advantage for Nicky would be that he would be much nearer the gallops for National Hunt horses, as apart from the wonderful paddock across the road, the Mandown

Gallops, the only ones available for him were an hour and a half's exercise or more away. The advantage for us would be having a much smaller yard, with room for about fifty horses, making it much easier to contain overheads. By the spring of 1992 the agreement was worked out, and we were able to do our partial swap on very good terms.

We found Windsor House much improved. Since we had left in 1965, the whole house had been transformed; Nicky had built on a brand new stable yard, with about thirty boxes, on the site of the old kitchen gardens, and there was an excellent hostel for the staff. We redesigned the kitchen and generally spruced the place up to suit ourselves. Although leaving Seven Barrows was a huge blow, we were still training, with the full support of our owners, and still had some nice horses in our hands – among them, of course, Hamas.

Over the rest of the summer he ran respectably in various races, and in September we were asked to use him as pacemaker for Lahib, also owned by Sheikh Hamdan, in the Queen Elizabeth II Stakes at Ascot. Ridden by Richard Hills, he set a good pace into the straight, at which point he hampered Selkirk, who should have won, enough to let Lahib up on the outside to win comfortably. Angus Gold then told me that he was going to be trained in Dubai, but I felt he was now showing such speed, even though he had won over a mile in his second race, that we ought to give him one more chance. I found a race for him in October at the Houghton meeting, the Bentinck Stakes over five furlongs, and he fizzed in; so he got a reprieve from the desert.

He wintered well, and the following year we ran him first in the Abernant Stakes at Newmarket; this was a Listed race over six furlongs, and I felt that he tired in the last furlong to finish fifth. We decided to give him another chance in the Duke of York Stakes at York (a Group Three race, again over six furlongs) and this time he won readily, beating among others a very good sprinter in Lochsong. On the morning of the race Mike Cattermole, a very astute judge and now a commentator, but at that time Willie Carson's agent, rang me up, and said, 'Do you fancy your horse today?' I said that I did; but, staying away from home as I was, I had not then seen the morning paper. He told me he could get 100–6 about Hamas; and even though I am not a betting man, I did well enough to send Mike a very nice case of claret afterwards as a present.

After this triumph Hamas ran two more moody races, first in the Temple Stakes at Sandown and then in the Cork and Orrery Stakes at Royal Ascot. Certainly Ascot was not his favourite course; in fact, he seemed to hate it, except when doing a marvellous job as pacemaker. The going then became firm, which suited him admirably, and I got permission from Sheikh Hamdan to run him in the July Cup at Newmarket's July meeting. I could not really fancy him on the basis of his previous two runs, but on the other hand I didn't rate the other sprinters very highly – with the exception of Vincent O'Brien's College Chapel, and he, I felt, would not like the firm ground. So it was worth a try; and indeed Hamas, always handy, and racing up the centre, won by three lengths, given a very positive ride by Willie Carson. It may have been a fluke, but he beat that lot of sprinters very easily – at 33–1! I wish I had had a bet.

Then came an announcement: 'Would Mr Peter Walwyn please come to the stewards' room?' I could anticipate what this was about; the horse had, after all, shown vastly superior form to his last two runs. Willie and I were marched in to give our explanations. When I was asked for my opinion, I looked at the stewards and it dawned on me that several of them had been divorced. Tongue in cheek, I replied: 'There is only one thing in life that makes more of a fool of a man than a woman, and that is a horse!' The explanation was quickly accepted.

Hamas produced another pair of moody races before being

packed off to Derrinstown, Sheikh Hamdan's stud in County Kildare. His stallion career started off very well, with over 71 per cent of his runners in 1999 winning or being placed. One of his successes was a little filly whom I bought at the December Sales for 2,500 guineas, called Regal Revolution. She won five of her races as a two-year-old, including the Dick Poole Stakes at Salisbury, a race that Mark Smyly and I started in memory of our great friend and stalwart owner, and the Firth of Clyde Stakes at Ayr. She did not train on, but she gave her owners a lot of fun, and was sold for 34,000 guineas at the end of her three-year-old career.

Because of the competition from Coolmore, at the end of 1999 Hamas was moved to stand at Branville in France. He was a very good horse on his day, but inconsistent; had he been less wayward, the sky would have been the limit. If only horses could talk, the connections would all be far better off.

It would be hard to get through all the unpredictable ups and downs of a trainer's life – or indeed any sort of life – without a sense of humour, and an element of fun and mayhem has certainly loomed large in ours. Racing is full of humorists, and one in particular for whom I had a great regard was Jeffrey Bernard, who first surfaced in our orbit in 1965, when he was a photographer and took a picture of me in the yard with Humble Duty. From then on he was in and out of our lives continually, bringing hilarious news of the scrapes he got into – especially with his wives and girlfriends. He wrote in *Private Eye* under the pseudonym of Colonel Mad, and one piece in particular made us howl with laughter. He was sent in the winter to Barbados, an island we have always avoided, as (a) it is expensive and (b) it is Newmarket-on-Sea, where you meet all the people you see all summer. From here he wrote an article containing the following passage:

Most sadly missed by all of us in Barbados this year is 'Big Pete' Walwyn, who with his charming wife Bonk is in Africa, leading an extremely hazardous expedition into the dark jungles where such intrepid men as Livingstone, Stanley, Ken Cundell and Doug Marks lost their lives searching for owners.

It is with a sense of deep regret and appalling loss that I have to inform readers that the expedition has not been heard or sighted since it set out from the cocktail bar of the Ocean Sports Hotel some two weeks ago. My African Correspondent tells me that a half-crazed native porter who was found on the steps of a Mission near Lake Victoria smoking a large Bolivar, and drinking whisky out of a flask with the initials P.W., reported, albeit somewhat in-coherently, that he had seen several members of the fierce Tumform tribe struggling to put a very tall white man into a cooking pot.

'Dis man,' the porter told his rescuers, 'he shout all the time bery bery loud. De golden-haired lady wid him, she say come along darling don't make de fuss and he shout I teach dese black bastards to make a meal of me and he say sumpting about gelding dem.'

Meanwhile a rescue operation has been mounted by Professor Benjamin Hanbury, which is why, as a local witch doctor put it, 'all de hope is fading pretty rapidly.'

When Jeffrey died, after coping so bravely with his terminal illness, we buried his ashes, with the help of the local vicar and his lookalike and wonderful stage portrayer Peter O'Toole, on the downs at the top of Faringdon road; he loved Lambourn, its people and its laughter, its pubs and its houses.

Throughout my career, though I have never felt myself to be particularly accident prone, I have had a few funny experiences and mishaps. I remember breaking my arm, just before we got married, in a bit of skylarking at Blewbury, and Bonk thinking I would have to walk down the aisle with it in plaster. Fortunately it came off in time – but not before a lot of jokes had flown around about its still being stiff . . .

In the 1980s I had a tumble out hunting with the Vale of the White Horse hounds, when I was cannoned into and fell off jumping a set of rails. Apparently I was knocked out and turning blue when a dear lady whom I knew well gave me the kiss of life. This apparently revived me quickly, but I was still rushed off to Malmesbury hospital for the night. When I was told who it was who had been so kind as to come to my rescue I had to borrow a mirror to see if I had any marks on my face, as the lady in question did have rather protruding teeth; but all was well. When Bonk came to pick me up, she saw the specialist, who said that I would be perfectly all right, but would have to take it easy for a few days. He also said that I might behave strangely in some ways: I might be very sleepy, or I might throw myself around a bit, and shout and scream. All she said was, 'What's strange about that? That's no different from usual.'

On another occasion I was up on the downs and was asked to help with a horse that we afterwards found out was a really nasty character. He was called Detroit Sam, and had a reputation for being extremely mulish and savage in the starting stalls. I was on foot, as I had just been schooling some jumpers, and didn't have a hunting crop with me; so when the horse propped, refusing to go forward, I gave a 'Huroosh!' At that it let fly with both hind legs, completely smashing my lower arm. I was whisked off to the Princess Margaret Hospital in Swindon, but the arm was so swollen that it was several days before they could operate on me. Eventually the time came, and plates and screws were put in, but the arm refused to heal and the doctors had to reset the bones. Still it would not heal, so it was decided to give me a bone transplant from my thigh. This was done by a brilliant surgeon called Dr Simonis at the BUPA hospital in Woking; it worked perfectly, and the arm has given me no trouble since.

Another horse who put me in hospital was a talented but soft three-year-old called Iamus that I was riding out as a hack. I loved doing this with difficult horses; it usually did them good, freshening them up to be taken all over the place, and on their own, not in a string. Suddenly he reared up, and when I gave him a corrective smack he fell down with me and trod all over me on the road. This caused a nasty cut on one ankle which would not heal, even with tight pressure bandages. Eventually it was decided that I should go to one of the Oxford hospitals and have the maggot treatment. This consisted of cleaning up the wound and inserting a layer of maggots sent in from a maggot farm at Bridgend, near Glamorgan. They would be left there, under a transparent dressing, for about three days. (This old-fashioned treatment dated back to the First World War, when it was discovered that badly wounded soldiers who had developed gangrene while lying on the battlefield would only recover if there were maggots in the wound; it was concluded that the maggots helped the healing process.) After the three days the maggots, which had been only about a quarter of an inch long when inserted, had grown to about two inches from their feasting on the rather mucky wound. They had completely cleaned it up and it healed beautifully.

My last brush with a hospital came about when I was presiding over the annual general meeting of the Vine and Craven Foxhounds at Hannington, near Basingstoke, in July 1997. I stepped away from the top table, not realising that it was on a platform, and with my papers under my arm fell heavily to the floor. I had not noticed that there was an old clay-pigeon trap, kept as a decoration, against the wall of the old barn we were in; the arm of this contraption was sticking out, and as I fell it drove into my thigh about six inches. There was a barb on it, designed to hold the arm of the machine; it was solid metal, and very sharp. I was fully conscious but pinned to the spot by this arm until some very helpful people came to my aid and undid the bolt on the arm so that I could be hurried unceremoniously off to Basingstoke Hospital in an ambulance, with the arm still stuck in me.

I had the offending weapon removed under general anaesthetic, and the next morning Bonk, who had been alerted the night before, came in with her brother Nick. Like any dutiful trainer's wife, she brought with her not grapes or flowers but my mobile phone; I might have been still hooked up to drips and oxygen, but I wanted to ensure the smooth running of the stable. No sooner had I pressed the 'send' button for the first call than sirens went off all around us, the oxygen supply to the intensive care department was cut off, heart defibrillators started working of their own accord, the lights went out in the operating theatre and the elderly patient in the next bed, who had not moved for a week, sat bolt upright as if a miracle had just been performed. The mobile telephone was confiscated; it seems they can do funny things to the computers which control vital equipment.

During the few days I was in the hospital – which I found as efficient as any I have been in – Pat Eddery conjured up all his magic, riding a brilliant race on Hattab to come from behind and win the Ruinart Stakes, a Listed race at Newbury. I don't think this did the peace and quiet of the hospital much more good than my telephone, as my shouts of encouragement echoed round the wards.

18

LAMBOURN: A RACING VILLAGE

Records of Lambourn go back as far as the Domesday Book of William the Conqueror, but it is believed that even before then, in the ninth century AD, Alfred the Great had a palace in Lambourn, probably on the site now occupied by Parsonage House, opposite the ancient church with its ziz-zag shaped west door lintel typical of Norman architecture. The surrounding slopes were ideal for grazing sheep, and the earliest hamlet of Lambourn was – in a name that lives on in the likes of Chipping Camden, Chipping Norton and Chipping Sodbury – originally Sheeping Lambourn, named after the main industry of those days.

It is unclear when Lambourn became a racing centre, but there were odd training stables scattered about early in the eighteenth century, and in the 1830s owners started to move their horses away from Newmarket to the Berkshire downs because the gallops in Suffolk became too firm in summer. The coming of the Lambourn Valley Railway, opened in 1894 (and closed in 1960), obviously speeded up the transport of horses and accelerated the attraction of owners to the locality. I have seen an old map of Upper Lambourn in the 1700s which marks a strip of land near the present straight mile on Mandown as 'The Raceway', and in Reginald Hebers' 'Historical List of Horfe-Matches' run in 1751 there are mentions of the 'best of four mile heats' taking place at Lambourn, presumably on Weathercock, the old racecourse – now ploughed up, but with the remains of an old building still there on top of the downs. Stork House, Waltham House and

Seven Barrows were some of the earliest stables, with Russley Park, where several nineteenth-century Derby winners were trained, not far away.

The incomers of the early twentieth century were not always welcomed without suspicion. In 1922 Randall Cramsie and his wife 'Dod' moved to train at Downs House in the High Street. One day Dod met the vicar, who said to her, 'Hello, where have you come from?', and then, 'Why have you come here?' On her reply, he retorted: 'They either come here to save their health, wealth, or reputation.' Some of them made their mark – Harry Cottrill and Captain Oswald 'Ossie' Bell were among those who patronised the village and had Classic winners; but right up to the end of the Second World War there were probably fewer than a dozen training establishments in Lambourn.

In early 1989 we had staying with us Dan Abbott, a friend and advertising agent, head of the well-known firm Abbott International. He complained that we did not advertise the village and its facilities enough; he cited as an example of what could be done Guy Harwood, who had made a great success of promoting himself and his attractive facilities. So, to try to respond to the problem he had identified, a committee of trainers was formed, which to my surprise elected me as its chairman. Thus was born the Lambourn Trainers' Association, which now has thirty-five members (only one trainer decided not to join us, preferring to paddle his own canoe – but he has now ceased training). The committee has remained virtually unchanged to this day, save for the lamented retirement of Jenny Pitman, a great Lambourn character and extraordinary personality. Having started out living in a caravan while working with her first husband Richard for Major Geoffrey Champneys, she worked her way up from the point-to-point yard she established and, after her marriage broke up, rose to the very heights of the profession: the only woman to have trained two

Grand National winners and two Cheltenham Gold Cup winners. She had some lovely horses in the old-fashioned jumping mould, and was a very positive member of our committee.

Also on the committee is my brother-in-law Nick Gaselee, one of the hardest workers I know. His training of the bad-legged and bad-winded Party Politics to win the 1992 Grand National was exemplary. Indeed, the horse would have probably won again the following year, when the race was abandoned after a very controversial start: he was apparently only cantering as they passed the stands on the first circuit, and going far better than he was when he won. Nick has been a tower of strength to us in Lambourn, and he and his wonderful wife Judy, who works equally hard at her thriving tent business, have greatly enhanced village life with their common sense and enthusiasm.

The other two members of the committee are Merrick Francis, who has been thoroughly supportive, despite having his hands amply filled by the task of running the very efficient Lambourn Racehorse Transport business, the foremost horse transport concern in the country; and Nicky Henderson, recently leading trainer at the Cheltenham Festival, who has settled into our old home at Seven Barrows as though he had been born in the place. It is thrilling for us to see him continue the long tradition of good horses being trained there.

Lambourn is an unusual community, to put it mildly. The whole village depends on racing; it is home to about 3,000 people and nearly 2,000 horses, and about half the former are involved directly or indirectly in the industry that revolves around the latter. As well as the 800 or so directly employed in the care of the horses, there are all the ancillary industries and their specialists, like saddlers, farriers and horsebox drivers, as well as, of course, the veterinary surgeons. The trainers get on very well together. We were once described by someone whom

I never met, and who has now left the village, as the 'valley of hate and spite', but this is completely untrue. (I always, jokingly, call Newmarket 'Sin City'.) We do have one or two residents who get themselves into the *News of the World* occasionally, but in general the standards of behaviour are high.

The newly fledged Lambourn Trainers' Association started out by asking Dan for advice, and the first thing he did was design us a logo. We then proposed to put up welcome and warning signs at the entrances to the village; at first the district council protested, but when we offered to pay for them ourselves they soon relented, and we are now known worldwide for promoting 'The Valley of the Racehorse'. When we formed the Association we asked the members what their main concerns were, and to a man they all said: 'Lack of accommodation for stable staff.' Any good trainer knows that if his staff are happily living in decent houses, they are far more likely to look after their horses well. Although some trainers do offer their employees subsidised accommodation, they are finding it harder to get appropriate properties. Wages may have been going up steadily, but house prices in the Home Counties have surged ahead out of all proportion to earnings. There is no real necessity at present for homes for the elderly, as there are already over 100 homes for retired people in the village, many of them occupied by people who were themselves, or whose dependants were, in the industry; the overriding priority has been to prevent the exodus from racing of so many young people who would otherwise have gone elsewhere to other jobs in areas where the housing is affordable, being completely unable even to contemplate paying the ridiculous prices being asked for property around Lambourn.

We had started an 'Open Day' on Good Friday, a day when (bar the death of Our Lord) nothing much happens, to try to save the Grand National, which at the time was undergoing one of the periodic crises that afflicted it during the 1970s and 1980s, and the fund raising was such a success that we redirected our efforts in the following years towards raising money for our newly formed charity, the Lambourn Valley Housing Trust. Today the 'Open Day' is a national event, with upwards of 10,000 people from all over the country flocking in to see their equine heroes at home.

In 2000 the day was yet again a huge success, with about thirty yards open, and massive crowds. Among the attractions were bungee jumping, schooling over hurdles and fences, and camel racing. I had to ride a very reluctant camel, which did not want to know. While I was still in my Arab costume, wearing my dishdasha, a lady came up to me and asked if I could speak to her very small son. He thought I was Jesus. I could hardly keep a straight face, but gave him a pat on his head, and said something like 'God bless you, my son.' I have been called many things in my life before, but never 'Jesus'.

The organisers of the Open Day are Mark Smyly, as chairman, and committee members Oliver Sherwood and Nicky Henderson. They and the secretary of the event, Sandra Nolan, put in prodigious amounts of work to make the whole thing operate smoothly, and the results bear witness to their dedication and talents. As a result of this success, we have been able to take real strides in addressing the housing problem for people working in racing. Against the tide of ever-increasing numbers of expensive matchbox houses built for commuters from Swindon and the south-east, and with a lot of help in the initial stages from Racing Welfare, we have bought land and built seventeen houses which are now being lived in by working staff, paying reasonable rents. In just over ten years since we launched the project, we have already raised over £1 million, wiped out the debt we incurred to help get the scheme off the ground, and are now looking at the next phase with a view to expanding our aims.

The other major achievement of the Lambourn Trainers' Association has been to secure the sponsorship of all the stables by Danka, an information technology firm based in Reading. The genesis of this enterprise dates back to 1993, when a great friend of ours, Anthea Gibson-Fleming, rang up: she had a friend staying on after Royal Ascot, Henry Bellingham, at the time MP for King's Lynn, and asked if he could have a look round the stables. After wandering around the horses, he came in for a drink, and asked what the main worries in racing were. I replied: VAT, and explained that owners in this country were unfairly treated with regard to tax, compared to their counterparts on the Continent. From the budget of 1983 owners in this country had been paying VAT at 17.5% on their training fees and the purchase price of horses, a much more onerous burden than the equivalent borne by our European competitors; on the Continent and in Ireland the standard rate of VAT was only 5% or lower. Was there anything that could be done?

Henry said that the only way was to get an influential lobby started to work for change. I therefore arranged for a strong group of professionals in the industry to meet at Bob McCreery's house in Newmarket, to discuss the whole issue. Among others we had Peter Mendham from the accountants Coopers & Lybrand; Chris Harper, a leading breeder; Bob himself, formerly a top amateur rider before becoming a leading breeder; and Henry Bellingham himself. Henry advised us to get in touch with Judith Chaplin, who in addition to being member of parliament for our constituency in Newbury was political adviser to the then Prime Minister, John Major. We duly contacted her; she expressed interest in our cause, and I was able to get her an invitation to meet the directors of Tattersalls, the bloodstock auctioneers, including their accountant Philip Potts and Michael Watt, one of their directors.

We took her around the back of the sales complex at

Newmarket, where the staff were at that moment mucking out boxes in preparation for the next batch of horses coming in; these would be for the December sale, the most important disposal sale of the year. We explained that the jobs of this considerable workforce in a highly labour-intensive industry could all be at risk, with the threat of a severe drain on all parts of the industry in this country, with owners, especially foreigners, moving their horses abroad to training bases where the tax rates were not so heavy.

We felt that Judith was impressed by our arguments, and she certainly grasped the nettle very quickly; further meetings followed, and it was not long before she was making good progress in pressing our case. I kept ringing her up, and she kept assuring me that things were well on target. The main obstacle was Customs and Excise, who have always had violent objections to any scheme which might reduce revenue to them.

Not everyone was optimistic about our chances of success. While I was in London, attending one of the apparently endless series of meetings on the subject, one of our local trainers rang Bonk up and said he thought that I was wasting my time, and would never get anything done. She told him that we had established a strong relationship with our MP and that there was every chance of a breakthrough; and indeed, things came to a very satisfactory conclusion when Judith rang me out of the blue in the early afternoon of Budget day 1994 to say that the whole deal had gone through and would be announced that afternoon in small print, right at the bottom of the Chancellor's statement. So I was able to ring the sceptical trainer and put his mind at rest; and, to be perfectly fair, he has been a great supporter of our efforts ever since.

The next step was to see how we could help meet the conditions of the bill, as the Treasury wanted owners to try to obtain sponsorship of their horses, to offset the lack of revenue occasioned by the concession of abolishing VAT on sales. We had a meeting of the LTA, and it was decided, as proposed by one of our members, Charlie Brooks, that we should try to find a company to sponsor *all* of us trainers in a group package deal, as it would be nearly impossible for individual trainers to obtain sponsors, especially for moderate horses.

Eventually, after interminable negotiations, the last stretching through the night and ending at eight o'clock in the morning, in February 1995 we concluded a three-year deal with a Reading word processor and photocopier firm, Danka. This involved carrying their logo on colours, paddock clothing, staff coats and horse boxes. The saddlers, clothing manufacturers and horsebox firms were immediately hard at work to make sure things were up and running before Cheltenham, and the local firm of lawyers was on overtime to get the contract signed and sealed.

Throughout this rapid but complex process we owed a huge debt of gratitude to our accountant, Robin Platt, who found Danka, and the company's chairman, Martin St Quinton. They have been pillars of strength, and thanks to them we achieved a deal that no other group of trainers has been able to match. Appropriately enough, it was Nick Gaselee who saddled the first televised winner under the Danka logo on 11 March, Kentish Piper at Chepstow; and not only did Alderbrook win the Champion Hurdle and Master Oats the Cheltenham Gold Cup for Kim Bailey shortly after that, but Jenny Pitman's Royal Athlete won the Grand National to cap an excellent first season for our sponsors. We are now negotiating a new deal, as Danka have had a poor time financially in the United States, and their former directors have now moved elsewhere; but already we have four potential new sponsors in the pipeline, and the trainers are committed to keeping the agreement intact.

Lambourn is now booming, but we must not let the planners think that we are a soft touch as a dormitory for Swindon and the pilots at Heathrow. We, the racing industry, are the main source of employment, especially now that farmers are cutting back on labour, because of modern machinery, soaring costs and ever-declining returns to the producer; and, as I tell all members of parliament that I see, we are a very important industry. Lambourn is, and always will be, a racing village.

19

COUNTRY SPORTS

In all the debates over the future of our countryside, one fact stands out. Virtually all those involved hate cruelty, and love and respect the animals they have to deal with. From birth we have all had animals round us, and the vast majority of us grow up learning to treat them properly.

Even in foxhunting, those who follow hounds hate the death of a good fox – bar the hunt staff, whose job it is to keep the hounds fit enough and hunting well enough to kill the fox quickly and cleanly, as usually happens. If ever we are lucky enough to be near the head of the hunt at the end of a run when a fox is caught, once we have seen the leading hound nip the fox in the back of the neck and turn him over instantly, we look away; it is not our job to interfere, and certainly not our wish to gloat over the kill. The contrast to the image put about by so many of our opponents, who think that we are all bloodthirsty, and froth at the mouth at the end of a hunt, could not be greater. We hunt to have fun; and to enjoy at its best the wonderful panorama of the countryside that has been laid out by so many generations of landowners, tenants and their employees.

I recall in particular one marvellous day with the Vale of the White Horse hounds from a meet at Leigh near Cricklade on Christmas Eve 1962. Jimmy Lindley, a fearless man across country, was on my father's dear old horse Sherry; Bonk was on a very good ex-racehorse of Peter Cazalet's which he had kindly given her; and I was riding a great big animal called Bendoon, lent to me by Tim Forster, who had just started training and was too busy to join us. At two o'clock it was pouring with rain, there was no sign of any foxes and we were sitting in the deluge near a big dairy building. Eventually the other two, ranged alongside me, said, 'Come on, this is no good, let's go home.' Luckily I didn't agree with them straight away. 'Steady on,' I said, 'you can see those hounds want to hunt, they are giving tongue all the time, even while we are waiting about.' All of a sudden a fox got up and away we went. After a very fast hunt, described afterwards by Colin Nash, master and superb huntsman of the Old Berkshire, as like a two-mile chase, with everyone's sticks up, the fox eventually went to ground just below Oaksey village. We had jumped for fun, and Sherry, always outpaced on the flat but a faultless jumper, was soon on terms over the fences. There had been a superb scent, which often happens before a lot of snow – and indeed the weather put paid to hunting for a long time afterwards through that awful winter. But that Christmas Eve was a day to recollect in a hot bath, with a good hunting tea inside you and your horse warmly bedded down.

There is a great deal of hypocrisy and double-think in the opposition to hunting. The people who condemn us are often the same people who will let the new puppy out in the city streets when it has done a mess on the carpet on Christmas Day, or throw a bitch and her newborn litter out on a motorway, because it is too much trouble to look after them. Contrast this behaviour with the loving care and respect that hunting people give to their horses and hounds and it surely makes no sense to brand us bloodthirsty and unfeeling.

The link between horse racing and hunting goes back to the very origins of steeplechasing, with the first recorded match between riders across country in 1752, when two brave men, Mr Cornelius O'Callaghan and Mr Edmund Blake, had a substantial wager as to which of them would beat the other in a race for their hunters. The contest took place over four and a half miles of natural country between St John's church at Buttevant and Doneraile in County Cork – hence the term 'steeplechase', the steeple of the church at the finishing point being a good visible marker when riding over what must have been very wild and hairy hedges. Even today, no other country in Europe has the varied landscape that we have here, except for Ireland, where horses are respected as much as they are in this country. Gradually the courses became more regular, and the original matches between two horses gave way to larger fields, and eventually the National Hunt code of rules was established to regulate the sport.

Flat racing had been going on since the time of Queen Boadicea, whose power base in East Anglia was not far from modern-day Newmarket; and the Romans raced at Chester, where the course has in its essentials hardly changed to this day. The Royal Family have always had a great love of the sport, and have enjoyed great success over the years, although lately the Royal Studs have been in decline, owing possibly to the policies of recent managers. However, there has been a distinct surge of optimism recently, and with the appointment of three new trainers, Roger Charlton, Richard Hannon and Michael Stoute, following on after Ian Balding and Dick Hern, there is every chance that Her Majesty the Queen may hit the high spots again with Classic horses.

Not only is there a strong bond between hunting and racing, but the connection between hunting and riding education in this country is very strong. Most of us learnt to ride on donkeys, or ponies, and then joined the Pony Club. This was and is divided into branches run by the hunts, and dispensed tuition typically at the hands of rather fierce-looking ladies, who voluntarily gave, and give, unstinting time and effort to teaching the next generation not only how to ride, but how to behave on horseback and among other riders and users of the countryside. Sadly, with the increasing domination of the motor car, over the twentieth century fewer and fewer children were brought up anywhere near horses, let alone among them as part of the working environment. Many of the young people coming into racing today aged sixteen have never ridden a horse before, and have to be taught from scratch. The other problem, of which I am only too acutely aware, as chairman of the trainers' committee at the British Racing School at Newmarket, is the size of the new entrants, with an average weight today of 8st 4lb – about two stone heavier than when I started in racing in the 1950s. Children are now better fed, which is of course to be welcomed, but once in their teenage years many spend too much time eating fast food and too little time getting any exercise at all, let alone any involving horses.

This widening division between the traditional ways of life in the country and the experience of many people growing up without intimate day-to-day knowledge of rural affairs has given rise to a lamentable hostility based largely on ignorance and, sadly, often also on jealousy of a supposedly privileged lifestyle. The pressure against the sports that we love has intensified, and was brought to a head by the election in 1997 of a Labour government whose new intake of MPs includes many urban-based left-wing members who have no idea of the ways in which the countryside works.

Many of us in racing were so worried that our leaders were not taking the initiative in working to save our sports that I felt it my duty, as a passionate defender of our way of life and an ordinary member of the community, to voice our feelings to them all. On 27 May 1997 I therefore wrote a personal letter to all members of the Jockey Club and British Horseracing Board, most of whom I knew, as follows:

Dear—

So many of us in the racing industry are, at best, perturbed and at worst horrified by the negative attitude on the possible ban on hunting with hounds by both the Jockey Club and the British Horseracing Board collectively.

We feel very strongly that so much employment will be severely curtailed or terminated, and the cost to the ancillary trades will be massive and the seed corn of our entire industry will be decimated.

So many saddlers, blacksmiths, veterinary surgeons, horsebox manufacturers and clothing suppliers will have to stop trading. The Jockey Club and British Horseracing Board must come out loud and strong in support of our stand, as point-to-pointing, the hunter trade, and the Pony Club will be shattered. The very roots of all we love and believe in in the countryside will be destroyed.

How will the racehorses that sadly have to be put down in training be disposed of?. The knackers and abattoirs don't want anything to do with them.

How will hunter-chasing survive? How will the certificate for a horse previously and regularly fairly hunted for 6 days be described in future? What volunteers will come to run point-to-points?

It is bad enough when the authorities persist in calling National Hunt racing in the summer 'Summer Jumping', although this has now been modified.

Don't think that the extremists will stop at hunting – think about horse-drawn caravan holidays, eventing, long distance riding, abuse of police horses and even more relevant, racing over fences. Too many people with a civil servant mentality have no idea of the proud heritage of our countryside. Let's stand up and be counted and not hesitate for one moment longer. We should have leadership and people being able to put their heads over the parapet.

I wrote this letter knowing that there was a Jockey Club meeting on the Monday before Royal Ascot, about three weeks before the Countryside Alliance rally in Hyde Park on 10 July.

The next few days were a revelation. The Jockey Club were nearly unanimous in their support, save for a very few predictable waverers who either did not reply or gave a very ambiguous answer. This was no more than I had expected; I had already put a toe in the water with several members and knew that I had overwhelming backing. By contrast, the response from the members of the British Horseracing Board was, with a few exceptions, very negative. One member, Sir Paul Fox, has now resigned. The Jockey Club meeting, according to several who were there, was a triumph, with the members suddenly galvanised into collectively realising the danger in which all our sports stood. In the face of this solid front the BHB eventually fell in behind them, so that the whole of racing was united behind a strong approach.

The Countryside Alliance rally in Hyde Park was a great success, with all the main racing bodies there in force, and the march in London in 1999 was an equally fantastic occasion. It is to be hoped that these massive demonstrations of concern have begun to make the government sit up and think. We have a long way to go, but if they don't want to divide the nation, they must realise that though the vocal spokespeople of the countryside may be relatively few in numbers, we have a huge base of support and are immovable in our resolve.

We have a heavy battle on our hands, but with so many devoted to the cause, the detractors will be hard pressed to carry the day. One thing remains certain; banning foxhunting will not save the life of a single fox, nor will the abolition of coursing keep a single hare alive.

20

THE FUTURE OF RACING

Horse racing in this country has been organised by volunteers for so long, and so successfully, that the sudden arrival of commercialism, bringing in its wake a completely new concept of the sport, seems to have taken it rather by surprise. Other countries have copied our traditions and practices to the extent that we have often asked ourselves whether we have our heads in the sand; certainly the Jockey Club, which had controlled racing for so many years, had come to be held in contempt by the more rebellious factions of the industry and the press. However, with the arrival on the scene of the British Horseracing Board, driven by the brilliant organising skills of Lord Hartington, opinions have begun to alter.

The BHB, however, a semi-democratic body, still appears a rather rudderless vessel. Peter Savill, recently appointed chairman, quickly ruffled a few feathers among the bookmakers and others who opposed his plans. Peter is a brilliant man, with the interests of the whole sport in his mind, but has never run a committee before and finds it difficult not to act on his own, instead of bringing his team around him to decide on a concerted course of action. It appears, however, that he is settling down now into the new appointment. It is important that the BHB speak with a united voice; for one thing, it is sad to see our wonderful sport riven by selfish interests when all we want to see is everyone pulling together; for another, government, who don't put money into the game, but take out far more compared to other countries, finds it difficult to understand what we want when different factions seem to be going off in different directions and making different demands.

Whatever one's view of the bookmakers, they are in legitimate business; having been given a licence to print money when betting shops were made legal in 1961, they have taken full advantage of subsequent relaxation in the rules. They are now realising that there may well be betting terminals in pubs and shops in the near future, which may well make their outlets even more unprofitable, and are determined not to give much away.

Anxieties about competition from overseas Internet betting and the government's decision shortly to disband the Horserace Betting Levy Board could give racing a very big boost, if only the government will give a lead, and decide to reduce betting duty to a realistic level. The rate should come down from 9 per cent at least to 5 per cent, or the bookmakers may well extend their overseas interests even more; in any event, it may well be the Irish government will reduce its rate of tax from 5 per cent to a much lower level. The theory that any offshore bookmakers are going to hand over amounts equivalent to what they would have been paying in duty has already been found lacking: so far Victor Chandler, who runs the biggest offshore betting operation, has so far chosen to put funds into prize money only at selected meetings, which does not benefit the general prize money pool, and only acts as more advertising for his firm.

I don't think that anyone who goes into a betting shop glances up to see who owns the shop, and there is a very good case for the Tote buying up as many more betting shops as it can possibly afford, in effect to create the makings of a Tote monopoly off-course. This has happened with devastating success in Australia, where much more money comes back into racing from betting, from a much smaller human and equine population, because the profits of the Tote go straight back into racing.

The government has already decided to privatise the Tote, at what price no one yet knows. The Tote was launched in 1927, with no backing from the government of its day, whose Chancellor of the Exchequer was Winston Churchill. The bill, backed and financed by a few enthusiasts and passed by a very narrow majority, established a monopoly on pool betting on racecourses. When shortly after its inception, led by the few people putting money in, it became profitable, they took their money out, and it is at the moment a 'mortmain' organisation – which, for anyone who doesn't understand French, means 'dead-hand': that is, the original investors having withdrawn their funds, today the Tote, though controlled by the government, is not in fact owned by anyone. For the government to say that if the Tote were to be sold the taxpayer would benefit is twisting words. The government would have to pass a bill through Parliament first to effect that, which in my opinion would be daylight robbery, and would be resisted by a lot of decent-minded MPs.

In any event, the sale of the Tote will take up to two years to get in motion, and in the meantime the BHB and the Jockey Club will have to devise a way to fund racing in place of the £60 million or so it receives from the Levy Board every year at the moment. This may well be done by the BHB exercising its right to the dissemination of the runners and riders, and the racecourses allowing the media rights which they own to be sold on a short lease, for the right amount of money.

Our main worry as trainers is the recruitment and retention of stable staff. For some reason the press feel that our employees are treated like slaves, but in most cases this is rubbish. Sadly, the new rules on modern apprenticeships are not so flexible as the old. Formerly, a young man would be signed up to a trainer as an apprentice for a minimum of three or five years in order to be taught his trade. If the boy grew too heavy to be a jockey, or did not quite fulfil his promise, one could raise his wages to the level of an ordinary lad. The three- or five-year system meant that trainers could bring a lad on slowly, and try to make a jockey out of him, if the potential was there. If someone did not have the potential to be a jockey, they were released from their apprenticeship ahead of time, enabling them to be paid a full wage. As things stand now, a trainer may find a promising boy and bring him on, only to find that after a year he is suddenly captured by a fashionable trainer, who may promise him rides, but really only wants him as cheap labour.

One idea I have is that winners of races not solely limited to apprentices should be able to run in handicaps without incurring a penalty, but only provided they are ridden by apprentice jockeys from their own stables, who would claim their 5lb or 7lb as appropriate. This would encourage trainers to put their own boys up, and would stimulate the apprentice system, as in any sport there is no better way to improve than to compete with people more experienced than oneself.

It is my personal opinion that the biggest stables in the country have too many horses, and that there should be a limit on the numbers in an individual yard of, say, 100. In America, where many top trainers divide their horses among several areas, the actual number of horses trained at each base will not exceed around fifty, making personal supervision more practical. A ceiling of 100 horses would encourage trainers to put their assistants in charge of satellite yards, and so spread the responsibility and improve the opportunities for younger would-be trainers to learn their craft. Further potential benefits would be that the dispersal of horses might help to contain the spread of disease, and also ease accommodation problems for staff around the big stables. I never wanted more than 100 horses at Seven Barrows, and only through giving in to a greedy impulse did I take on more in a separate yard for a short time.

How many horses can a trainer cope with, going around stables in the traditional way, however good his staff are, without keeping employees at their work until 7.30 or 8 p.m.? As it is, racehorses must be tended and exercised at weekends; and the more strain that is put on the staff, the worse the already deteriorating recruitment problem is going to become.

I do feel that we should try to reward better the staff who work in the stables at weekends. In the summer of 2000, we had racing on eighteen Sundays in a row. This may well suit the racecourses and the authorities, but how will trainers cope? We have only half staff at weekends anyway; and now a lot of those who are on duty may have to take their horses racing. In a stable such as that I referred to earlier, with just eight staff to look after 100 horses on a Sunday, what could they do with them? If they were lucky, the box would be opened and corn, hay, and water would be thrown in; but as for proper attention, that would be virtually impossible. I have already mentioned my idea that the racecourses, who want Sunday racing so much, might give the staff who actually were at work in the yard on a Sunday a sum, say £25, for each runner from the yard. There is already a £300 allowance for runners on a Sunday, but this goes to the owner and does not filter through to the lads working at home, and if a one-horse owner were asked to pay something to the staff at home when his horse was running, he would have a fit. This scheme would target those who have to stay at home and work in the yards over the weekends.

We have the finest racing in the world, with the highest levels of integrity, and are copied by all other racing countries; but the sport remains heavily underfunded; and efforts to address this problem bring new problems in their wake. Sponsorship, of course, has great potential, and I have already described the efforts we made in the Lambourn Trainers' Association to establish our own scheme; but we became rather concerned when a bookmaker attempted to arrange sponsorship of Kieren Fallon. I and my committee in Lambourn felt that this was a bad move. Where would Fallon's loyalties lie? With the owners who retained him, or with the bookmaker, who was probably paying him more than they were for the advertising? Luckily the BHB has now addressed this issue, stipulating that no owner, trainer or jockey can be sponsored by a bookmaker. Even though it is now almost universally accepted that the image of bookmakers has improved out of all recognition in recent years, the implications of such a deal would still be very complex. If Fallon had ridden an injudicious race, tongues would have been set wagging, and the public would have been bound to say, 'No wonder, he is in the pay of the bookmakers.' I do feel, too, that any jockey's sponsorship deal should include the payment of a percentage towards the owners who put them up, and also the stable staff, who have to work at home throughout the winter when so many of the flat race jockeys are enjoying themselves in sunny climes abroad.

The next few years are going to be crucial, but I believe there are so many good brains in the sport that ways will be found to iron out our difficulties. We also have a sound tradition of integrity that will stand us in good stead. There are still cases where drugs can be given at the wrong time, and to the wrong horse, but that is human error, and racing as a whole stands in sharp contrast to some other sports where crooked elements seem to have wormed their way in to the heart – as, for example, in the scandals surrounding cricketers being paid to throw games, or the prevalence of drug use by cyclists and track athletes. Thanks to our excellent security systems and the brilliant forensic laboratory at Fordham near Newmarket, we are able to deter many would-be wrongdoers. Horse racing remains a sport to be proud of.

EPILOGUE

In 1999 we had been back at Windsor House for seven years and were well settled and happy; but through the spring we had been having long discussions with our great friend David Oldrey about our future, and wondered about whether it was a good time to give up training.

Jim Ryan, the veteran American trainer and another friend of ours, once said that no man ever committed suicide or thought of retiring when he had a good two-year-old in his barn – and we had one, Khasayl; but one swallow does not make a summer, and we realised that it would be a surprise if we got a very good horse again. We had a lot of luck and a lot of success doing the most fascinating job; but we felt that at our age it was unlikely that we would get any new young owners, as they seem to prefer the whizz-kids of their own generation among the training ranks. We were reliant on a few wonderful owner–breeders, and Sheikh Hamdan. He had been the most marvellous owner, but although he was still very supportive, we knew that we were not likely to get the very best yearlings. The Godolphin operation, too, seemed to be getting stronger all the time, since Sheikh Mohammed had started the scheme by picking out some of the best of his exposed horses and taking them away from their English trainers to a private stable which he set up, first in Newmarket, then in Dubai, in France at Evry, and now in California too. (Evry, a racecourse near Paris established less than twenty years ago, was shunned by the French trainers because they said it was too far from the capital.

If only they were used to the travelling we in this country have to do!) The Société d'Encouragement was delighted: Sheikh Mohammed had installed new all-weather gallops, and rebuilt the whole place as a training centre, taking David Loder over from Newmarket to train the Godolphin two-year-olds. However, the French exercise has seemed to have been a bit of a disaster, with a lot of young horses succumbing to injury; and now the whole operation is suddenly folding, and returning to Stanley House at Newmarket, empty since John Gosden decided to move his string to Manton in the autumn of 1999.

With all these new developments, and with Marcus Tregonning's career blossoming in Sheikh Hamdan's own new complex at Kingwood House stables above Lambourn, we felt it was time to take more of a back seat. We talked things over with our estate agent, Mark Wiggin of Lane Fox and Co., whose firm have looked after us since we were married in 1960; he, as usual, was extremely helpful, and advised us that we could find someone to rent the stables and stable cottage, and continue to live in the house, probably the nicest house in Lambourn, with our beautiful garden and beloved dogs.

I rang up Marcus Armytage, one of the *Daily Telegraph*'s team of talented racing journalists, and asked him if he would come and see us on Friday morning, 27 August. I told him our news, and he asked for an exclusive interview about it all, to appear in the *Telegraph* next morning. The die was cast.

The worst thing was telling the staff on the Friday evening. Ron Thomas, who had been with us for over twenty-nine years, was wonderful. He said that he had been worried about the future for some time, but quite understood. I too was concerned about the future of some of our employees; we had six lads who had been with us for over twenty years. I need not have worried, because they knew their work backwards, and so were able to get good new jobs straight away. Ron, who was still only fifty-five, said that he would not want to work for another trainer; but luckily Jamie Osborne, just starting up in Peter Nelson's old yard, was keen to have him, and already the partnership is getting on well. Ralph Beckett, who had been with us for three and a half years, took on the stables and cottage at the end of the yard, and has so far done extremely well with the twenty or so horses he has started out with; it is very satisfying to see the stable continuing its winning thread!

The autumn seemed to speed by, and our good two-year-old Khasayl won us our last race at Redcar, the ATL Stakes on 2 October, with a prize of very nearly £100,000. Our jockey was that very popular and able rider from the West Country, Tim Sprake, who was sadly involved in a ghastly car accident shortly after the end of our season. We are glad to hear that he is recovering, albeit slowly.

I felt that having been so lucky, and won a lot of races, there was not much else to achieve. I will miss the winners, especially of our favourite races, such as the twenty-one we took at Royal Ascot – which, with better jockeyship here and there, could have been more. We won't miss days like the one on which Bonk drove for about three hours, plus another hour spent in a traffic jam, to get to Folkestone for a meeting in October. When we got there, they had run out of sandwiches, there were no racecards available, and only by the kindness of one of the directors were we able to get refreshments in their box. We then had to watch our horse being given a very negative ride, and to add insult to injury, getting beaten with a last-stride effort by Pat Eddery!

For many years there has been a small number of people whom I have disliked, because, in my opinion, they have done us wrong. I have always had an inkling that it would be good to have a bus to take them all over Beachy Head. It would not be very big; it would have a regulator to make sure it would go at a uniform speed, and it would have no brakes. It would be a double-decker, and the top storey, with the best view, would be reserved for the main culprits. Willie Carson would have an upstairs seat; Alec Wildenstein would definitely be the driver, and the doors would be firmly locked to make sure the inmates could not escape. At the December sales at Newmarket, in the small club of which I am a member, I was presented with such a bus, two feet long, with enough seats for all the people who they thought should be in it. It was a wonderful idea, dreamed up by Christo Phillipson and Hugh McCalmont, whose wives have complained since that they felt their husbands were using up all their energy, like tiresome schoolboys, getting this vehicle ready. I have altered the passenger list a bit, and have certain persons on standby, and the bus now sits in pride of place on the window seat in our dining room. It has caused a lot of laughter, with several other people being suggested as possible passengers.

On 7 November we had our tack sale. This was a very sad day, as we had collected a lot of racing saddlery over the years, but the auctioneers and our staff did a brilliant job. In the middle of it the auctioneers had to abandon proceedings, as a couple of scruffy-looking gypsies arrived, complete with a coloured horse and flatbed cart. They turned out to be our dear friends Mark Smyly and Jim Cramsie, who had driven up the high street, amazing the village people with their antics. This cabaret really cheered us up.

Just after that, an astonishing letter appeared in the *Racing Post*, which really touched us.

A TRUE GENTLEMAN WITH A GREAT SENSE OF FUN
Working with the auctioneers at the Windsor House tack sale recently was the saddest day of my life, and that goes for the rest of us. In addition to Mr Walwyn being a true gentleman, he was the guv'nor and it has been a privilege to know and work for him. He had the respect of all.

I had been with him for 29 years, and six other lads for over 20 years, and that says it all, especially when modern trainers can't get staff to stay for longer than a few. The guv'nor is one of those rare breeds who appreciated that loyalty had to go both ways, and no one could bear greater witness to that than the young Pat Eddery, particularly when Mr Daniel Wildenstein questioned his ability.

Seven Barrows and Windsor House were a family, and both the guv'nor and Mrs Walwyn made it so. Nothing was too much trouble, especially if we needed help, morally, financially or otherwise.

Mr Walwyn's achievements for the Lambourn community over the years are legendary, and he has been the driving force behind so many projects but, typically, he never sought out praise.

I sincerely hope that, one day soon, this great gentleman will be recognised with an award for what he has achieved for others.

It has been an honour to work for such a man, and I will miss his humour, his sense of fun and his most generous nature.

We all wish him and Mrs Walwyn a long, successful and happy retirement.

Ron Thomas, Wantage, Oxon

This generosity was typical of the sort of people that we employed, and who became our friends and colleagues.

To my continued amazement, tributes from people all over the world had started to pour in from the moment we announced our retirement. In November we were very kindly invited to the annual Cartier awards for racing, generously given by Monsieur Arnault Bamberger and his firm at a dinner in London. I suggested to Bonk that it would be fun to go, as we had not been before, and it seemed to be a very good evening in the making. When we arrived at the party, we noticed that there appeared to be a host of people whom we knew. I was placed between Lady 'Chicky' Oaksey and Anna Deedes, wife of the managing director of the *Daily Telegraph*, Jeremy, and had a thoroughly pleasant and relaxed dinner – until the end of the meal when Harry Herbert, the master of ceremonies, was about to start his awards address. All of a sudden there was a tug on my shoulder from the table behind us, and a dear friend, Peter O'Sullevan, leant forward, and said: 'I do hope you have got your speech ready.'

I was flabbergasted. I looked across at Bonk, who winked at me with a beaming smile. A lot of wonderful people were giving me the *Daily Telegraph* Lifetime Award of Merit, and had apparently organised for friends to record their feelings on camera in secret. This was a complete surprise to me, and I realised I had been utterly fooled; all the recording had been done while I was away for two days at Newmarket on meetings at the Animal Health Trust and British Racing School, and the cameras had invaded the yard for their filming. I was overwhelmed, especially by some very funny footage of incidents in our lives – including an episode in Corfu where, rather bored by a humourless cabaret, I had nipped round backstage and been allowed to don a Greek guard's uniform, in which I did my own version of the entertainment.

Then, about two weeks later, I received a further presentation at the Derby Awards, of the George Ennor Trophy for Outstanding Achievement. This too came as a great surprise, although in this case at least I was told about it in advance of the ceremony!

One morning in the middle of November I walked into the house, after riding out, to get my breakfast and look through the usual pile of letters that awaited me in the middle of the table.

The top one was from my bank manager. It was one of those nasty ones, saying that my overdraft was over the limit again. I exploded, as I seldom feel that banks are very helpful nowadays, and certainly never give anything away to their customers. Bonk said, 'Sit down and read the rest of the post.'

There in front of me was a letter from our great friend Christopher Spence, informing me that the Stewards of the Jockey Club, of which he was Senior Steward, had decided to appoint me an honorary member of the club. I could not have been more astonished. Whatever some of the press say, membership of the Jockey Club is the greatest honour that can be bestowed on anyone in racing, and I never imagined that it could come to me. The Jockey Club is respected, admired and copied all over the world. The members may be, as the press is fond of saying, 'self-selected', but their accomplishments in different fields are many and distinguished, and their collective talents lend the body a high degree of competence. Very few trainers have been made honorary members, and I am very privileged to have been asked to join the likes of Noel Murless and Dick Hern among the select few. It is my intention now to put back into the Club and racing a little of what I have got out of it.

We have had the most wonderful lives. Not long ago a fellow trainer said to me, 'Whatever are you going to do when you retire?'

I said, 'We are going to do all the things we want to do.'

'But,' he said, 'haven't you always done that?'

PETER WALWYN'S
BIG-RACE WINNERS

1965

Mabel (J. Mercer) Yorkshire Oaks, York (prize money £4,465)

1967

Be Hopeful (L. Piggott) Prix du Calvados, Deauville (£2,997)

Crozier (F. Durr) Doncaster Cup, Doncaster (£2,292)

1968

Crozier (D. Keith) Jockey Club Stakes, Newmarket (£2,309)

Crozier (D. Keith) Grand Prix de Vichy, Vichy (£8,446)

1969

Lucyrowe (D. Keith) Masaka Stakes, Kempton (£1,578)

Crozier (D. Keith) John Porter Stakes, Newbury (£2,845)

Town Crier (D. Keith) Victoria Cup, Ascot (£3,277)

Shoemaker (D. Keith) Player Wills Derby Trial,
    Leopardstown (£4,045)

Lucyrowe (D. Keith) Ebbisham Stakes, Epsom (£3,440)

Town Crier (D. Keith) Queen Anne Stakes, Royal Ascot
    (£2,235)

Lucyrowe (D. Keith) Coronation Stakes, Royal Ascot (£4,539)

Red Velvet (D. Keith) Princess Margaret Stakes, Ascot (£1,848)

Frontier Goddess (J. Mercer) Warren Stakes, Goodwood
    (£1,164)

Rose Arbour (J. Mercer) Rous Memorial Stakes, Goodwood
(£1,022)

Lucyrowe (F. Durr) Nassau Stakes, Goodwood (£3,112)

Red Velvet (D. Keith) St Hugh's Stakes, Newbury (£806)

Frontier Goddess (D. Keith) Yorkshire Oaks, York (£5,825)

Humble Duty (D. Keith) Lowther Stakes, York (£2,825)

Darlington (G. Lewis) Melrose Handicap, York (£2,176)

Seventh Bride (D. Keith) Fifinella Stakes, Epsom (£1,133)

Humble Duty (D. Keith) Cheveley Park Stakes, Newmarket
(£10,187)

Seventh Bride (D. Keith) Princess Royal Stakes, Ascot
(£2,105)

1970

Humble Duty (L. Piggott) One Thousand Guineas,
Newmarket (£21,015)

Shoemaker (D. Keith) Grand Prix de Printemps, St Cloud
(£19,250)

Humble Duty (D. Keith) Ebbisham Stakes, Epsom (£3,427)

Humble Duty (D. Keith) Coronation Stakes, Royal Ascot
(£4,577)

Rock Roi (G. Lewis) Warren Stakes, Goodwood (£1,772)

Humble Duty (D. Keith) Sussex Stakes, Goodwood (£12,087)

Rock Roi (G. Lewis) Gordon Stakes, Goodwood (£4,134)

Shoemaker (D. Keith) Prix Gontaut Biron, Deauville (£9,306)

Humble Duty (D. Keith) Wills Mile, Goodwood (£7,343)

Linden Tree (D. Keith) Observer Gold Cup, Doncaster
(£19,698)

1971

Ouda (F. Durr) Newbury Spring Cup, Newbury (£1,721)

Linden Tree (D. Keith) Chester Vase, Chester (£3,350)

Tamergene (D. Keith) Ebbisham Stakes, Epsom (£1,514)

Rock Roi (D. Keith) Paradise Stakes, Ascot (£842)

Rock Roi (D. Keith) Ascot Gold Cup, Royal Ascot
(disqualified)

Ortis (D. Keith) Hardwicke Stakes, Royal Ascot (£9,645)

Rock Roi (D. Keith) Goodwood Cup, Goodwood (£3,614)

Rock Roi (D. Keith) Doncaster Cup, Doncaster (£3,645)

Ortis (D. Keith) Valdoes Stakes, Goodwood (£938)

Guillotina (D. Keith) Houghton Stakes, Newmarket (£1,968)

1972

Rock Roi (D. Keith) John Porter Stakes, Newbury (£4,189)

Jakomima (D. Keith) Musidora Stakes, York (£2,532)

Rock Roi (D. Keith) Prix du Cadran, Longchamp (£23,048)

Golden Treasure (P. Eddery) Kingsclere Stakes, Newbury
(£1,824)

Rock Roi (D. Keith) Ascot Gold Cup, Royal Ascot
(disqualified)

Lunchtime (P. Eddery) Dewhurst Stakes, Newmarket
(£13,340)

Guillotina (P. Eddery) Prix de Royallieu, Longchamp
(£10,894)

1973

Red Berry (P. Eddery) Kingsclere Stakes, Newbury (£1,465)

Loyal Guard (P. Eddery) Bessborough Handicap, Royal
Ascot (£3,252)

Habat (P. Eddery) Norfolk Stakes, Royal Ascot (£5,199)

Tudor Rhythm (P. Eddery) Britannia Stakes, Royal Ascot
(£3,946)

One Over Parr (P. Eddery) Lancashire Oaks, Haydock
(£5,098)

King's Park (P. Eddery) Convivial Stakes, York (£3,135)

Brook (P. Eddery) Hungerford Stakes, Newbury (£2,956)

Habat (P. Eddery) Mill Reef Stakes, Newbury (£1,026)

Tudor Rhythm (J. Mercer) Yellow Pages Autumn Cup,
Doncaster (£3,423)

Hilo Girl (P. Eddery) Blue Seal Stakes, Ascot (£2,445)

Habat (P. Eddery) Middle Park Stakes, Newmarket (£25,346)

Charlie Bubbles (P. Eddery) Clarence House Stakes, Ascot
(£1,032)

1974

Understudy (P. Eddery) Union Jack Stakes, Aintree (£817)

Habat (P. Eddery) Two Thousand Guineas Trial, Ascot
(£2,676)

Polygamy (P. Eddery) One Thousand Guineas Trial, Ascot
(£2,640)

Numa (P. Eddery) Craven Stakes, Newmarket (£3,229)

Charlie Bubbles (P. Eddery) Free Handicap, Newmarket
(£4,040)

Tudor Rhythm (P. Eddery) Gordon Richards Stakes,
Sandown (£2,337) (dead heat)

English Prince (P. Eddery) White Rose Stakes, Ascot (£3,615)

Lady Rowe (D. Cullen) Glenlivet Handicap, Newmarket
(£3,610)

English Prince (P. Eddery) Predominate Stakes, Goodwood
(£1,996)

Polygamy (P. Eddery) Oaks, Epsom (£40,639)

Royal Aura (P. Eddery) Queen's Vase, Royal Ascot (£4,402)

Red Cross (P. Eddery) Chesham Stakes, Royal Ascot (£3,243)

English Prince (P. Eddery) King Edward VII Stakes, Royal
Ascot (£10,727)

English Prince (Y. Saint-Martin) Irish Derby, Curragh
(£74,945)

Grundy (P. Eddery) Granville Stakes, Ascot (£1,611)

One Over Parr (P. Eddery) Globik Stakes, Goodwood
  (£2,544)
Grundy (P. Eddery) Sirenia Stakes, Kempton (£621)
Red Cross (P. Eddery) Mill Reef Stakes, Newbury (£10,884)
Record Token (P. Eddery) Vernon's Sprint, Haydock
  (£13,611)
Grundy (P. Eddery) Champagne Stakes, Doncaster (£9,443)
Mayhill (P. Waldron) Duke of Edinburgh Stakes, Ascot
  (£2,685)
Grundy (P. Eddery) Dewhurst Stakes, Newmarket (£26,271)
Bygone (P. Cook) Houghton Stakes, Newmarket (£2,152)
Corby (P. Eddery) Horris Hill Stakes, Newbury (£6,855)

1975
No Alimony (P. Eddery) Craven Stakes, Newmarket (£3,288)
Charlie Bubbles (P. Eddery) Newbury Spring Cup, Newbury
  (£1,746)
Consol (P. Eddery) Guardian Classic Trial, Sandown (£2,938)
One Over Parr (P. Eddery) Cheshire Oaks, Chester (£3,737)
Patch (P. Eddery) Lingfield Derby Trial, Lingfield (£7,413)
Foiled Again (F. Morby) Sandleford Priory Stakes, Newbury
  (£1,639)
No Alimony (P. Eddery) Predominate Stakes, Goodwood
  (£2,134)
Taros (J. Mercer) Clive Graham Stakes, Goodwood (£1,668)
Grundy (P. Eddery) Irish Two Thousand Guineas, Curragh
  (£64,063)
Consol (P. Eddery) Royal Whip, Curragh (£2,745)
Grundy (P. Eddery) Epsom Derby, Epsom (£106,465)
Corby (P. Eddery) Prix du Lys, Longchamp (£10,118)
Charlie Bubbles (P. Eddery) Hardwicke Stakes, Royal Ascot
  (£12,345)
Grundy (P. Eddery) Irish Derby, Curragh (£64,063)

Grundy (P. Eddery) King George VI & Queen Elizabeth
 Stakes, Ascot (£81,910)
Hard Day (Miss F. Vittadini) Diamond Ladies' Race, Ascot
 (£2,072)
One Over Parr (P. Eddery) Virginia Water Stakes, Ascot
 (£1,431)
Pasty (P. Eddery) Lavant Stakes, Goodwood (£1,598)
Mayhill (P. Eddery) Yorkshire Oaks, York (£13,192)
Pasty (P. Eddery) Lowther Stakes, York (£3,576)
Patch (P. Eddery) Great Voltigeur Stakes, York (£9,119)
Consol (P. Eddery) Geoffrey Freer Stakes, Newbury (£8,098)
Mayhill (P. Eddery) Park Hill Stakes, Doncaster (£9,065)
Pasty (P. Eddery) Cheveley Park Stakes, Newmarket
 (£21,956)
State Occasion (P. Eddery) Horris Hill Stakes, Newbury
 (£6,618)

1976
Oats (P. Eddery) Blue Riband Trial, Epsom (£4,388)
Red Regent (P. Eddery) City & Suburban Handicap, Epsom
 (£3,748)
Free State (P. Eddery) Esher Cup, Sandown (£2,586)
Record Token (P. Eddery) Victoria Cup, Ascot (£4,144)
Record Token (P. Eddery) John O'Gaunt Stakes, Haydock
 (£5,031)
Crow (P. Eddery) Ormonde Stakes, Chester (£9,912)
Illustrious Prince (P. Eddery) Glasgow Stakes, York
 (£3,594)
Orange Bay (P. Eddery) Hardwicke Stakes, Royal Ascot
 (£14,412)
Avgerinos (P. Eddery) Granville Stakes, Ascot (£3,154)
Red Letter Day (P. Eddery) Princess Margaret Stakes, Ascot
 (£2,553)

Dactylographer (P. Eddery) South Coast Stakes, Lingfield (£2,427)

Avgerinos (P. Eddery) Solario Stakes, Sandown (£3,229)

Red Regent (Mr N. Gaselee) Moët & Chandon Silver Magnum, Epsom (£2,463)

Anchorite (R. Cochrane) Stanley Leisure Stakes, Haydock (£7,635)

Sporting Yankee (P. Eddery) William Hill Futurity, Doncaster (£36,398)

1977

Millionaire (P. Eddery) Warren Stakes, Epsom (£4,552)

Orange Bay (P. Eddery) Jockey Club Stakes, Newmarket (£4,991)

Oats (P. Eddery) Ormonde Stakes, Chester (£9,912)

Orange Bay (P. Eddery) Aston Park Stakes, Newbury (£2,991)

Red Letter Day (P. Eddery) International Stakes, Kempton (£2,934)

Rectitude (P. Eddery) Ebbisham Stakes, Epsom (£7,054)

Gypsy Dancer (P. Eddery) Leisure Stakes, Lingfield (£3,850)

Millionaire (P. Eddery) Queen's Vase, Royal Ascot (£8,220)

Classic Example (P. Eddery) King Edward VII Stakes, Royal Ascot (£14,215)

Busaca (P. Eddery) Lancashire Oaks, Haydock (£11,811)

Red Regent (P. Eddery) Concentra Pokal, Frankfurt (£11,320)

Busaca (P. Eddery) Yorkshire Oaks, York (£21,250)

Free State (P. Eddery) Wills Mile, Goodwood (£10,780)

Sporting Yankee (P. Eddery) March Stakes, Goodwood (£3,821)

Bolak (P. Eddery) Solario Stakes, Sandown (£3,402)

Formidable (P. Eddery) Mill Reef Stakes, Newbury (£19,094)

Orange Bay (P. Eddery) Cumberland Lodge Stakes, Ascot
  (£7,310)
Formidable (P. Eddery) Middle Park Stakes, Newmarket
  (£36,614)
Camden Town (P. Eddery) Clarence House Stakes, Ascot
  (£2,519)
Dactylographer (P. Eddery) Sandwich Stakes, Ascot
  (£2,742)
Vitiges (P. Eddery) Champion Stakes, Newmarket (£38,609)
Dactylographer (P. Eddery) William Hill Futurity, Doncaster
  (£42,766)

1978

Camden Town (P. Eddery) Rosebery Stakes, Stockton
  (£2,322)
Seraphina (P. Eddery) Nell Gwyn Stakes, Newmarket
  (£6,249)
Leonardo da Vinci (P. Eddery) Wood Ditton Stakes,
  Newmarket (£2,632)
Saros (P. Eddery) City & Suburban Handicap, Epsom
  (£4,428)
Leonardo da Vinci (P. Eddery) White Rose Stakes, Ascot
  (£5,833)
Classic Example (P. Eddery) Jockey Club Stakes, Newmarket
  (£10,442)
Suni (P. Eddery) Lingfield Oaks Trial, Lingfield (£8,607)
Paico (P. Eddery) Aston Park Stakes, Newbury (£2,944)
Crow (P. Eddery) Ormonde Stakes, Epsom (£25,206)
Camden Town (P. Eddery) Jersey Stakes, Royal Ascot
  (£9,628)
Rhineland (P. Eddery) Britannia Stakes, Royal Ascot
  (£6,253)
Kampala (P. Eddery) Beeswing Stakes, Newcastle (£12,217)

Seraphina (P. Eddery) Blue Seal Stakes, Ascot (£3,194)

Proven (P. Eddery) Fakenham Handicap, Newmarket (£3,210)

Proven (N. Howe) Irish Sweeps Handicap, Newmarket (£8,973)

1979

Untitled (P. Eddery) Masaka Stakes, Kempton (£3,048)

Proven (P. Eddery) Rosebery Handicap, Kempton (£7,197)

Formidable (P. Eddery) John O'Gaunt Stakes, Haydock (£10,330)

New Berry (P. Eddery) Glasgow Stakes, York (£4,227)

Jellaby (P. Eddery) Brigadier Gerard Stakes, Sandown (£10,576)

Little Annie (P. Eddery) Warwick Oaks, Warwick (£2,439)

Spanish Dancer (P. Eddery) Steventon Stakes, Newbury (£2,085)

1980

Kampala (P. Eddery) Victoria Cup, Ascot (£9,942)

Western Star (P. Eddery) Lupe Stakes, Goodwood (£3,002)

Cracking Form (Miss F. Vittadini) Diamond Ladies' Race, Ascot (£2,750)

Kampala (P. Eddery) Hungerford Stakes, Newbury (£14,540)

Spanish Dancer (P. Eddery) Lintas London Handicap, Ascot (£3,856)

Spanish Dancer (P. Eddery) Irish Sweeps Handicap, Newmarket (£12,752)

1981

Travel On (J. Mercer), Cherry Hinton Stakes, Newmarket (£14,910)

Cracking Form (Miss F. Vittadini) Diamond Ladies' Race,
Ascot (£2,850)
Kampala (P. Eddery) Rose of York Stakes, York (£3,980)
Halsbury (J. Mercer) Cesarewitch Handicap, Newmarket
(£27,815)

1982
Sancta (P. Eddery) Steventon Stakes, Newbury (£3,007)
Fitzpatrick (N. Howe) Newbury Autumn Cup, Newbury
(£9,494)

1983
Hill's Pageant (J. Mercer) Duke of Cambridge Handicap,
Newmarket (£5,212)
Hill's Pageant (J. Mercer) Concentra Pokal, Frankfurt
(£10,390)

1984
Wagoner (T. Ives) Doncaster Cup, Doncaster (£18,747)
Fitzpatrick (J. Mercer) Tennent Trophy, Ayr (£3,739)
Khozaam (J. Mercer) Granville Stakes, Ascot (£6,388)
La Tuerta (J. Mercer) Singapore Airlines Handicap, York
(£8,439)
Stalker (J. Mercer) Gimcrack Stakes, Newmarket (£35,334)
Khozaam (P. Eddery) Washington Singer Stakes, Newbury
(£6,399)
Triagonal (P. Eddery) Atalanta Stakes, Sandown (£7,400)
Nesting Time (J. Mercer) Premio Delleana, Milan (£6,176)

1985
Nashia (J. Mercer) St Hugh's Stakes, Newbury (£7,674)
Stalker (J. Mercer) Middle Park Stakes, Newmarket (£34,744)
Luqman (N. Howe) Mill Reef Stakes, Newbury (£17,034)

1986

Sperry (P. Eddery) Cork & Orrery Stakes, Royal Ascot
(£18,950)

Plaid (P. Eddery) Granville Stakes, Ascot (£6,440)

1987

Framlington Court (D. Browne) Charisma Hurdle, Kempton
(£8,956)

Turfah (B. Thompson) Jubilee Handicap, Kempton (£16,596)

Just Kala (N. Howe) Prix La Sorelina, Bordeaux (£10,582)

Framlington Court (D. Browne) Free Handicap Hurdle,
Chepstow (£5,733)

1988

Waterfield (P. Eddery) Doncaster Shield, Doncaster
(£10,477)

Waterfield (P. Eddery) Aquascutum Silver Cup, Lingfield
(£15,036)

Simon Rattle (N. Howe) Sprinter Preis, Munich (£10,204)

1989

Alsabiha (P. Eddery) Masaka Stakes, Kempton (£7,180)

Ottergayle (P. Eddery) Newbury Spring Cup, Newbury
(£7,876)

Sure Gold (P. Eddery) William Hill Handicap, York
(£21,721)

1990

Hateel (W. Carson) Aston Park Stakes, Newbury (£7,876)

Relief Pitcher (P. Eddery) Festival Stakes, Goodwood
(£14,759)

Rawnak (R. Cochrane) King Charles II Stakes, Newmarket
(£11,394)

Husyan (W. Carson) Brigadier Gerard Stakes, Sandown
(£21,222)

Farm Street (C. Asmussen) Croydex Handicap, Epsom
(£13,875)

Hateel (W. Carson) Bessborough Handicap, Royal Ascot
(£14,913)

Tadwin (W. Carson) Northumberland Sprint Trophy,
Newcastle (£12,135)

Hateel (W. Carson) Old Newton Cup, Haydock (£22,710)

Husyan (W. Carson) Scottish Classic, Ayr (£27,162)

Mukaddamah (W. Carson) Champagne Stakes, Goodwood
(£18,494)

Thaidah (M. Roberts) Rose of York Stakes, York (£8,155)

Jallad (W. Carson) Convivial Stakes, York (£7,440)

Relief Pitcher (P. Eddery) Grand Prix des Fonds Européen,
Deauville (£22,810)

Dominio (R. Cochrane) St Hugh's Stakes, Newbury (£10,770)

Tadwin (W. Carson) Hopeful Stakes, Newmarket (£11,648)

Relief Pitcher (P. Eddery) State of New York Stakes, Belmont
Park (£50,311)

1991

Rami (R. Cochrane) Leicestershire Stakes, Leicester (£11,550)

Takaddum (W. Carson) Meyer Perry Handicap, Newmarket
(£11,940)

Hateel (W. Carson) Northern Dancer Handicap, Epsom
(£17,255)

Takaddum (G. Baxter) Tote Credit Silver Bowl, Haydock
(£19,900)

Takaddum (G. Baxter) Cecil Frail Handicap, Haydock
(£19,900)

Mukaddamah (W. Carson) International Stakes, Curragh
(£23,928)

Salatin (W. Carson) Sandwich Stakes, Ascot (£9,688)

Northern Hal (L. Piggott) Preis der Stadt, Baden-Baden (£10,380)

1992

Hamas (W. Carson) Bentinck Stakes, Newmarket (£9,706)

1993

Hamas (W. Carson) July Cup, Newmarket (£106,365)

Hamas (W. Carson) Duke of York Stakes, York (£21,978)

Tablah (W. Carson) Blue Seal Stakes, Ascot (£10,234)

1994

Munwar (R. Hills) Haynes Hanson & Clark Stakes, Newbury (£6,323)

1995

Munwar (W. Carson) Fielden Stakes, Newmarket (£11,199)

Munwar (W. Carson) Lingfield Derby Trial, Lingfield (£30,820)

1997

Hattab (R. Hughes) Beefeater Handicap, Sandown (£7,491)

Hattab (P. Eddery) Ruinart Stakes, Newbury (£12,178)

1998

Nadwah (R. Hills) Queen Mary Stakes, Royal Ascot (£27,040)

Regal Revolution (J. Lowe) Firth of Clyde Stakes, Ayr (£18,592)

1999

Khasayl (R. Hills) Firth of Clyde Stakes, Ayr (£11,094)

Khasayl (T. Sprake) NTL Stakes, Redcar (£99,949)

PETER WALWYN'S
YEAR-BY-YEAR WINNING RECORD

1960–61	3 hurdle races, 1 steeplechase
1961	4 winners on the flat
1961–62	2 hurdle races, 2 steeplechases
1962	12 winners on the flat
1963	19 winners on the flat, 1 hurdle race
1963–64	2 hurdle races, 3 steeplechases
1964	16 winners on the flat
1964–65	1 hurdle race, 1 steeplechase
1965	24 winners on the flat
1966	37 winners on the flat
1967	45 winners on the flat
1968	50 winners on the flat
1969	70 winners on the flat, most winners, most winning and place money
1970	55 winners on the flat
1971	62 winners on the flat
1972	57 winners on the flat
1973	87 winners on the flat, most winners since before the Second World War
1974	97 winners on the flat, most winners, first time leading trainer and in Ireland
1975	125 winners on the flat, most winners, second time leading trainer and in Ireland
1976	111 winners on the flat, most winners
1977	111 winners on the flat, most winners

1978	70 winners on the flat
1979	44 winners on the flat
1980	78 winners on the flat
1981	52 winners on the flat
1982	48 winners on the flat
1983	26 winners on the flat
1984	48 winners on the flat
1985	42 winners on the flat, 1 hurdle race
1986	43 winners on the flat, 8 hurdle races
1987	37 winners on the flat, 1 hurdle race
1988	31 winners on the flat
1989	38 winners on the flat
1990	49 winners on the flat, 4 hurdle races
1991	24 winners on the flat, 3 abroad
1992	22 winners on the flat
1993	17 winners on the flat
1994	31 winners on the flat, 1 steeplechase
1995	28 winners on the flat
1996	18 winners on the flat
1997	31 winners on the flat
1998	16 winners on the flat
1999	8 winners on the flat

Total winners
Flat winners: 1,783
Steeplechases: 8
Hurdle races: 23